PENGUIN BOOKS

SEXUAL ANARCHY

Elaine Showalter is chairperson of the department of English at
Princeton University and the author of *A Literature of Their Own:
Women Writers from Brontë to Lessing* and *The Female Malady:
Women, Madness, and English Culture, 1830–1980*. She has lectured widely throughout the United States and England on
women's writing, Victorian medical history, and literary theory,
and has edited *These Modern Women: Autobiographies of Women in
the 1920s* and *The New Feminist Criticism: Essays on Women, Literature, and Theory*.

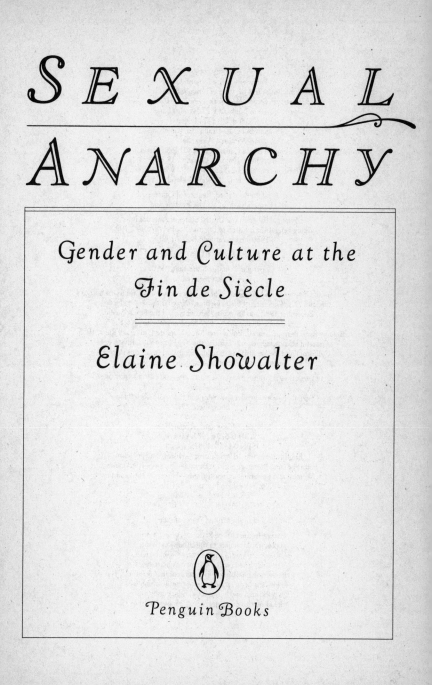

SEXUAL ANARCHY

Gender and Culture at the Fin de Siècle

Elaine Showalter

Penguin Books

PENGUIN BOOKS
Published by the Penguin Group
Viking Penguin, a division of Penguin Books USA Inc.,
375 Hudson Street, New York, New York 10014, U.S.A.
Penguin Books Ltd, 27 Wrights Lane,
London W8 5TZ, England
Penguin Books Australia Ltd, Ringwood,
Victoria, Australia
Penguin Books Canada Ltd, 2801 John Street,
Markham, Ontario, Canada L3R 1B4
Penguin Books (N.Z.) Ltd, 182–190 Wairau Road,
Auckland 10, New Zealand

Penguin Books Ltd, Registered Offices:
Harmondsworth, Middlesex, England

First published in the United States of America by
Viking Penguin, a division of Penguin Books USA Inc., 1990
Published in Penguin Books 1991

1 3 5 7 9 10 8 6 4 2

Portions of Chapters 4 and 10 appeared previously in different form in the author's
articles "The Greening of Sister George," Nineteenth-Century Fiction,
35, December 1980 and "Syphilis, Sexuality, and the Fin de Siècle,"
in Sex, Politics, and Science in the Nineteenth-Century Novel,
edited by Ruth Bernard Yeazell, Baltimore: Johns Hopkins University Press, 1985.
Grateful acknowledgment is made to the Regents of the University of
California and the English Institute for permission to use this material.
Illustration credits appear on pages xi and xii.

THE LIBRARY OF CONGRESS HAS CATALOGUED THE HARDCOVER AS FOLLOWS:
Showalter, Elaine.
Sexual anarchy : gender and culture at the fin de siècle/Elaine
Showalter.
p.   cm.
Includes bibliographical references.
ISBN 0-670-82503-4 (hc.)
ISBN 0 14 01.1587 0 (pbk.)
1. English literature—19th century—History and criticism.
2. Feminism and literature—Great Britain—History—19th century.
3. Women and literature—Great Britain—History—19th century.
4. Sex role in literature. I. Title.
PR468.F46S56   1990
820.9'9287'09034—dc20   89–40697

Printed in the United States of America

For Michael Cadden

Acknowledgments

This book has grown out of my teaching and research at Princeton, where it has crossed the borderlines of the genres, the generations, and the disciplines, and I owe warm thanks to the many friends who have helped me think it through. Thanks especially to Michael Cadden, whose friendship and interest lasted through hundreds of hours of talking about gender in the office, the Student Center, and the Annex. Special thanks, too, to Richard Kaye, Wayne Koestenbaum, and John Perry, who inspired me by taking these ideas so seriously, supplying a steady stream of clippings, pictures, and references, and generously sharing ideas from their ongoing work in gender studies. David Faulkner, Chris Go-Gwilt, Marjorie Howes, Andrew Miller, Catherine Milsum, Jeff Nunokawa, Robert Spoo, and Helen Sword, preceptors and co-conspirators in my undergraduate course in "Literature of the *Fin de Siècle*," helped form the intellectual community out of which new ideas could grow, as well as the Dracula Film Club for rainy nights. Gayle Wald was a superb research assistant whose imagination and ingenuity often took me in new directions. Many Princeton undergraduates, especially Miki Dedijer, Rob Ginsberg, Walter Jean, Cindy Klein, Phil Pearson, Janet Sarbanes, Susan Schmeiser, Gary Sunshine, Melissa Sydeman, Tanya Herrera, David Zabel, and Paul Zablocki, contributed important insights, connections, and always a sustaining combination of skepticism and enthusiasm. The participants in the Salzburg Seminar on "Gender and the Humanities" in the summer of 1988, especially James Boon, Laurence Senelick, and Jeffrey Weeks, were supportive critics and enlivening companions. Colleagues at Princeton and elsewhere—Charles Bernheimer, Joseph Boone, Richard Dellamora, Sander L. Gilman, Sandra M. Gilbert, Elliot Gilbert, Daniel Jaeger-Mendelson, Roy Porter, Deborah Nord, Joyce Carol Oates, Andrew Ross, Garrett Stewart, David Van Leer, and Judy Walkowitz shared their time, research, expertise, and advice. Most of all, my husband, English Showalter, is the one person who reads all the drafts, sees me through every power failure, and makes me welcome the millennium if we can ring it in together.

Contents

Contents

Table of Illustrations

SEXUAL
ANARCHY

ONE

Borderlines

Suspended above the courtyard of the Pompidou Center in Paris is the Génitron, an electric sign-clock flashing the number of seconds left in the twentieth century. Inaugurated in January 1987 by François Mitterrand, the Génitron is a time machine that conducts its relentless countdown over the heads of the milling international fauna of les Halles, the hustlers, punks, dealers, con men, mystics, musicians, strongmen, fire-eaters, rappers, breakers, addicts, sidewalk artists, and sidewalk dwellers who seem already to represent the specters of the apocalypse. As the novelist Angela Carter observes, "the *fin* is coming a little early this *siècle*."

The Génitron makes spectators uncomfortable, for the terminal decades of a century suggest to many minds the death throes of a diseased society and the winding down of an exhausted culture. In his gloomy and embittered treatise on *Degeneration* (1892), the Austrian Max Nordau proclaimed that "in our days there have arisen in more highly developed minds vague qualms of a Dusk of the Nations, in which all suns and all stars are gradually waning, and mankind with all its institutions and creations is perishing in the midst of a dying world."[1] From urban homelessness to imperial decline, from sexual revolution to sexual epidemics, the last decades of the twentieth century seem to be repeating the problems, themes, and metaphors of the *fin de siècle*. Latter-day Nordaus like Allan Bloom, William Bennett, or John Silber preach against a new American Dusk, in which the breakdown of the family; the decline of religion; the women's liberation and gay rights movements; the drug epidemic; and the redefinition of the humanities merge to signal a waning culture. For some years already we have become accustomed to the electric signs of apocalypse, or rather those troubling signals of "Apocalypse From Now On," as Susan Sontag puts it, that seem characteristic of late-twentieth-century life—dire predictions of disasters that never exactly happen, or perhaps have invisibly happened already—the greenhouse effect, the stock market crash, the nuclear threat, AIDS, terrorism, crime, urban decay, crack.[2] After post-industrialism, post-modernism, post-feminism, and post-historicism, we now hear that the end of the century means the end of art, the end of nature, or the end of history.[3]

The ends of centuries seem not only to suggest but to intensify crises, as the 1989 bicentennial of the French Revolution and the astonishing events in Eastern Europe reminded us. History warns that after the revolution comes the terror and decadence. When the term *fin-de-siècle* originated in France in the 1880s to define this state of mind, it spread rapidly throughout Europe and the United States; "the word," wrote Nordau, "has flown from one hemisphere to the other, and found its way into all civilized languages."[4] (The term being currently proposed for late-twentieth-century culture is "endism.")[5] But why should the ends of centuries have special meanings and feelings or manifest common patterns? After all, the century markers are only imaginary borderlines in time; there is even disagreement as to when—December 31, '99? December 31, '00?—the new century begins. As Thomas Mann wrote in "The Magic Kingdom," "Time has no divisions to mark its passage. There is never a thunderstorm or blare of trumpets to announce the beginning of a new month or year. Even when a new century begins, it is only we mortals who ring bells and fire off pistols."

Could there be cycles in time like cycles in the weather, like hurricanes and earthquakes, which are chaotic but not random? In a famous book, Frank Kermode argued that "the sense of an ending" is a myth of the temporal that affects our thought about ourselves, our histories, our disciplines, and our fictions: "We project our existential anxieties on to history; there is a real correlation between the ends of centuries and the peculiarity of our imagination, that it chooses always to be at the end of an era."[6] The crises of the *fin de siècle*, then, are more intensely experienced, more emotionally fraught, more weighted with symbolic and historical meaning, because we invest them with the metaphors of death and rebirth that we project onto the final decades and years of a century. Myths and metaphors cannot be separated from our historical understanding of the fin-de-siècle experience, for they are part of it, not merely decorative flourishes in an objective historical description, but constituitive of the experiences themselves.

This book is about the myths, metaphors, and images of sexual crises and apocalypse that marked both the late nineteenth century and our own *fin de siècle,* and its representations in English and American literature, art, and film. The 1880s and 1890s, in the words of the novelist George Gissing, were decades of "sexual anarchy," when all the laws that governed sexual identity and behavior seemed to be breaking down. As Karl Miller notes, "Men became women. Women became men. Gender and country were put in doubt. The single life was found to harbour two sexes and two nations."[7] During this period both the words "feminism" and "homosexuality" first came into use, as New Women and male aesthetes redefined the meanings of femininity and masculinity. There were fears that emancipated women would bear children outside of marriage in the free union, or worse, that they would not have children at all. In the wake of Ibsen, women's oppression became the theme of successful plays by Arthur Pinero, Oscar Wilde, Harley Granville-Barker, and George Bernard Shaw, and novels by Thomas Hardy, George Meredith, and George Moore.

The *fin de siècle* was also a period of sexual scandals. In England, they ranged from the trial and acquittal of the notorious brothel-keeper Jeffries in 1884, and the sensational journalistic series on child prostitution of W. T. Stead, "The Maiden Tribute of Modern Babylon," in 1885, to the exposé of the Cleveland Street male brothel in 1889. All of these scandals changed the level of public awareness about sexuality and engendered a fierce response in social purity campaigns, a renewed sense of public moral concern, and demands, often successful, for restrictive legislation and censorship. They were occasions when gender roles were "publicly, even spectacularly, encoded and enforced."[8] Especially there was a call to reaffirm the importance of the family as the bulwark against sexual decadence. "In all countries the purity of the family must be the surest strength of a nation," wrote the Reverend W. Arthur in 1885.[9] The emergence and medicalization of the modern homosexual identity in the 1880s reached widespread public attention with Oscar Wilde's trial and conviction in 1895. Indeed, many Englishmen regarded the homosexual scandals of the 1880s and 1890s, up to Oscar Wilde's trial, as certain signs of the immorality that had toppled Greece and Rome. "If England falls," one clergyman warned, "it will be this sin, and her unbelief in God, that will have been her ruin."[10] A public furor over prostitution and the sexual epidemic of syphilis changed the discourse of sexuality, the body, and disease.

In the late twentieth century, too, threats of sexual anarchy have generated panic and backlash against the sexual liberalism of the 1960s and 1970s. Concerns about the sexual abuse of children and the increasing frequency of occurrences of rape have focused on censoring art and banning pornography rather than on examining the social construction of male sexual violence. Fears about the drastic changes in women's sexual choices have taken the form of anti-abortion campaigns rather than plans for child support, parenting leaves, or daycare. Anxiety about women's educational and economic advances and the effects of women's paid labor on traditional marital structures have led to a renewed idealization of the family, domesticity, and maternity. The AIDS epidemic has fueled homophobia and an emphasis on monogamy and celibacy rather than a commitment to sex education and information about safer sexual practices.

These responses are also typical of the *fin de siècle*. In periods of cultural insecurity, when there are fears of regression and degeneration, the longing for strict border controls around the definition of gender, as well as race, class, and nationality, becomes especially intense. If the different races can be kept in their places, if the various classes can be held in their proper districts of the city, and if men and women can be fixed in their separate spheres, many hope, apocalypse can be prevented and we can preserve a comforting sense of identity and permanence in the face of that relentless specter of millennial change.

Sexual difference was only one of the threatened borders of the *fin de siècle*, and sexuality only one of the areas in which anarchy seemed imminent. The 1880s were a turbulent decade in English history. The making of vast industrial fortunes was balanced by the organization of trade unions and the founding of the British Labour party. Imperialist adventure in Africa, where diamonds were discovered in the Transvaal in 1880, occurred while urban poverty and homelessness in England received dramatic attention. Hopes for the Empire were undermined by acts of political terrorism committed by anarchists and Irish nationalists. Even while the age of imperialism was at its height, there were also fears of degeneration and collapse. England was often compared to decadent Greece and Rome, and there were parallel fears of the rise of captive peoples.

Racial boundaries were among the most important lines of demarcation for English society; fears not only of colonial rebellion but also of racial mingling, crossbreeding, and intermarriage, fueled scientific and political interest in establishing clear lines of demarcation between black and white, East and West. After General Gordon's defeat by an Islamic fundamentalist, the Mahdi, at Khartoum in 1885, many saw signs that the Empire was being undermined by racial degeneration and the rebellion of the "lower" races. Late Victorian science, especially the new science of physical anthropology, devoted itself to establishing the legitimacy of racial differentiation and hierarchy, and to demonstrating the "degenerations that threatened when these boundaries were transgressed."[11]

There was a major crisis in class relations as well. At the end of the 1870s, England and Western Europe in general were hit by an economic depression, and in the 1880s the term "unemployment" first came into use. In the inner city lived the "residuum" of the chronically poor and hard-core unemployed. This netherworld was seen to live in slums, breeding disease, ignorance, madness, and crime, problems some eugenicists felt were so intractable that the poor should not be allowed to reproduce. The theory of urban degeneration furthermore held that poverty led to a general deterioration of the race. "Everywhere no doubt," wrote H. M. Hyndman in his essay "English Workers as They Are" (1887), "there is a certain percentage who are almost beyond hope of being reached at all. Crushed down into the gutter, physically and mentally by their social surroundings, they can but die out, leaving, it is hoped, no progeny as a burden on a better state of things."[12]

Metaphors of race were also used to describe class relationships. While other races seemed distant and exotic, the working class was close at hand. William Booth's *In Darkest England* (1890) and Margaret Harkness's novel *In Darkest London* (1891) drew parallels between the problems of the African jungle and the urban jungle where homelessness, poverty, hunger, drunkenness, and sexual barbarity could be seen every day. In an eloquent comparison of Stanley's vast African forest, with its pygmies, traders, and cannibals, to the labyrinth of London, with its stunted people and its predators, Booth, the leader of the Salvation Army, asked: "As there is a darkest Africa is there not also a darkest England? Civilisation, which can breed its own barbarians, does it not also breed its own pygmies? May we not find a parallel at our own doors, and discover within a stone's throw of our cathedrals and palaces similar horrors to those which Stanley has found existing in the great Equatorial forest? . . . The ivory raiders who brutally traffic in the unfortunate denizens of the forest glades, what are they but the publicans who flourish on the weakness of our poor? . . . As in Africa it is all trees, trees, trees with no other world conceivable, so is it here—it is all vice and poverty and crime."[13] Everything that was "dark, labyrinthine, threatening, and benighted," Deborah Nord notes, could be located in "the East—whether Burma, India, or the East End of London."[14] Thus Conrad, among others, draws significant parallels between the Thames and the Congo, between the heart of darkness and an England which has also "been one of the dark places of the world."

While for most of the nineteenth century the urban boundaries between the classes were clearly demarcated, with the poor restricted to working-class districts of the East End, urban homelessness and general unemployment made the borderline between the classes startlingly visible. In London, by 1887, the homeless had taken to camping out in Trafalgar Square and St. James's Park, arousing both compassion and fear. As the social scientist Charles Booth explained, "This state of things attracted attention. The newspapers published accounts of it, and public imagination was aroused. Here at any rate was genuine distress. Some charitable agencies distributed tickets for food or lodging, others the food itself, taking cart-loads of food into the Square."[15] On the other hand, many shopkeepers felt threatened by the influx of homeless and indigent, who scared customers away. They demanded that the police deal with the situation and threatened that they would otherwise hire their own guards to clear the streets.[16] The pressure resulted in a violent clash on "Bloody Sunday" in November 1887, as police cleared the squares and park. This netherworld of darkest England thus presented the perpetual threat of class revolution; any minute, it was feared, workers might rise up in revolt.

While the "lower races" were safely distant in Africa and India, and the poor usually well out of sight, men could not hide in the same way from the threat of a revolution by women. The crisis in race and class relations in the 1880s had a parallel in the crisis in gender. "That both women and 'natives' simultaneously began to manifest frightening drives toward independence just as England's great century of empire drew to its uneasy close," Sandra Gilbert and Susan Gubar point out, "would, of course, have sealed the fin-de-siècle connection between these two previously silent and disenfranchised groups."[17] And many

Victorians, such as Karl Pearson, saw "two great problems of modern social life" as "the problem of women and the problem of labour."[18] Feminism, the women's movement, and what was called "the Woman Question" challenged the traditional institutions of marriage, work, and the family. In the 1880s, moreover, feminist reform legislation, as Peter Gay notes, "began to dismantle England's time-honored patriarchal system."[19] A series of legislative acts materially improved women's legal status: the Married Women's Property Act of 1882 and the Guardianship of Infants Act in 1886. In France, too, women's right to divorce was reestablished in 1884. Women also challenged the system of higher education, and their efforts to gain admission to university lectures at Oxford and Cambridge were met with strong opposition. The Oxford Union voted overwhelmingly against admitting women to the B.A. degree in 1896, and there were riots at Cambridge in opposition to women's admission. The different political interests of men and women created a severe strain in relations between the sexes. "To many late nineteenth and early twentieth century men," Gilbert and Gubar observe, "women seemed to be agents of an alien world that evoked anger and anguish, while to women in those years men appeared as aggrieved defenders of an indefensible order."[20]

The resistance to feminist initiatives made it seem as if a female takeover were imminent. In fact, however, the fin-de-siècle rhetoric of invasion was out of proportion to the reality. For most of the period, the English suffrage movement was in what Lady Frances Balfour called "the doldrum years." In 1884, suffragists had hopes that the Reform Bill would include a women's amendment; more than 40 percent of the M.P.s elected in 1880 were pledged to support it. But Gladstone opposed the amendment, and carried the Liberal Party with him. After the amendment's defeat, women's suffrage was more or less a dead issue until the beginnings of militancy in 1905. Women were certainly no economic threat either. Overall, women in the workforce earned only 50 percent of what men earned, and only 8 percent of trade union membership was female. And the universities were far from feminized. By 1897, there were only 844 women in all the English universities put together; in England there were only 87 women doctors, in France, 95.

Why then were these few privileged and exceptional women so alarming for men to contemplate? As the political historian Carole Pateman has observed, women have traditionally been perceived as figures of disorder, "potential disrupters of masculine boundary systems of all sorts."[21] Women's social or cultural marginality seems to place them on the borderlines of the symbolic order, both the "frontier between men and chaos," and dangerously part of chaos itself, inhabitants of a mysterious and frightening wild zone outside of patriarchal culture.[22]

But the process of upheaval, the redefinition of gender that took place at the turn of the century, was not limited to women. Gender crisis affected men as well as women, and the fantasies of a pitched battle for sexual supremacy typical of the period often concealed deeper uncertainties and contradictions on both sides. It is important to keep in mind that masculinity is no more natural, transparent, and unproblematic than "femininity." It, too, is a socially constructed role, defined within particular cultural and historical circumstances, and the *fin de siècle* also marked a crisis of identity for men. The nineteenth century had cherished a belief in the separate spheres of femininity and masculinity that amounted almost to religious faith. In revolutionary periods, the fear of social and political equality between the sexes has always generated strenuous counter-efforts to shore up borderlines by establishing scientific proof for the absolute mental and physical differences between men and women. As the historian Thomas Laqueur comments with relation to the French Revolution, "wherever boundaries were threatened arguments for fundamental sexual differences were shoved into the breach."[23] Thus by the *fin de siècle*, a post-Darwinian "sexual science" offered expert testimony on the evolutionary differences between men and women. While women's "nurturant domestic capabilities fitted them for home and hearth," . . . men had evolved aggressive, competitive abilities "that fitted them for public life."[24] The sexual borderline between the masculine and the feminine represented the dangerous vanishing point of sexual difference. As Bram Stoker, the author of *Dracula*, wrote, "the ideal man is entirely or almost entirely masculine and the ideal women is entirely or almost entirely feminine. Each individual must have a preponderance, be it ever so little, of the cells of its own sex, and the attraction of each individual to the other sex depends upon its place on the scale between the highest and lowest grade of sex. The most masculine man draws the most feminine woman, and vice versa; and so down the scale till close to the borderline in the great mass of persons, who, having only developed a few of the qualities of sex, are easily satisfied to mate with anyone."[25]

Yet many men found their part of the equation as difficult to sustain as women did theirs, and the source of as much anxiety. Opportunities to succeed at home and in the Empire were not always abundant; the stresses of maintaining an external mask of confidence and strength led to nervous disorders, such as neurasthenia; suppressing "feminine" feelings of nurturance and affection created problems for many men as well. What was most alarming to the *fin de siècle* was that sexuality and sex roles might no longer be contained within the neat and permanent borderlines of gender categories. Men and women were not as clearly identified and separated as they had been, as *Punch* lamented in April 1895: "A new fear my bosom vexes; / Tomorrow there may be no sexes!" Havelock Ellis confirmed this anxiety when he wrote in *The Psychology of Sex* that although "we may not know exactly what sex is, . . . we do know that it is mutable, with the possibility of one sex being changed into the other sex, that its frontiers are often mutable, and that there are many stages between a complete male and a complete female."[26] Where, men asked themselves, were they placed on the scale of masculinity? Were they dangerously close to the borderline?

Thus while many critics and historians have described this period as a battle *between* the sexes, a period of sexual antagonism that came from male resentment of women's emancipation, I would argue that it was also a battle *within* the sexes. Men, too, faced changes in their lives and sexual identities. In England, there was "a crisis in the 1890s of the male on all levels—economic, political, social, psychological, as producer, as power, as role, as lover."[27] In France, where the feminist movement had been active since the 1890s, "at the advent of the twentieth century, fear of women's sexual and economic liberation or perhaps an imaginary fear—gave rise to renewed antifeminism, expressed as a masculinity crisis . . . The crisis of masculinity marked an awakening consciousness of what it meant to be a man. In the context of developing individualism, men become aware of their sexual difference, their physical and moral specificity."[28] In the United States, Michael Kimmel argues, there was a crisis in masculinity after the Civil War which took three forms: an anti-feminist backlash, a movement for male supremacy, and male feminism; and these modes of response can also be seen in other national settings.[29]

Opposition to the women's movement in an attempt to preserve traditional definitions of sex roles was an obvious reaction. In England and the United States, men organized antisuffrage groups, often with ladies' auxiliaries. Some went much further and blamed rebellious women and female emancipation for the decline and fall of the Western world. In France, anti-feminist literature by such writers as Georges Donen, Emile Zola, Albert Cim, and Maurice Barrès linked what was seen as the insidious power of New Women with social degeneracy.[30] Fin-de-siècle misogyny was most dramatically and vividly apparent in painting. There images of female narcissism, of the femme fatale and the sphinx, of women kissing their mirror images, gazing at themselves in circular baths, or engaging in autoerotic play mutate by the end of the century into savagely "gynecidal" visions of female sexuality. These images of women are part of the pattern Bram Dijkstra has called "idols of perversity."[31] In Ludwig von Hofmann's *The Valley of Innocence* (1897), for example, a huge adolescent girl plays with the naked body of a toylike man. Beside her is a knife and a pile of decapitated male bodies, while a parade of other tiny men wait their turn for the massacre. Among the most famous images of the period are Gustave Klimt's gilded, predatory women. The popularity of exhibits of art from fin-de-siècle Vienna and the revival of Art Nouveau in the last decade suggest the continuing fascination with the figure of the sexually voracious femme fatale, which has entered popular culture as well; in the opening scenes of Rodney Dangerfield's hit film *Back to School* (1986), the pop-eyed hero walks into a lavish party in his own home and surprises his arty, gold-digging wife in the arms of another man. "Excuse me," the interrupted lover haughtily remarks, "Your wife was just showing me her Klimt."

While one response to female power was an exaggerated horror of its castrating potential, another response was the intensified valorization of male power, and expressions of anxiety about waning virility. Teddy Roosevelt was one of many fin-de-siècle politicians who connected his imperialist politics with an image of robust masculinity: "There is no place in the world for nations who have become enervated by the soft and easy life, or who have lost their fibre of vigorous hardness and masculinity."[32] In France, the masculinity crisis "found positive expression in the affirmation of virile values, physical, cultural, and moral. We see the development of sports, the praise of athletic figures, the new stadium gods who displayed their beautiful muscular bodies before women spectators."[33] At the same time, Zola lamented the weakening virility of a feminized France.[34] In England, psychiatrists identified a new kind of male neurotic, the "borderliner." Andrew Wynter's popular medical text, *The Borderlands of Insanity*

(1877), described the potential degeneration of borderline men in "Mazeland," "Dazeland," and "Driftland," whose minds felt the lack of "directing" or "controlling power." Freed from the controls of patriarchy, especially from service in the army, and uncertain of their role, Wynter warned, young men from the middle and upper classes would find their minds "first stiffen from disuse and then rot from the decay of a vitality which is never properly brought into play."[35]

Men in Dazeland and Mazeland might actually welcome the crisis in gender as an escape from their own sexual burdens. Another way of understanding the crisis is to see it as generated from within and reflecting stresses and tensions in the rigid construction of masculine roles. By the 1890s, indeed, the system of patriarchy was under attack not only by women, but also by an avant-garde of male artists, sexual radicals, and intellectuals, who challenged its class structures and roles, its system of inheritance and primogeniture, its compulsory heterosexuality and marriage, and its cultural authority. Others, primarily educators, social reformers, and sexual libertarians, identified themselves as male feminists, seeing the women's movement as an answer to their own problems. The French novelists (scornfully called the *"vaginards"*), such as Villiers de L'Isle Adam in *L'Eve future* (1888) and Jules Dubois in *L'Eve nouvelle* (1896), heralded the new age of women.

But the male rebellion against patriarchy did not necessarily mean a commitment to feminism. While the male avant-garde of the 1880s "were critical of the patriarchal order in which they lived and heralded its end," they often "looked with fear towards the new feminist order."[36] This paradox is at the heart of fin-de-siècle culture. Indeed, strongly anti-patriarchal sentiments could also coexist comfortably with misogyny, homophobia, and racism.

A significant aspect of the construction of masculinity was the institution of "Clubland," the network of men's clubs which served all social classes and provided alternatives and substitutes for domestic life. Clubland reinforced the spatial as well as the social boundaries separating men and women. As the historian Brian Harrison explains, "this was an age of bachelors, or of married men who spent a large part of their lives as if they were bachelors: the London clubs— recruited from a number of ancillary male institutions in the public schools, Oxford and Cambridge colleges and professional institutions—catered amply for their needs."[37] In England, the clubs were primarily extensions of the male communities of the public schools and universities. Peter Gay points out that "leading anti-feminists lived in . . . the privileged enclaves of men's colleges, men's holidays, men's professional brotherhoods, all symbolized and perpetuated in men's clubs, and they found it painful to contemplate their boyish world being invaded by the females whom their favorite institutions had deliberately, so far successfully, excluded."[38]

Clubland operated as a lifetime training ground for men wishing to exclude women. Aggressively and urbanely heterosexual, even rakish, in their discourse, the clubs were the stronghold and headquarters of opposition to women's suffrage and practiced an "intermittent and localised misogyny."[39] A boy accustomed to intense male friendships and anti-feminist assumptions in the atmosphere of the public schools was "fully equipped to play his part in keeping women out" when he reached the university; and "the Oxford college was itself a small club" where the social and intellectual habits of public school could be continued. The London gentleman could spend his entire life moving through "a maze of clubs," athletic, political, and social; and professions from medicine and the law to "the best club of all—the House of Commons," also imitated the structure of Clubland.[40] Finally, the exclusion of women was not restricted to the upper and middle classes. Women were generally not permitted in public houses, and in 1897 only one of the 512 groups in the Working Men's Clubs and Institute Union admitted women as members.[41]

A few male feminists protested against the world of the clubs. In the spring of 1879, Ibsen proposed that women be allowed to vote in the meetings of the Scandinavian Club in Rome, where he was living. In his speech on the proposal, Ibsen derided male fears of women's participation: "Is there anyone in this gathering who dares assert that our ladies are inferior to us in culture, or intelligence, or knowledge, or artistic talent? I don't think many men would dare suggest that. Then what is it men fear? I hear there is a tradition here that women are cunning intriguers, and that therefore we don't want them. Well, I have encountered a good deal of male intrigue in my time . . ."[42] He was voted down.

Literacy and professional women, too, were concerned about their access to the male club world. During the 1880s, a number of women's professional clubs were formed, including the feminist Pioneer Club, which mixed the social classes and sponsored lectures on literature and politics. The Club became sufficiently controversial to attract the

Punch parodists; in November 1894, *Punch* cleverly adapted Whitman's "Pioneers! O Pioneers!" to satirize "literary dames" chanting:

> We primeval fetters loosing,
> We our husbands taming, vexing we and worrying Mrs. GRUNDY
> We our own lives freely living, we as bachelor-girls residing,
> Pioneers! O pioneers![43]

Some women sought admission to the male clubs. In her essay "Women and Club Life," the poet Amy Levy observed that "not long ago, indeed, a motion was brought forward for the admission of women to the Savile Club. Its rejection must be a matter of regret to all women engaged in literature and education; but the fact that such a motion was brought forward and considered is of itself significant."[44] She was optimistic that women would be admitted before very long. A full century later, however, women were still fighting in the courts for admission to the male sanctuaries of Clubland, from the Athenaeum in London to the Century Club in New York, the Bohemian Grove in Washington, the Ethan Allen Club in Vermont, and the Ivy Club at Princeton University. In 1983, Lewis Lapham, the editor of *Harper's*, insisted on the need to maintain distinct and permanent boundaries between the genders, in this case by excluding women from the Century Club: "The clarity of gender makes possible the human dialectic. Let the lines of balanced tension go slack and the structure dissolves into the ooze of androgyny and narcissism."[45]

But Clubland could not really separate the messy "ooze of androgyny" from the "clarity of gender." Fin-de-siècle Clubland existed on the fragile borderline that separated male bonding from homosexuality and that distinguished manly misogyny from digusting homoeroticism. "The fears of clubland," Peter Gay observed, ". . . were fears not of being castrated but of being compelled to grow up, of having to abandon persistent adolescent ties with their distinctly, though largely unconscious, homoerotic pleasures."[46] In Caryl Churchill's contemporary play *Cloud 9*, set in Africa in 1880, Clive tells his friend Harry, "There is something dark about women that threatens what is best in us. Between men the light burns brightly." But when Harry responds by embracing him, Clive is disgusted. "The most revolting perversion. Rome fell, Harry, and this sin can destroy an empire." The light that burned brightly between men could also be the sin that destroys an empire. In her important book *Between Men: English Literature and Male Homosocial Desire* (1985), Eve Sedgwick pointed to the double bind of masculine identity that structures the spectrum of relationships between men. "For a man to be a man's man," Sedgwick noted, "is separated only by an invisible, carefully blurred, always-already-crossed line from being 'interested in men.' "[47]

Following the pioneering work of Michel Foucault, many historians of sexuality now argue that male homosexuality and the male homosexual role are "inventions" of the late nineteenth century. The concept of homosexuality began to take shape in the 1880s in the work of John Addington Symonds and Richard von Krafft-Ebing and in the research of Victorian sexologists such as Havelock Ellis. As Foucault writes in *The History of Sexuality*, "the nineteenth-century homosexual became a personage, a past, a case history, and a childhood, in addition to being a type of life, a life form, and a morphology, with an indiscreet anatomy, and possibly a mysterious physiology. Nothing that went into his total composition was unaffected by his sexuality."[48] Homosexuality became a medical problem, a pathology, even a disease; and medical and scientific speculations about homosexuality attempted to establish clear borderlines and labels, to draw "an impassable border between acceptable and abhorrent behaviour."[49]

The effort to create boundaries around male homosexuality was also carried out in the legal sphere. The burgeoning homosexual subculture that had begun to develop in England in the 1870s and early 1880s was both identified and outlawed by the Labouchère Amendment to the Criminal Law Amendment Act of 1885, which made all male homosexual acts, private or public, illegal: "Any male person who, in public or private, commits, or is a party to, the commission of, or procures or attempts to procure the commission by any male person of any act of gross indecency with another male person, shall be guilty of a misdemeanour, and being convicted thereof shall be liable at the discretion of the court to be imprisoned for any term not exceeding two years, with or without hard labour." This was the law under which Oscar Wilde would be convicted and sentenced to two years of hard labor at Reading Gaol.

Nevertheless, fin-de-siècle efforts to define and control homosexuality, and to bound it off from masculinity in general, were not successful, and may have had the effect of strengthening homosexual bonds. As Jeffrey Weeks explained, "it seems likely that new forms of legal regulation, whatever their vagaries in application, had the effect of bringing home to many the fact of their difference and thus creating a new community of knowledge, if not of life and feeling, amongst many men with homosexual leanings."[50] Foucault maintained that this paradoxical effect is inevitable because the official definition, marginalization, and control of a particular group such as homosexuals always creates a "reverse discourse," an identity around which a sub-culture might begin to form and to protest. Thus, once homosexuality had been singled out in the late nineteenth century, "it begins to speak on its own behalf, to forge its own identity and culture, often in the self-same terms by which it had been produced and marginalised, and eventually to challenge the very power structure which had pro-duced and marginalised it."[51] The record of this culture emerges in the "decadent" art and literature of the *fin de siècle*.

While this book is largely a history of sexual change in the late nineteenth century, it is thus also a study of late-nineteenth-century literature. The two go together; for, as Nancy Armstrong observes, "the history of the novel cannot be understood apart from the history of sexuality,"[52] and the history of sexuality is also constructed in the pages of fiction. Turn-of-the-century characters have become part of our cultural mythology. From the moments of their creation, Sherlock Holmes, Jekyll and Hyde, Dracula, Dorian Gray, the Time Traveller, and Mr. Kurtz leapt out of the pages of their books into popular culture. We know them whether or not we have read the books in which they first appeared. Like Dracula, they are the undead of the *fin de siècle*, legendary creations who never stay at rest and whose myths have been rewritten and revisioned in our own time.

Moreover, one of the most dramatic changes at the *fin de siècle* was the transformation of the publishing world and the way literary myths were disseminated to readers. In his history of the profession of au-thorship in the nineteenth century, Nigel Cross pointed out that between 1880 and 1895 the publishing world saw such changes as the introduction of syndication, the founding of the Society of Authors [1884], the rise of the literary agent, and the proliferation of magazines and the popular press.[53] Another major change was the disappearance of the Victorian three-volume novel, which had been designed for family readership and had been a staple of the Victorian home. Three-volume novels were priced artificially high—the standard price was thirty-one shillings sixpence, or about forty dollars in contemporary terms—so that most middle-class readers could not afford to buy them. The triple decker was maintained by "a cartel of publishers and circulating libraries who depended on its high price for their stable profit margins."[54] A large circulating library such as Mudies or Smiths could buy up virtually the entire run of a novel, thus guaranteeing the publisher and the author an income. Three-volume novels were also handy to distribute. A poor subscriber could pay a fee entitling him or her to take out only one volume at a time; in a family, father could begin to read volume one, and pass the volumes around the family through wife and daughters as he finished.

Since they were designed for family circulation, Victorian novels were obliged to be respectable and chaste, and several male English novelists in the 1880s protested against the three-volume form as an aesthetic straitjacket. In a controversial essay of 1885 called "Literature at Nurse," George Moore protested against the censorship, decorum, and restraint on the novelist's art imposed by the dictatorship of the libraries and family readership. But the death of the three-decker was primarily economic and followed a decision by the lending libraries themselves in 1894. From 193 triple-decker novels published in 1884, the number dropped to merely four by 1897. Novelists rejoiced at the demise of a genre that had constrained and inhibited them. "It is fine to see how the old three-volume tradition is being broken through," wrote George Gissing in 1885; "one volume is becoming commonest of all. It is the new school, due to continental influence. Thackeray and Dickens wrote at enormous length . . . their plan is to tell everything and leave nothing to be divined. Far more artistic, I think, is the latter method of merely suggesting; of dealing with episodes, instead of writing biographies."[55]

Just as they were designed for family reading and public circulation, the volumes in their stout bindings were themselves physically associated with the Victorian nuclear family: father, mother, and child. But the slim, exquisitely bound novels of the *fin de siècle*, with their gilded covers and Beardsley designs, suggested a very different image of character and sexuality: the celibate, the bachelor, the "odd woman," the dandy, and the aesthete. New sexual and fictional combinations characterized the narrative milieu of the 1880s, as Rhoda Broughton noted in eyeing "the brand-new books . . . in threes, in twos, in ones."[56] Unsuitable for family consumption, these books were more likely to be read alone and perhaps even under the covers. Sex and the single book became the order of the day.

Another dramatic change in the English novel was the striking, although temporary, eclipse of women writers. It was a fact of mid-

Victorian literary life that women novelists were both talented and successful. Novels, wrote the critic W. R. Greg, were "almost as indispensible a portion of the food of English life as beef or beer; and no producers are superior to women in this line either as to delicate handling or abundant fertility."[57] But after 1880, women novelists, while ever more numerous in the marketplace, entered a period of critical decline. After George Eliot's death in 1880, male professional jealousies erupted in critical abuse of women's emasculating effect on the English novel. While Havelock Ellis could still praise Hardy in 1883 by comparing him to Eliot, since, as Ellis observed, "it seems now to stand beyond question that the most serious work in English fiction . . . has been done by women," a decade later such comparisons were odious.[58] By the 1890s, women novelists were viewed as shriveled prudes whose influence hindered a virile masculine genre. In her study of feminism and fiction at the turn of the century, Patricia Stubbs lamented that "at the very moment when literature was beginning to break free from the moral stranglehold of Victorian sexual ideology, the novel was dominated for the first time and quite accidentally by male writers."[59]

One of the questions I ask in this book is whether this domination was indeed accidental. Could it have been that after a century in which English women had shaped the novel, there was a twenty-year period in which no talented women appeared? Or was the male domination of the novel after 1880 an aspect of the crisis in masculinity that intensified sexual struggle? The answers begin with the funeral of George Eliot in 1880 and with the reaction by both women and men against female dominance and the Victorian novel. The scriptures of sexual difference had been part of the infrastructure of Victorian fiction, which had "produced a great tradition of narrative controlled by difference, by the discrete separation of subject and object, public and private, active and passive—categories intimately linked to the radical dualism of masculine and feminine."[60]

George Eliot's novels were the finest example of this narrative form. But when sexual certainties broke down, fictional certainties changed as well. The disappearance of the three-decker suggested a movement away from subjects, themes, and forms associated with femininity and maternity. In describing a popular Victorian woman novelist, for example, Henry James saw her books as "a little family, in sets of triplets."[61] The three-part structure dictated a vision of human experience as linear, progressive, causal, and tripartite, ending in marriage or death. When there were no longer three volumes to fill, writers could abandon the temporal structures of beginning, middle, and end, and the procreative and genealogical fables of inheritance, marriage, and death that had been traditionally associated with women writers and Victorian realism. Instead, fin-de-siècle narrative questioned beliefs in endings and closures, as well as in marriage and inheritance. As endings opened up, the genre of the fantastic also introduced the theme of split personality at the same time that psychoanalysis was beginning to question the stable and linear Victorian ego. Thus many of the stories of the *fin de siècle* are also case histories which describe deviance, rebellion, and the abnormal. Like Freud's accounts of hysterical patients, they are fragmented, out of chronological sequence, contradictory, and incoherent. Rather than being told by the omniscient narrator of Victorian realism, they are told by multiple narrators, or by characters who reveal their own feelings towards the hero or heroine in the course of telling the tale.

Many of the correspondences between the end of the last century and the end of our own will already have become apparent. The 1980s and 1990s also compulsively tell and retell the stories of the 1880s and 1890s, in contemporary versions of Victorian novels, in film and TV adaptations, in ballets and musicals, and in all the myriad forms of popular culture from Count Chockula breakfast cereal to men's clothes on the label Jekyll and Hyde. Yet in retelling these stories we transmit our own narratives, construct our own case histories, and shape our own futures. In the chapters to follow, I deal with myths, texts, and images rather than issues: the single woman, the New Woman, the battle between literary kings and queens, sexual surgery and sexual epidemics, decadence and the apocalypse. The parallels between the sexual anarchy of the *fin de siècle* and the gender crises of our time are tempting, and it is tempting, too, to fall into despair as we contemplate the erosion of hard-won rights and the perpetuation of hard-fought wrongs in an atmosphere of moral panic. Yet if we can learn something from the fears and myths of the past, it is that they are so often exaggerated and unreal, that what looks like sexual anarchy in the context of *fin-de-siècle* anxieties may be the embryonic stirrings of a new order.

T W O

Odd Women

Sexual anarchy began with the odd woman. The odd woman—the woman who could not marry—undermined the comfortable binary system of Victorian sexuality and gender roles. Starting with the English census of 1861, a steadily increasing surplus of unmarried women over men had created a sense of national alarm. In a widely read essay in the *Westminster Review* called "Why Are Women Redundant?" the journalist William R. Greg called attention to the "enormous and increasing number of single women in the nation, a number quite disproportionate and quite abnormal; a number which positively and relatively is indicative of an unwholesome social state."[1] The odd woman was the one left over, the uneven number, the spinster who could not find a husband to pair off with her. The term the *fin de siècle* invented for her gives the sense of both her nonconformity and her commodification. Writing to a friend about his novel *The Odd Women* (1891), George Gissing explained, "the title means 'Les Femmes Superflues'—the women who are *odd* in the sense that they do not make a match; as we say 'an odd glove.' "[2]

Odd women were a social problem. Thousands had to earn their own living, rivaling men for employment, Greg pointed out, instead of "spending and husbanding the earnings of men." Deprived of the "natural duties and labours of wives and mothers," they had to "carve out artificial and painfully-sought occupations for themselves;" and overall, instead of fulfilling women's destiny by "completing, sweetening, and embellishing the existence of others," they were compelled to "lead an independent and incomplete existence of their own."

Greg's solution to the problem was government-sponsored emigration of single women to the colonies, where English women were a scarce commodity, and where they might therefore find husbands. He opposed the expansion of women's employment opportunities, however, because it might "surround single life . . . with such a pleasant, ornamented, comfortable path" that marriage would be perceived as only one option among many and encourage an unnatural celibacy.

Fin-de-siècle feminists interpreted the statistics of female oddness very differently. They used the surplus of unmarried women to prove that women's traditional domestic roles were outmoded and that social policies which denied them higher education, alternative roles, professional opportunities, and votes were self-defeating and cruel. If women could no longer expect to be supported by husbands, they would have to be educated and trained to support themselves. In an essay called "How to Provide for Superfluous Women" (1869), Jessie Boucherett argued that the best plan was to allow unmarried women "to engage freely in all occupations suited to their strength . . . thus converting them into useful members of society."[3] Feminist reform organizations such as the Society for Promoting the Employment of Women, founded in 1859, tried to find new occupational fields for untrained middle-class women—those hardest hit by the demographic change, since their only traditional employments, governessing and teaching, had become professionalized and overcrowded. The Female Employment Society attempted to make office and clerical work, as well as some manual jobs, such as printing, telegraphy, and hairdressing, respectable for middle-class women. Emily Davies and others led the campaign to open the university examinations to women, while Elizabeth Garrett, Sophia Jex-Blake, and Elizabeth Blackwell organized the fight for women's admission to medical schools.

While feminist reformers concerned themselves primarily with middle-class women, they were also aware of the different problems facing working-class women. An investigator of the Select Commission on the Shop Hours Regulation Bill, for example, reported in 1886 that "the majority of shop assistants look upon marriage as their one hope of release, and would, as one girl expressed it, 'marry anybody to get out of the drapery business.' "[4] Feminist reformers' concern for working women manifested itself most dramatically in sympathy for the prostitute who might have been driven to the streets because she had no alternative kind of work.

Why this sudden attention to the single woman? The unmarried woman was obviously not a new phenomenon, and anxieties about a surplus of single women had emerged in England many times before, especially after wars and in other periods of gender crisis. At the end of the seventeenth century, for example, women concerned about a "male shortage" had petitioned Parliament for a tax on all men who remained single after the age of twenty-one. What, then, made the odd women of the *fin de siècle* so conspicuous, troubling, and dramatic?

The answer lies in the period's construction of unmarried women as a new political and sexual group, not just an absence or cipher in the social body, but a constituency with potential opportunities, powers, and rights. First of all, unmarried women, or *femes soles*, were targeted as the initial beneficiaries of the women's suffrage movement. While married women seemed to be excluded from enfranchisement by the common law doctrine of coverture, adult single women, it could be argued, needed to vote since they were legally unrepresented. Furthermore, the vote "became both the symbol of the free, sexually autonomous woman and the means by which the goals of a feminist sexual culture were to be attained."[5] For Josephine Butler and other leaders of the women's movement, the vote was the best way to end prostitution, facilitate divorce, and raise public morals.

A second factor in the attention devoted to odd women derived from new definitions of sexuality. Moving away from a mid-Victorian notion of female "passionlessness," or sexual anaesthesia, advanced late-nineteenth-century thinkers acknowledged women's capacity for sexual pleasure and discussed the psychological and biological harmfulness of celibacy. One of the significant factors in this change was the recognition of female sexual desire, both as a physical function and as a health requirement. Physicians promoted the idea that women needed sexual intercourse just as men did, and that "the evil results of abstinence are especially noticeable in women."[6] In 1882, for example, Dr. Charles Taylor, an American obstetrician, warned that unmarried women needed to protect their health by finding other outlets for their "unemployed functions," or suffer the consequences of "disturbance" and "weakness."[7]

Although Taylor's recommendations for his sexually unemployed women involved exercise and reading rather than, say, masturbation, lesbianism, or premarital sex, this view of the dangers of celibacy was difficult for many Victorian women to accept. Educated to believe that women's chief superiority to man lay in her greater spirituality and passionlessness, even advanced feminist thinkers of the *fin de siècle* found it difficult to reconcile their vision of a new social order with an acceptance or endorsement of female sexuality. The social purity campaigns of the 1880s, such as the twenty-year effort to repeal the Contagious Diseases Acts, which finally succeeded in 1886, the campaign for incest legislation that began in 1885, and the revelations of child prostitution in Stead's "The Maiden Tribute of Modern Babylon" (1885) had left women traumatized by their discoveries of abusive male sexuality. Repealers "tended to view sex not merely as male-defined, but as *male*, while women were promoted as the agents regulating immorality—powerful but asexual guardians of the nation's morals."[8]

By the turn of the century, there were feminists and suffragists who saw celibacy as a "silent strike" against oppressive relations with men. The suffragette leader Christabel Pankhurst saw female celibacy as a political response to men's corrupt sexual behaviors and widespread venereal infections. "There can be no mating between the spiritually developed women of this new day and men who in thought and conduct with regard to sex matters are their inferiors," she wrote.[9] Some feminists argued that an "unhusbanded class of women" was necessary for "the task of raising the fair sex out of its subjection."[10] They maintained that celibacy was not harmful to women, but indeed healthful, and that "woman is physically complete" without sex: "Though she is a necessity to man, he is not necessary to her."[11] Writers such as Frances Swiney maintained that sexual intercourse was inherently an abusive and dangerous act and that sperm was a virulent poison composed of alcohol, nicotine, and venereal germs. Swiney further believed that men were a "defective variation" of the female gene and that intercourse should take place only for purposes of reproduction at widely-spaced intervals of two or three years.[12]

More moderate feminists endorsed celibacy on ideological, medical, or spiritual grounds, or advocated it as a temporary political strategy. Beatrice Webb wrote in her diary that it might be needful for a generation of women to sacrifice their sexuality to a cause, for women "with strong natures to remain celibate; so that the special force of womanhood—motherly feeling—may be forced into public work."[13] For her cousin Margaret Harkness, who came to London alone to earn her living as a journalist at the age of twenty-three, a single life allowed both social usefulness and independence. "So few women have enough character to live an unmarried life," she wrote to a friend, "or not sink into a nobody, or still worse into a general nuisance. I think an unmarried woman living a true life is far nobler than a married woman."[14]

By the 1880s it was possible for middle-class single women like Webb and Harkness to work, to find housing, and to find a community of friends.[15] Between marriage and celibacy, however, there were few sexual alternatives for respectable women. Heterosexual affairs were the realm of the prostitute; lesbianism was not recognized in public or medical discourse. By 1884, only four cases of lesbian homosexuality had been reported in European and American medical literature, and all were transvestites. The Labouchère Amendment of 1885 did not mention lesbianism, and J. A. Symonds devoted only two pages of his *Problem in Greek Ethics* to it. Nevertheless, close long-term attachments between women, whether the "romantic friendship" or the "Boston marriage," were both acknowledged and accepted. And although lesbianism had relatively little official place in medical discourse, it was a topic in literature and art, obviously well understood by a general audience. In Eliza Lynn Linton's *The Rebel of the Family* (1880), for example, Bell Blount, the "Lady President for the West Hill Society for Women's Rights," lives with another woman, her "good little wife," kisses the innocent heroine with "strange warmth," and preaches on "the best and truest love that the world can give— the love between women without the degrading and disturbing influence of man." By the mid-1880s, sexologists began to pay more attention to the phenomenon of lesbianism, although they saw it as morbid and masculine. Krafft-Ebing included lesbianism among the sexual perversions he discussed in *Psychopathia Sexualis* (1889), placing homosexual women along a scale from "invisible" to highly masculinized. He maintained that "Uranism may nearly always be suspected in females wearing their hair short, or who dress in the fashion of men, or pursue the sports and pastimes of their male acquaintances; also in opera singers and actresses who appear in male attire on the stage by preference." Lesbianism was also seen as linked with feminism. In his essay on homogenic love, Edward Carpenter observed "that the movement among women towards their own liberation and emancipation, which is taking place all over the civilised world, has been accompanied by a marked development of the homogenic passion among the female sex."[16]

The popular image of the odd woman conflated elements of the lesbian, the angular spinster, and the hysterical feminist. The mannish woman orator was an especially popular satiric figure in popular novels:

"It would not be obvious to a stranger," wrote Rhoda Broughton in *Dear Faustina* (1897), "that it is not a slender man who is preparing to address the little group, so austerely masculine is the just-grey-touched thick short hair parted on side, the coat, the tie, the waistcoat." To claim the pulpit or the podium was in itself such a transgression of "womanly" modesty that the most ladylike feminist campaigners seemed decidedly out of place and odd. "There is something repugnant to the ordinary Englishman in the idea of a woman mounting a platform and facing the noisy, gaping, vulgar crowd of an election meeting," wrote Mary Jeune in the 1890s.[17] The tireless anti-feminist campaigner and novelist Eliza Lynn Linton scornfully described the various speakers at a women's emancipation meeting in *The Rebel of the Family*: the "lady from America" who "did her business in a workmanlike manner, with no more agitation, shyness or embarrassment than if she had been a man"; the well-dressed and polished "specimen of a female public orator" whose "case-hardened self-sufficiency was as ugly as a physical deformity"; and the mannish woman with "close-cropped hair, a Tyrolese hat . . . a waistcoat and a short jacket."

Linton also coined the phrase "shrieking sisterhood" to describe feminist activities and speakers. "One of our quarrels with the Advanced Women of our generation," she wrote, "is the hysterical parade they make about their wants and their intentions . . . for every hysterical advocate 'the cause' loses a rational adherent and gains a disgusted opponent."[18] As late as 1907, the term was still in wide use, as one suffragist lamented: "It stares at us from letters to the newspapers almost daily."[19] It was an easier explanation to see women's desire for emancipation as a form of unbalance in the reproductive system and mind than to take it seriously; and the argument was doubly useful because it also showed how dangerous to the public would be "the incorporation of these instabilities into the structures of political life."[20] In opposing the women's suffrage bill in 1871, a Tory parliamentarian argued that if women had the vote, "our legislation would develop hysterical and spasmodic qualities."[21]

With such a flourishing literature, visual tradition, and medical discourse about female oddness, one might well ask about the odd man. "What has become of the marrying man?" one essayist asked in 1888. "Is he not becoming as extinct as the dodo? Will not future generations of geologists gloat over the infrequent discovery of his precious bones in rare rocks? Already he is hard to find and coy to catch."[22] Many Victorian men married late or never, lived a bachelor existence, and spent their adult lives with only male friendships. The odd man, however, was not seen as a problem. His life could be one of dignity and honor, or, while he was young, of adventure and challenge. While Sarah Grand satirized anti-feminist men as the "bawling brotherhood," misogyny seemed much more natural than feminism.[23] And masculine oddness, of course, did not entail celibacy. "How many men *have you known* who have reached the age of 30, and been absolutely celibate? What in England among the middle classes should you say was the proportion of celibate men?" wrote Olive Schreiner to Karl Pearson in 1886.[24] There is no record of Pearson's reply, but we may guess its contents.

Odd men also explained that they were unwilling to link themselves with emancipated women who might have needs and ambitions of their own. Beatrice Webb recorded in her diary a conversation she had about marriage with Alfred Marshall, a Cambridge professor who was "the single most effective enemy of degrees for women."[25] According to Webb, he held that "woman was a subordinate being, and that, if she ceased to be subordinate, there would be no object for a man to marry. That marriage was a sacrifice of masculine freedom, and would only be tolerated by male creatures so long as it meant the devotion, body and soul, of the female to the male. . . . Contrast was the essence of the matrimonial relation: feminine weakness contrasted with masculine strength: masculine egotism with feminine self-devotion. 'If you compete with us we shan't marry you,' he summed up with a laugh."[26]

Moreover, if men did not marry, Grant Allen explained, it was not because they were odd but because they had so many more interesting things to do: "In America, the young man has gone West. In England, he is in the army, in the navy, in the Indian Civil Service, in the Cape Mounted Rifles. He is sheep-farming in New Zealand, ranching in Colorado, growing tea in Assam, planting coffee in Ceylon; he is a cowboy in Montana, or a wheat-farmer in Manitoba, or a diamond-digger at Kimberley, or a merchant at Melbourne; in short, he is everywhere and anywhere, except where he ought to be, making love to the pretty girls in England. For, being a man, I, of course, take it for granted that the first business of a girl is to be pretty."[27]

If the marrying man was becoming "extinct as the dodo," a bachelor explained in an essay in *Temple Bar* called "Why Men Do Not Marry," in 1888, it was not because he was odd. "I am thirty-one years of age," he wrote. "I am a dancing and dining man; I am not a slave to a club; I am no misogynist; I am moderately well-to-do in my profession and could marry if I chose. But, on the whole, I prefer to remain single. Why?" It was because he was too comfortable living the single life, too reluctant to lower his standard of living for the sake of female companionship. "I consider the domestic dinner gruesome," the bachelor confessed. "I prefer to keep a horse; I prefer a comfortable annual trip to the Continent, or to America; I prefer pictures and china, shilling cigars and first-rate hock."[28]

It's an appealing picture, and one can well imagine that if odd women were allowed more business than being pretty, they too might have preferred travel, dining at the club, and comfortable surroundings to preparing the domestic dinner. Indeed, in a poem called "A Ballad of Religion and Marriage," the novelist Amy Levy predicted a future in which the concept of universal marriage and domestic drudgery would decline along with religious faith:

> Monogamous, still at our post,
>   Recently we undergo
> Domestic round of boiled and roast,
>   Yet deem the whole proceeding slow,
>
> Daily the secret murmurs grow;
>   We are no more content to plod
> Along the beaten paths—and so
>   Marriage must go the way of God.
>
> Grant, in a million years at most,
>   Folk shall be neither pairs nor odd—
> Alas! We shan't be there to boast
>   "Marriage has gone the way of God!"[29]

In addition to Levy, other odd women writers described the lives of single women in single rooms. Isabella O. Ford's *On the Threshold* (1895), Ella Hepworth Dixon's *The Story of a Modern Woman* (1894), Annie Holdsworth's *Joanna Trail, Spinster* (1894), and Netta Syrett's *Nobody's Fault* (1896) envisioned possibilities for women outside of marriage. But while feminist novelists wrote about odd women, it is a significant paradox that "the literary beneficiaries of nineteenth-century feminism were men rather than women."[30] The answer may be in both the internal and external pressure for this literature to be representative, to speak for Woman. Reviewers of the novels insisted on seeing them as the products of a collective consciousness. As W. T. Stead put it, "The Modern Woman novel is not merely a novel written by a woman, or a novel written about women, but it is a novel written by a woman about women from the standpoint of Woman."[31]

The connection between oddness and oratory and the subtext of lesbianism shape two of the most interesting novels men wrote about the nineteenth-century women's movement, Henry James's *The Bostonians* (1886) and Gissing's *The Odd Women* (1891). Both novels deal with the questions of feminist celibacy, "womanliness," and sexual repression, but also with more submerged male agendas about competition with women for power and speech.

In writing *The Bostonians*, James chose a topic he felt was "very national, very typical": "I wished to write a very *American* tale," he noted in 1883, "a tale very characteristic of our social conditions, and I asked myself what was the most salient and peculiar point in our social life. The answer was: the situation of women, the decline of the sentiment of sex, the agitation on their behalf."[32] He also chose to depict a Boston marriage, "one of those friendships between women which are so common in New England." When he had completed it, James though it "the best fiction I have ever written," yet it also proved his most disappointing novel, one from which he had "expected so much and derived so little."[33] A lengthy review in the *Women's Journal* of 1886 called it nothing but a caricature of the suffrage movement, and his own brother William charged him with ridiculing Elizabeth Peabody as the suffragist Miss Birdseye, whose blurred features, "dim little smile," and many-pocketed loose dress bespeak her status as a "confused, entangled, inconsequent, discursive old woman," a monitory image of what befalls women who take up public speech. James himself came to feel that he had not realized the potential of his American tale. In a letter to William he said he regretted having displeased some of his readers with generalizations about the character of Boston and joked that he might have "to write another. 'The Other Bostonians.' "[34]

The idea of "the other Bostonians," a kind of ghost novel or double within James's text, is fascinating, especially since the novel itself suggests so many possible readings and endings. In a plot that critics have described as a "satiric replay of the Civil War on the battlefields of sex," James sets up an erotic triangle of competition between a Boston feminist, Olive Chancellor, and a Southern conservative, Basil Ransom, for the love of Verena Tarrant, a young woman orator. Alike in their rigidity, Basil and Olive have very different outlets and ideologies. While both see their age as decadent and demoralized, they have comically opposite agendas for its repair. Olive looks to "the influx of the great feminine element" to shape up her society, while Basil laments the degree to which it is already "womanized," and lacking "masculine tone." Basil is the "stiffest of conservatives," who looks like "a column of figures," aspires to write for the *Rational Review,* and considers women "have no business to be reasonable"; Olive preaches a kind of romantic feminism based on oppression and suffering: "The unhappiness of women! The voice of their silent suffering was always in her ears, the ocean of tears that they had shed from the beginning of time seemed to pour through her own eyes. Ages of oppression had rolled over them; uncounted millions had lived only to be tortured, to be crucified. They were her sisters, they were her own, and the day of their delivery had dawned." Olive believes that women must redeem the age and that men must step back; Basil believes that women "should not think too much, not feel any responsibility for the government of the world."

Depending on their own alignments, critics have seen Basil either as a rescuing prince or as a cruel misogynist and Olive as either a noble figure or a "latent lesbian with a deep-seated sexual neurosis."[35] James describes Olive in the standard terms used for the odd and militant spinster; she has "absolutely no figure," is unable to laugh, and seems horrified by sex. To Basil, she "was so essentially a celibate that he found himself thinking of her as old," although in fact they are about the same age. Olive's feminism is related to her class status in a way that James presents as rarefied and unnatural. The celibacy of the Back Bay heiress seems to symbolize the sterility of an old Yankee aristocracy no longer viable in the post-war environment. Olive and her sister feminists lament their lack of success with shopgirls, who are stubbornly romantic about their suitors, and always "cared far more about Charlie than about the ballot." Olive's longing for a "friend of her own sex with whom she might have a union of souls" seems equally arid and unreal.

Moreover, her feminism is tied up with her ecstatic and neurotic longing for martyrdom: "the most secret, the most sacred hope of her nature was that she might some day . . . be a martyr and die for something." Like other nineteenth-century women intellectuals, such as Florence Nightingale and Margaret Fuller, Olive longs to become the feminist messiah, the woman whose suffering will redeem her sex.

The language James uses to describe her feelings suggests Olive's envy of the men who had had the chance to fight in the Civil War: "It seemed to her at times that she had been born to lead a crusade." Joan of Arc is her symbol of feminist militant martyrdom and ardor; and to her smitten gaze, Verena looks "as if, like Joan, she might have had visits from the saints." As James notes, her plan is to supply Verena's eloquence with "facts and figures," so that she will be "armed at all points, like Joan of Arc (this analogy had lodged itself in Olive's imagination)." Joan of Arc was indeed a significant imaginative figure for Victorian feminists and especially for single women. "That kind is not to be possessed by one man; she belongs to a cause," the novelist Florence Converse wrote of Joan of Arc in *Diana Victrix* (1897). Vernon Lee's lover, Kit Anstruther-Thompson, was painted by John Singer Sargent as a modern Joan "wearing her cloak like a breastplate."[36] During the suffrage campaign, Joan of Arc was used as an archetypal figure of holy and righteous militance by women attempting to "reinhabit the empty body of female allegory, to reclaim its meanings in behalf of the female sex."[37] Beatified on April 16, 1909, St. Joan represented the chastity, courage, and persecution of female militancy. She was also a border case—a figure who defied gender categories, who both transcended and represented femininity. In France in the 1880s and 1890s, she was claiming a cult and, in England and the United States, had become as much the "patron saint of a sex" as of a country.[38]

In Olive's mind, the female crusader, like St. Joan, must be a virgin as well as a martyr; celibacy is the price she must pay for leadership. "Priests . . . never married, and what you and I dream of doing," she tells Verena, "demands of us a kind of priesthood." Verena must give up sexuality and love: "Thou shalt renounce, refrain, abstain!" Yet in James's view, for Olive herself, celibacy, renunciation, and abstinence have led to a kind of sterility. As much as she longs to speak, she is "awkward and embarrassed and dry," while the flirtatious Verena overflows with words.

Olive and Basil seem to be battling for Verena's body, but in another sense they are battling for her voice. Basil sees the freedom of emancipated female speech as particularly subversive. He finds "the age too talkative," "querulous, hysterical," "chattering" and feminized. He wants women to be "private and passive." If he marries Verena, he thinks to himself, "he should know a way to strike her dumb." He intends Verena to turn her "ranting" in public into charming conversation at the dinner table; and significantly when he appears to carry her off before her great speech at the Boston Music Hall, she is struck dumb by his presence and scarcely needs to be muffled in the hood of her velvet cloak as he takes her away. Much of Basil's determination to capture and silence Verena comes from his discomfort with her success at a time when he is struggling to get his writing published. Significantly, as Josephine Hendin points out, after a long love scene in Central Park in which he reduces Verena to silence, "Basil has his first success at publication."[39] Female chattiness must be transformed into submissive sexuality if men are to hold the field.

There is a hint at the end of the novel, however, that Olive, having loved, lost, and suffered, has also overcome silence. When Verena leaves with Basil, Olive must take her place on the platform. Her moment of speech is offered up as martyrdom, presenting herself to the disappointed audience to be "hissed and hooted and insulted," "trampled to death and torn to pieces." But in fact, when she mounts the platform, like "some feminine firebrand of Paris revolutions," "the hush was respectful." Olive can now speak for the movement; she can realize her long-stifled personal longing for eloquence. In losing Verena, Olive gains her own voice and fulfills her destiny.

George Gissing's attitudes towards Victorian feminism were very mixed, and one critic called him "a woman-worshipping misogynist with an interest in female emancipation."[40] His attraction to feminism was primarily one of self-interest. "My demand for female 'equality,' " he wrote to his friend Edouard Bertz, "simply means that I am convinced there will be no social peace until women are intellectually trained much as men are. More than half the misery of life is due to the ignorance and childishness of women . . . I am driven frantic by the crass imbecility of the typical woman. That type must disappear, or at all events become altogether subordinate." Furthermore, Gissing identified with "oddness," difference, and alienation as social characteristics. He viewed himself as an outsider—a "born exile," as his biographer Gillian Tindall puts it—doomed by his class, his sexuality, and his art. Thus he was sympathetic towards the plight of marginal women.

On the other hand, he was always profoundly skeptical about the possibility of fulfilling permanent relationships between men and women. In his personal life, the conflict between his impossibly romantic ideals of women and a strong self-destructive impulse led him to make disastrous emotional and marital commitments. His first wife was a young prostitute he had attempted to reform, even stealing money (and going to prison) when he was eighteen to help her; his second was an alcoholic who bore him two sons, but finally had to be institutionalized. Gissing's attitudes towards feminists were colored by his prejudices about feminine attractiveness and "normality." In October 1888, during a trip to Paris, he went to hear the feminist-anarchist Louise Michel speak on "Le rôle des femmes dans l'humanité." While Gissing was struck by her ideas and by the vision of free womanhood, he also found her personally unattractive—plain, badly dressed, coarse, and "unwomanly."

In *The Odd Women*, Gissing had the brilliant idea of revising James's sexual triangle to show what might happen when the independent feminist herself is courted by a sexually attractive man; it's as if Basil Ransom were to try to seduce Olive rather than Verena. Like Olive Chancellor, Rhoda Nunn, the explicitly named heroine of Gissing's novel, is a self-declared odd woman: "So many *odd* women—no making a pair with them," Rhoda declares. "The pessimists call them useless, lost, futile lives. I, naturally, being one of them, take another view." She has taken vows of chastity and service, and she compares herself and her choice of celibacy in the women's movement to the Christian saints: "There will have to be a widespread revolt against sexual instinct. Christianity couldn't spread over the world without the help of the ascetic ideal, and this great movement for women's emancipation must also have its ascetics."

At the beginning of the novel, Rhoda's position is an uncompromisingly radical one. She fiercely opposes marriage as an institution and is hostile towards men, whom she regards as untrustworthy and dishonorable. What silences women, she argues, is not sexual frustration, but rather the myth of romantic love; sentimentality; jealousy; and anguish over male betrayal. Rhoda believes that her oddness gives her both exemplary power and rhetorical force and that her integrity and powers of leadership depend on her remaining single: "My work is to help those women who by sheer necessity must live alone—women whom vulgar opinion ridicules. How can I help them so effectually as by living among them, one of them, and showing that my life is anything but weariness and lamentation?" Rhoda believes, too, that the feminist movement will never progress unless women can become "hard-hearted" and separate their emotions from practical decisions: "It isn't personal feeling that directs a great movement in civilization." She is harsh and unsympathetic to those who fall by the wayside, such as Bella Royce, who has been seduced and abandoned by a married man. But her friend Mary Barfoot, with whom she directs a business school for women, takes a different view, arguing that a feminism that has sacrificed compassion to the desire for power will ultimately fail: "To work for women one must keep one's womanhood."

Rhoda's principles are put to a severe test when she falls in love with the cynical ex-radical Everard Barfoot. Barfoot, of course, is not celibate and has indeed had a child with a working-class girl. Strongly attracted to Rhoda, he is primarily motivated by the desire for conquest. To subjugate the militant virgin would be a delicious victory; and while he is both genuinely drawn to Rhoda and impressed by her strength and intelligence, the pleasure of domination never escapes him. When he looks at her full but "impregnable" lips, tries to capture her "strong, shapely" hand, or gazes into her "fine eyes," he thinks of her as an odd woman, a collector's item, "an unfamiliar sexual type . . . hinting at the possibility of subtle feminine forces that might be released by circumstances." What appeals to him most is the thought of her "unconditional surrender," a surrender which is to be both ideological and sexual: "delighting in her independence of mind, he still desired to see her in complete subjugation to him, to inspire her with unreflecting passion."

Rhoda has always assumed that only the working classes are slaves to their sexuality; while "the daughters of eduated people" are capable of self-discipline, "working-class girls," as Mary Barfoot declares, "are absorbed in preoccupation with their animal nature"; or, as Everard brutally puts it, they are "mere lumps of flesh." Yet to Rhoda's shock and humiliation, it is not as easy to suppress her sexuality and desire for love from a man as she had hoped. Gissing makes clear that she is a passionate woman and that it is hard for her to deal with her feelings. In her romance with Everard Barfoot, Rhoda realizes that she is capable not only of intense desire but also of agonizing jealousy; she is humbled to recognize that for all her education and elegance, she is as susceptible to her "animal nature" as the shopgirls she disdains. In the end, Rhoda refuses to marry Barfoot, having recognized his superficiality; but her life is irrevocably changed.

Gissing contrasts this story with the parallel plot of the unhappily married woman, the shopgirl Monica Madden, who marries a reclusive older man, Edmund Widdowson, in order to escape her drudgery and to provide for her indigent spinster sisters. Unable to bear her husband's possessiveness and narrowness, Monica embarks on a disastrous

romance with a younger man and meets the classic fate of the adul-
teress, death in childbirth. Thus the odd woman and the odd couple
dramatize the problems of reconciling theory and practice in the realm
of human emotions.

Contemporary feminist readers of the novel criticized Gissing's pessimistic conclusions. In a review for the *Illustrated London News* in
1893, the journalist Clementina Black expressed disappointment in
the unhappy outcome of the love affair of Everard and Rhoda: "We
feel, as we read, that between two persons so clear-sighted, so out-
spoken, and so fully aware of the pitfalls of married life, the natural
end would be a real marriage—that is to say, an equal union, in which
each would respect the freedom and individuality of the other, and
in which each would find the completest development."

Yet, like James, Gissing hints that sexuality and loss are necessary
for a truly compassionate social movement; as Samuel Butler rewrites
Tennyson, "'Tis better to have loved and lost than never to have lost
at all." Mary Barfoot warns Rhoda that she must not become a fanatic
about oddness or odd women will die out: "After all, we don't desire
the end of the race." In order for Rhoda to preserve her integrity and
yet for the movement of odd women not to seem sterile, the Madden
sisters and Rhoda adopt Monica's child. Thus there is a kind of magical
collective maternity at the end; the fallen woman has left them her
daughter to raise, a baby who may grow up to be "a brave woman."
This solution to the maternal needs of odd women and to the
perpetuation of a celibate generation echoed real-life solutions of Victorian women. The social worker Mary Carpenter adopted a five-year-
old child when she was fifty-one and rejoiced in having "a little girl
of *my own*, . . . ready made to hand, and nicely trained, without the
trouble of marrying." Later the militant suffragette Charlotte Despard
adopted the illegitimate daughter of a cavalry officer.[41] But as Martha
Vicinus points out in her study of independent Victorian women,
"middle-aged single women simply could not change their life-styles
to fit the imperative demands of children," and these adoptions, seem-
ingly so miraculous a solution, rarely were successful.[42]

In many respects, representations of the single woman do not seem
to have changed much since the *fin de siècle*. In a modern novel inspired
by Gissing, Gail Godwin's *The Odd Woman* (1975), the heroine Jane
Clifford protests against Rhoda's self-destructive sublimation of sexuality into a cause: "You've proved your admirable point—that in the
nineteenth century you are able to forego the legal form of marriage

to preserve your independence. And he had proved he loves you enough to give up his prized bachelorhood and marry you. Why not get married and do more interesting things than destroy your love with ideologies?" An unmarried professor of English and Women's Studies, Jane Clifford seems to have many more options than Rhoda or Olive. In addition to her professional status, she has the advantage of having read Gissing, and she is even preparing a lecture on *The Odd Women*: "She had chosen Gissing for an opener because of his unrelenting pessimism. It was one of the few nineteenth-century novels she could think of in which every main female character who was allowed to live through the last page had to do so alone. The book's ending depressed her utterly, and she was eager to fling it into a classroom of young women (and men?) who still believed that they would get everything and see how they would deal with Gissing's assurance that they would not." Yet Jane herself ends in solitude, having broken off her love affair with a married professor of art history; and her friend, the militant feminist Gerda Mulvaney, editor of the radical newspaper *Feme Sole*, is hard-hearted and coarse. Godwin seems to be indicating that despite the success of women novelists, women professors, feminist journals, and women's studies, little has changed.

The film version of *The Bostonians* in 1984, produced by the team of Ismail Merchant and James Ivory and written by Ruth Prawer Jhabvala, retells James's story, but like Godwin's novel, is even less optimistic about the prospects of the modern odd woman. The film version is explicit where James is ambiguous, changing the nuances of his text into much stronger anti-feminist fare for the Reagan decade. Whereas James is consistently critical of Basil Ransom, the film casts him as Christopher Reeve, who brings his film persona as Superman to bear on the battle of the sexes with an Olive who is older than the character in the book, clearly lesbian and neurotic, and played by Vanessa Redgrave, an actress associated with a number of other radical and eccentric roles. The women's feminism, the film suggests through Redgrave's performance, through the deployment of suggestive visual images, and through its use of music, is really a hysterical displacement of sexual longings. In a brilliant touch, the filmmakers pick up on a minor detail in the novel for the opening frames of the film: that of the great organ in the Boston Music Hall, which "lifted to the dome its shining pipes and sculptured pinnacles, and some genius of music or oratory erected himself in monumental bronze at the base." Only in listening to music have Olive and Verena found an outlet commensurate to their revolutionary passions; "as they sat looking at the great florid, sombre organ, overhanging the bronze statue of Beethoven, they felt that this was the only temple in which the votaries of their creed could worship." As Merchant and Ivory represent it, however, the mammoth organ which dominates the opening minutes of the film becomes a punning visual metaphor for the spectacularly phallic Basil Ransom, who comes to rescue Verena from Olive's shrivelled embrace. When Olive speaks at the Boston Music Hall, her words are, ironically, a man's: Jhabvala gives her the words of William Lloyd Garrison.[43]

Debates over female oddness that took place in the 1880s will also sound very familiar to contemporary American readers. Once again, we are hearing that women are becoming redundant, that there is a frightening shortage of men, and that the feminist movement betrayed women by encouraging them to postpone marriage for a career. Once again we are hearing that men are unwilling to marry women who cherish ambitions like their own and who may compete with them. In 1986, a group of Yale sociologists issued a study claiming to prove that feminists postponing marriage for career risked permanent spinsterhood. "According to the report," *Newsweek* explained in an article called "Too Late for Prince Charming," "college-educated women who are still single at 30 have only a 20 percent chance of marrying. By the age of 35 the odds drop to 5 percent. Forty-year-olds are more likely to be killed by a terrorist. They have a minuscule 2.6 percent possibility of tying the knot."[44] Follow-up articles like "Single Women: Coping with a Void" on the front page of *The New York Times* reinforced the sense of crisis.[45] In a letter to the *Times*, one woman sarcastically thanked the editors "for running that neat article on how single women feel sorry for themselves. What I really liked about it was how it wasn't the least little bit slanted. After all, 'void,' 'stigma,' 'aging brings acceptance,' 'rabid' feminist response—these are all neutral terms."[46] The *Newsweek* story, as many feminists pointed out, seemed "to regard the specter of singlehood for women as conservatives view the advent of AIDS among male homosexuals: as a fitting curse brought on by the transgressions of the 'victims.' "[47] The sexual anarchy of women seeking higher education, serious careers, and egalitarian spouses, it hinted, had engendered its own punishment. An avalanche of movies and television shows about hard-driving career women stopped in their fast tracks by babies drove home the message that post-feminist motherhood, not a career, was the real prize.

In an essay for *The New York Times Magazine* called "Why Wed? The Ambivalent American Bachelor," Trip Gabriel explored the reasons for men's reluctance to marry, reasons very similar to those offered by the bachelor writing in *Temple Bar* a century before. "The word they use is 'scary,' " Gabriel noted of the bachelors on "the supply-side curve." While they had told themselves that they were waiting to marry until the right woman came along, many of these men gradually realized that they were never going to be ready to commit themselves to marriage. Single life was too comfortable, although sexual adventure, in the age of AIDS, was no longer much of a temptation. Many of the men Gabriel interviewed were using sports to fill the space in their lives left by the absence of wives and families: "Many men today are more obsessed with working out than they ever were as schoolboys. Some bachelors seem to have effected a simple exchange: the vicissitudes and uncertainties of a single man's sex life for the known payoffs of athletics."[48]

Articles like these, which are recycled in the press, blame the unrealistic expectations generated by the women's movement for the loneliness, singleness, and oddness of career-oriented women, while they accept the most narcissistic behavior of men as natural and unchangeable. They also act as a not-too-subtle form of propaganda aimed at frightening women away from feminism. Loneliness and fear of male violence are all-too-real factors of women's lives at the end of the twentieth century, and anger at both feminism and men seems like a natural outlet for these feelings. As Judith Walkowitz and Judith Newton commented, "contemporary feminists have still not determined how to articulate a feminist sexual politics that simultaneously addresses the possibilities of female sexual pleasure and the realities of sexual danger, and the ideological splits which generated tension among early feminists are still being played out today."[49] There is a renewed emphasis in the 1980s on women as sexual victims in cases of sexual harassment, rape, wife abuse, and incest. Feminist campaigns against pornography have divided the women's movement. The most extreme statements in the campaign have come from Andrea Dworkin, who argued in her study *Intercourse* (1987) that sexual intercourse is the basis and symbol of women's oppression. In language strongly reminiscent of the 1880s purity campaigners, Dworkin described intercourse as "the pure, sterile, formal expression of men's contempt for women," but envisioned "freedom from intercourse" as an unlikely social development "because there is a hatred of women, unexplained, undiagnosed, mostly unacknowledged, that pervades sexual practice and sexual passion."[50]

But while Andrea Dworkin campaigns relentlessly against intercourse and pornography in "Amerika," other women who also call themselves feminists believe that women are still sexually repressed and that many aspects of women's lives and feelings are different from the norms of the late-nineteenth century. As Linda Gordon and Ellen DuBois note, "the increasing tendency to focus almost exclusively on sex as the primary area of women's exploitation, and to attribute women's sexual victimization to some violent essence labelled 'male sexuality' is even more conservative today, because our situation as women has changed so radically." Women today, they eloquently remind us, "have possibilities for sexual subjectivity and self-creation today that did not exist in the past. We have a vision of sexuality that is not exclusively heterosexual, nor tied to reproduction. We have a much better physiological understanding of sexual feeling, and a vision of ungendered parenting. We have several strong intellectual traditions for understanding the physiological and social formation of sexuality. Perhaps most important, we have today at least a chance at economic independence, the necessary material condition for women's sexual liberation. Finally, we have something women have never enjoyed before—a feminist past, a history of 150 years of feminist theory and praxis in the area of sexuality."[51]

The changes in women's lives brought about by feminism have made the status of the unmarried woman at the end of the twentieth century very different from that of a Rhoda Nunn, an Olive Chancellor, or a Verena Tarrant a century before. Female singleness no longer has to mean celibacy; and, at least for the time being, the "spectre of death or disease from back-street abortion, of shame and dire social perils for the 'fallen women' who conceived when single . . . no longer [haunts] the sexual encounters of unmarried and sexually active women."[52] Moreover, single motherhood is a real if difficult option for those who desire it and, increasingly, a standard family pattern among black women. Single women may not be odd at all in the future but rather the majority, as they are already in some cultures and some countries. These new patterns may look like sexual anarchy when they are compared to the still-potent Hollywood images of the American family, but they are clearly part of a new sexual system emerging at the *fin de siècle*.

THREE

New Women

Be bold and yet be bold,
But be not overbold,
Although the knell is tolled
Of the tyranny of old,

And meet your splendid doom
On heaven-scaling wings,
Woman, from whose bright womb
The radiant future springs!
(John Davidson, "To the New Woman") (1894)

Unlike the odd woman, celibate, sexually repressed, and easily pitied or patronized as the flotsam and jetsam of the matrimonial tide, the sexually independent New Woman criticized society's insistence on marriage as woman's only option for a fulfilling life. "On the eve of the twentieth century," the French historian Michelle Perrot observed, "the image of the New Woman was widespread in Europe from Vienna to London, from Munich and Heidelberg to Brussels and Paris."[1] In the United States, too, the New Woman, university-educated and sexually independent, engendered intense hostility and fear as she seemed to challenge male supremacy in art, the professions, and the home.[2] Politically, the New Woman was an anarchic figure who threatened to turn the world upside down and to be on top in a wild carnival of social and sexual misrule. Journalists described her in the vocabulary of insurrection and apocalypse as one who had "ranged herself perversely with the forces of cultural anarchism and decay."[3] In an essay comparing the New Woman to the anarchist women of the French Revolution and the *pétroleuses* of the Paris Commune of 1871, a critic for the *Quarterly Review* saw her as a woman warrior: "In her wide-spread, tumultuous battalions . . . she advances, with drums beating and colours flying, to the sound also of the Phrygian flute, a disordered array, but nowise daunted, resolute in her determination to end what she is pleased to define as the slavery of one-half the human race."[4]

In 1888, the novelist Mona Caird wrote a series of columns for the London *Daily Telegraph* called "Is Marriage a Failure?" in which she argued that marriage as an institution was based on the economic dependence of the wife and that it restricted the freedom of both sexes. Over twenty-seven thousand readers wrote in with their comments, most in strong agreement. With their new opportunities for education, work, and mobility, New Women saw that they had alternatives to marriage. And another novelist, Ella Hepworth Dixon, explained, "If young and pleasing women are permitted by public opinion to go to college, to live alone, to travel, to have a profession, to belong to a club, to give parties, to read and discuss whatsoever seems good to them, and to go to theatres without masculine escort, they have most of the privileges—and others thrown in —for which the girl of twenty or thirty years ago was ready to barter herself for the first suitor who offered himself and the shelter of his name."[5]

As women sought opportunities for self-development outside of marriage, medicine and science warned that such ambitions would lead to sickness, freakishness, sterility, and racial degeneration. In France, the *femme nouvelle* was often caricatured as a *cerveline*, a dried-up pedant with an oversized head; an androgynous flat-chested *garçonnet*, more like a teenage boy than a woman; or a masculine *hommesse*. Alarmed by the wave of feminist activity which swept France from 1889 to 1900, including twenty-one feminist periodicals and three international congresses; and the highly publicized decline in the national birthrate, doctors, politicians, and journalists united in condemnation of the New Woman and in celebration of the traditional female role. "Feminists are wrong when they turn women away from the duties of their sex," wrote Victor Jozé in the journal *La Plume*, "and when they turn their heads with illusory emancipatory ideas, which are unrealizable and absurd. Let woman remain what Nature has made her: an ideal woman, the companion and lover of a man, the mistress of the home."[6]

In England, male anxiety focused on the biological imperative of reproduction and on what the poet John Davidson called "the bright womb from which the future springs." Doctors maintained that the New Woman was dangerous to society because her obsession with developing her brain starved the uterus; even if she should wish to marry, she would be unable to reproduce. "The bachelor woman," wrote G. Stanley Hall, ". . . has taken up and utilized in her own life all that was meant for her descendants, and has so overdrawn her account with heredity that, like every perfectly and completely developed individual, she is also completely sterile. This is the very apotheosis of selfishness from the standpoint of every biological ethics."[7] In his presidential address to the British Medical Association in 1886, Dr. William Withers Moore warned that educated women would become "more or less sexless. And the human race will have lost those who should have been her sons. Bacon, for want of a mother, will not be born."[8] Discussing the New Woman who has "gone out to labour in the world," the scientists Geddes and Thomson warned even more apocalyptically that such women "have highly developed brains but most of them die young."[9]

The New Woman was also the nervous woman. Doctors linked what they saw as an epidemic of nervous disorders including anorexia, neurasthenia, and hysteria with the changes in women's aspirations. Women's conflicts over using their gifts, moreover, would doom them to lives of nervous illness. As Dr. T. Clifford Allbutt commented, "the stir in neurotic problems first began with the womankind." By the 1890s, he continued, "daily we see neurotics, neurasthenics, hysterics and the like . . . every large city is filled with nerve-specialists and their chambers with patients."[10] It was estimated that there were fourteen neurasthenic women for every neurasthenic man, one hysterical man to twenty hysterical women.[11] In his preface to *Jude the Obscure* (1895), Thomas Hardy confidently describes his heroine, Sue Bridehead, as "the woman of the feminist movement—the slight, pale 'bachelor' girl—the intellectualized, emancipated bundle of nerves that modern conditions were producing, mainly in cities." In the same year, in their *Studies on Hysteria*, Sigmund Freud and Joseph Breuer noted that hysterical girls were likely to be "lively, gifted, and full of intellectual interests." Among their patients in Vienna were "girls

What the New Woman Will Make of the New Man!,
Punch, 1895.

who get out of bed at night so as secretly to carry on some study that their parents have forbidden for fear of overworking"; and women of "powerful intellect" and "sharp and critical common sense" like "Anna O."

The battle against the New Woman was waged as intensely in the pages of *Punch, The Yellow Book,* and the circulating library as in the clinic. Scarcely an issue of *Punch* appeared without a cartoon or parody of New Women (Figure 1). In *The Yellow Book,* too, both male and female aesthetes wrote alarming stories about the "fatal repercussions . . . when women attempt to take the initiative, particularly in marriage, or attempt to assert themselves emotionally."[12] In 1882 an anonymous novel called *The Revolt of Man* described the war between the sexes led by insurgent New Women. In a matriarchal England of the twentieth century, women have become the judges, doctors, lawyers, and artists, while men are kept in complete subordination, taught to cultivate their beauty in order to be chosen in marriage by successful matrons. The heroine of the novel is a liberal politican, taking up the cause of the subjection of men and pleading eloquently in Parliament that "there is more in life for a man than to work, to dig, to carry out orders, to be a good athlete, an obedient husband, and a conscientious father."

The author of *The Revolt of Man* was Walter Besant, an active clubman, journalist, novelist, and founder of the Society of Authors. A staunch antifeminist, Besant brings to the foreground two revealing anxieties about a female-dominated society. His first anxieties are Oedipal: he fears that in a reversal of the Victorian marriage market, young men will be forced to marry women old enough to be their mothers. Much of the novel deals with the terrifying specter of "toothless hoary old women" claiming young men in marriage, and the slogan of the revolutionary movement is "Young men for young wives!" Besant's other anxieties are professional. He mocks the sexual reversals and absurd conventions the art of a feminist or matriarchal society would create. Portraits of women show them "represented with all the emblems of authority—tables, thrones, papers, deeds and pens," while men "were painted in early manhood" and their "hair was always curly." Paintings at the Royal Academy depict "lovely creamy faces of male youth," or "full-length figures of athletes, runners, wrestlers, jumpers, rowers and cricket-players." One self-taught male artist secretly submits a rugged painting of an old man, but he is caught, his pictures are burned, and he goes mad. Literature consists of romantic and uplifting ballads written by women to indoctrinate men: "The Hero of the Cricket Field" or Lady Longspin's "Vision of the Perfect Knight," "Hymns for Men," or "The Womanhood of Heaven: or, the Light and Hope of Men." In the theater, the feminist society prides itself on having perfected the drama by prohibiting farce, consigning tragedy to oblivion, suppressing ballet, and pronouncing laughter vulgar. The New Drama is "severe and even austere."

Besant's primary message is that women "cannot create . . . at no time has any woman enriched her world with a new idea, a new truth, a new discovery, a new invention" or "composed great music." But rather than claiming responsibility for these sentiments himself, he puts his diatribe against female creativity in the mouth of an elderly woman professor of Ancient and Modern History at Cambridge, Dorothy Ingleby. It is she who urges the young men to restore knowledge "by giving back the university to the sex which can enlarge our bounds." "The sun is masculine—he creates," Professor Ingleby lectures. "The moon is feminine—she only reflects."

We might read the novel as a sharply satiric critique of sexism which works by reversing the roles; but it did not seem to occur to Besant that women resented their stereotyped representation in art and their exclusion from the professions just as much as men would. Besant could only imagine a society of complementary roles, of dominance and subordination; and his intention is not to expose the stagnation of male art, education, politics and culture but indeed to warn against their infiltration by women. Taking all his examples of what a sexually oppressive society would be like from the Victorian subordination of women, he writes entirely without irony of a future in which men must band together in revolt to reestablish patriarchal dominance and an androcentric religion. The revolt of men chillingly reinstates religious fundamentalism: "There was a general burning of silly books and bad pictures; and they began to open the churches for the new worship, and more and more the image of the Divine Man filled women's hearts." After the male rebellion, women are firmly put in their post-feminist places, places they actually prefer:

> No more reading for professions! Hurrah! Did any girl ever really like reading the law? No more drudgery in an office! Very well . . . no anxiety about study, examinations, and a profession . . . unlimited time to look after dress and matters of real importance. . . . Then was born again that sweet feminine gift of coquetry.

Besant was proud of the reception of his book: "*The Revolt of Man* I brought out anonymously. It shows the world turned upside down. Women rule everything and do the whole of the intellectual work; the Perfect Woman is worshipped instead of the Perfect Man. The reception of the book was at first extremely cold; none of the reviews noticed it except slightingly; it seemed as if it was going to fail absolutely. Then an article in the *Saturday Review*, written in absolute ignorance of the authorship, started all the papers. I sent for my friend the editor to lunch with me, and confessed the truth. When I say that the advanced woman has never ceased to abuse the book and the author, its success will be understood."[13]

Ironically, it has been the indignation and abuse of feminist readers that has enabled mean-spirited books like *The Revolt of Man* to outlive their historical moments, while feminist satires have been forgotten. Fin-de-siècle women writers did not write feminist "revenge scenarios" comparable to Besant's in which men are enslaved and exploited.[14] There were, however, a range of feminist texts that imagined women victorious. For an opposite view that uses the same concepts and metaphors as Besant, but to a very different purpose, we might turn to Mary Cholmondeley's futuristic play *Votes for Men* (1909). While Besant uses a fantasy of role reversal to play on men's fears, Cholmondeley uses it to make a case for women's suffrage by showing men how they would feel if they were treated as the subordinate sex. In her fantasy, New Women have won the vote, used control of the birthrate to take control of the government, and disenfranchised men. The young Prime Minister Eugenia argues patiently with her husband Harry who wants to join the Men's Reinfranchisement League; she raises the issue of male hysteria and the "brawling brotherhood"; she deplores the caricatures of male suffragists in *Punchinella*; she sympathizes with the problems of surplus men who cannot find wives; and she worries with him about male powerlessness in general. All of these details reverse aspects of women's situation and its masculine representations. But even in writing a propaganda play for the suffrage movement, Cholmondeley cannot repress her own dark self-critical speculations on power. Her female Prime Minister is more empathetic and generous than Gladstone, but she holds on to power just the same. As Harry sadly remarks, "Those who have the upper hand cannot be just to those who are in their power. They don't intend to be unfair, but they seem unable to give their attention to the rights of those who cannot enforce them." Thus, in the end, Harry gives in to Eugenia's pleading and goes off to become President of the Anti-Suffrage League, having fully internalized the psychology of the colonized.

Feminist views of the New Woman also came from such writers as Mona Caird, who adopted the satirical techniques of Besant and other Clublanders in order to demonstrate the absurdity of sexual roles. In 1899, Caird wrote an essay for a symposium in *The Ladies' Realm* on the topic "Does Marriage Hinder a Woman's Self-Development?" Rather than arguing the case, she demonstrated it in a witty role-reversal, asking how a man's self-development and career "would fare in the position, say, of his own wife." John Brown is devoted to his family and to his housekeeping chores; but sometimes "he wonders, in dismay, if he were a true man." As a young unmarried man, he cherished "a passion for scientific research," but his experiments did not go well, and his father "pointed out how selfish it was for a young fellow to indulge his own little fads, when he might make himself useful in a nice manly way, at home." Meanwhile, when his sister Josephine "showed a languid interest in chemistry," the family rushed to support her, fitted up a spare room as a laboratory, and cheerfully endured mess and explosions. "John, who knows in his heart of hearts that he could have walked round Josephine in the old days, now speaks with manly pride of his sister, the Professor." She has an "awestruck" family and husband, who protect her from worry and interruptions; he has to snatch a few moments of spare time from the household for his research, and worries that "a man's constitution was not fitted for severe brain-work." When he has an idea, his wife gently mocks it; and he grows faded and old, hoping vaguely "that presently, by some different arrangement, some better management on his part, he would achieve leisure and mental repose to do the work that his heart was in."[15]

In the enormous number of feminist utopian writings that proliferated in the *fin de siècle*, women did speculate about a future world of sexual equality. As Anne Mellor comments, "feminist theory is essentially utopian."[16] But the women's utopias are egalitarian and much more concerned with practical matters, with the division of labor and the care of children, than with anarchy, revolt, or matriarchal rule. Jane Hume Clapperton's *Margaret Dunmore, or a Socialist Home* (1885), for example, set out minute details of the regulation of a communal home in which men and women would share the housework. Charlotte Perkins Gilman's various utopian writings examined the possibilities for social systems that would free women from drudgery and give them control of their bodies.

The dominant sexual discourse among New Women, as among other late-nineteenth-century feminists, reproduced and intensified stereotypes of female sexlessness and purity. Some New Women writers applied the terminology of Darwinian science to the study of male sexuality and discovered biological sins that could lead to general retrogression. "Man in any age or country is liable to revert to a state of savagery," wrote Mona Caird. Henrietta Müller argued that "male hypersexuality" and female self-restraint would eventually lead to a society in which women reigned.[17] Taking to heart Darwinian arguments about women's self-sacrifice for the good of the species, and sustained by the Victorian belief in women's passionlessness, many New Women envisioned themselves as chaste yet maternal heralds of a higher race. In their stories, female sexuality is purged, projected, or transcended through activism.

But a small group of New Women were also beginning to speak out for the reality and importance of female sexuality. In the United

States, the free-lover Victoria Woodhull and the married-women's-rights activist Elizabeth Cady Stanton spoke out in behalf of the naturalness of female sexual desire. In England Olive Schreiner and Eleanor Marx, among others, did research on female sexuality, discussed their own experiences together and with sexologists like Havelock Ellis, and championed a future of mutual desire. By the turn of the century, Stella Browne and other feminist contributors to the *Freewoman* argued for sexual liberation along with women's legal emancipation: "Let us admit our joy and gratitude for the beauty and pleasure of sex," wrote Stella Browne in *The Freewoman* in 1912. "It will be an unspeakable catastrophe if our richly complex feminist movement with its possibilities of power and joy, falls under the domination of sexually deficient or disappointed women, impervious to facts and logic and deeply ignorant about life."

The most advanced male thinking about New Womanhood came from those late-Victorian radicals who had developed socialist, feminist, or utopian critiques of marriage. Britain's first socialist party, the Democratic Federation, was founded in 1881, and the spread of socialist ideas and massive growth in trade union membership led to the formation of the Independent Labour Party in 1892. But British socialism in the 1880s was far from coherent in its ideology. It included intellectuals and artists, like H. G. Wells and Sidney and Beatrice Webb, who founded the Fabian Society in 1884; the counterculture protest of sexual radicals like Edward Carpenter and the Fellowship of the New Life; and the Socialist League of Karl Marx, Edward Aveling, and Frederick Engels. Each of these groups developed its own position on the woman question, the marriage question, and sexuality.

The Marxists saw women's opposition as a byproduct of capitalism that would disappear when women had equal rights as workers. In *The Origin of the Family, Private Property, and the State* (1884), Engels declared that "the supremacy of the man in marriage is the simple consequence of his economic supremacy, and with the abolition of the latter will disappear of itself." After the overthrow of capitalism, Engels believed, there would be a new generation of free men and women who would make their own sexual rules: "a generation of men who never in their lives have known what it is to buy a woman's surrender with money . . . a generation of women who have never known what it is to give themselves to a man from any other considerations than real love . . . When these people are in the world, they will care precious little what anybody today thinks they ought to do; they will make their own practice . . . and that will be the end of it." Similarly, in *The Woman Question* (1886), Eleanor Marx and Edward Aveling argued that in a socialist state, in which private property would have been abolished and women would enjoy the same educational and vocational opportunities as men, "monogamy will gain the day. There are approximately equal numbers of men and women, and the highest ideal seems to be the complete, harmonious, lasting blending of two human lives. Such an ideal, almost never attainable today, needs at least four things. These are love, respect, intellectual likeness, and command of the necessities of life." In such a society, there would be no need for either divorce or prostitution. [18]

While some activists, such as Robert Blatchford, believed that all their energy should go into "the accomplishment of the industrial change" and that "the time is not ripe for socialists, as socialists, to meddle with the sexual question," [19] the sexual radicals, such as the homosexual theorist Edward Carpenter, shared a socialist perspective but placed much more importance on freedom of sexual expression. Carpenter saw the personal and the political as inseparable and believed that sexuality could be the basis of social change. The feminist movement, which he strongly supported, represented a model of sexual politics that he hoped would be followed by a movement for the emancipation of homosexuals.

The most significant debates on the question of sexuality took place in the Men and Women's Club, an organization that met in London from 1885 to 1889. Founded by Karl Pearson, a young Darwinist and socialist instructor of mathematics at University College, it brought together twenty middle-class feminist and socialist intellectuals to discuss everything from Buddhist nuns to contemporary marriage. The male members of the Club, primarily Cambridge friends of Pearson's, were university-educated professionals who were trying to develop a new scientific language for human relationships based on Darwinian and eugenic thought. The female members were mainly reformers and philanthropists. All except two of them were single. Only Henrietta Müller, a militant feminist and "man-hater," had been university-educated. They were earnestly debating a "new sexuality." They were "exploring sexual possibilities . . . and searching for a new language of desire," trying to construct "new narrative forms that would encompass complex thought and feeling." [20]

The most distinguished member of the women's group was the South

African novelist and essayist Olive Schreiner, one of the visionaries of her generation. With the publication of her novel *The Story of a South African Farm* in 1883, Schreiner had become a celebrity. Glad-stone sent his compliments; George Moore and Oscar Wilde were eager to meet her; Rider Haggard found her novel, along with those of Stevenson, to be among the most meaningful of the age; the young aesthete Ernest Dowson annotated his copy in private homage to Schreiner's realism; and socialist radicals greeted her as one of their own. *African Farm*, according to Gilbert and Gubar, "through its prototypical portrait of the New Woman . . . helped to establish both the intellectual basis and the rhetorical tropes of turn-of-the-century feminism."[21] In her lifelong commitment to the woman question, Schreiner anticipated and inspired many of the feminist ideas of the twentieth century; her book *Woman and Labor* (1911) was among the first efforts to work out the relationship between feminism and capi-talism. Her utopian vision of sexual love allowed for complete spiritual, intellectual, and physical expression for both women and men. She was appalled by Henrietta Müller, the most militant woman in the Club, who "thinks we will have to rule over men in the future as they have ruled and trodden on us in the past."[22] Her pacifism and her views on the racial problem in South Africa also placed her ahead of her time.

Despite Schreiner's efforts, however, the quasi-scientific discourse of the male radicals, echoing concepts of late Victorian "sexual sci-ence," both intimidated the women members and made it harder for them to overcome their inhibitions and begin to discuss their own sexuality. Emma Brooke protested against the "distinctly dominant tone" Pearson took in talking to women, and Henrietta Müller even-tually resigned, explaining angrily to Pearson that it was "the same old story of the man laying down the law to the woman and not caring to recognize that she has a voice, and the woman resenting in silence, and submitting in silence."[23] In 1889, unable to reach a common position, the Men and Women's Club broke up, not only because of feminist resistance, but also because, as Judith Walkowitz has shown, "men were dissatisfied with the women's performance" and with *their* resistance to the language of scientific reason.

Moreover, the men saw the sexual revolution only in terms of heterosexuality and women's roles. They could only focus on "woman" as the problem in modern sexuality and had no vocabulary in which to discuss masculine subjectivity. "You have studied and thought out so deeply the position of woman," Schreiner reproached Pearson; "Why have you not given the same thought to man?"[24] Pearson's paper on "The Woman Question" was all very well, but as Schreiner pointed out, it assumed that one could understand sexuality by discussing "woman, her objects, her needs, her mental and physical nature, and man only in as far as he throws light upon her question. This is entirely wrong."[25] In *The Morality of Marriage*, Mona Caird pointed out that men, too, needed to change: "Nature has indicated fatherhood to man as much as she has indicated motherhood to woman, and it is really difficult to see why a father should not be expected to devote himself wholly to domestic care; that is, if we are so very determined that one sex or the other should be sacrificed EN MASSE."[26]

While men were focusing on the Woman Question, women raised the Man Question. Was the age producing a New Man, the companion who would share their lives and who would evolve by their side? Schreiner was optimistic about the idea that a New Man was emerging to join the New Woman and that together they would create an ideal society. "Side by side with the New Woman," she wrote, ". . . stands the New Man, anxious to possess her on the terms she offers."[27] Much utopian New Women fiction, from Sarah Grand to Charlotte Perkins Gilman, was about the vision of the New Man, often an artist or a writer. In George Egerton's "The Regeneration of Two," the heroine establishes a free marriage with a poet. In Sarah Grand's *The Beth Book*, Beth MacLure meets and cares for an invalid artist: "It was all as congenial as it was new to her, this close association with a man of the highest character and the most perfect refinement. She had never before realized that there could be such men, so heroic in suffering, so unselfish, and so good."

In reality, however, men and women were widely separated on many issues. New Women did not think that they could depend on men for political and emotional support. "I really cannot stand this perpetual boasting on the part of men as to how much they have done for us," Elizabeth Wolstoneholme Elmy wrote to a friend in 1893, "when I know with what terrible difficulty each little bit has been extracted from them—always excepting the few brave, noble, generous men-helpers for whom no words of praise are enough."[28] Many of the conflicts between the positions of New Men and New Women surfaced around the issue of the free sexual union. Men who thought about the future of sexual relations under socialism assumed that economic dependency was the chief, if not the only, obstacle to women giving up the legal protection of marriage. Karl Pearson wrote enthusiastically about its possibilities in 1887: "I hold that the sex-relationship, both as to form and substance, ought to be a pure question of taste, a simple matter of agreement between the man and [the woman] in which neither society nor the state would have any need or right to interfere. The economic independence of both man and woman would render it a relation solely of mutual sympathy and affection; its form and duration would vary according to the feelings and wants of individuals. This free sexual union seems to me the ideal of the future, the outcome of Socialism as applied to sex."[29]

But the socialist ideal of the free sexual union assumed that men and women had equal stakes in the relationship, whereas the unaddressed problem of the legitimacy and care of children put women at much greater risk of abandonment. Women had more to lose in compromising their sexual reputation than men did. Schreiner could not even receive calls from professional colleagues like Rider Haggard without her landlady bursting in with suspicious questions.[30] A sexual relationship, whether legal or free, meant pregnancy for the woman. Contraception was strictly controlled by doctors (who themselves had the smallest families among professionals), despite the beginnings of a secular birth-control movement. And even more important, the rational ideal ignored or wished away emotional issues of fidelity, jealousy, and insecurity. In the sexual utopia after socialism, both Pearson and Carpenter would argue, jealousy and heartbreak would not exist. Where there was no possession and no commitment, there could be no betrayal and no loss. In his thinking about the "form and duration" of the free sexual union, Pearson seemed to have assumed that it would end as it had begun, by "mutual" consent, and not because one partner would stop loving first.

Women took a more pessimistic view of the potential damage of abandonment. Olive Schreiner had developed many of her own ideas in her correspondence with Pearson. "The most ideal marriage at the present day," she wrote in 1886, "seems to me to be the union of two individuals, strongly sympathetic, who after deep thought enter in the sexual relationship. There should be no bond or promise between them; for the *sake of children* a legal contract should be, I think, formed. The less said about love and life-long continuance together the better . . . The union will be, as long as each one feels they are expanding or aiding the other's life."[31] But when she talked to women suffering from the pain of abandonment, Schreiner felt that the concept of free love was a "devilish thing" that had to be modified.

The gender divisions around the issue of the free sexual union were central to Gissing's plot in *The Odd Women*. The struggle between Everard and Rhoda is symbolized by his wish to make her accept a "free union" rather than marriage, and her insistence on a full legal commitment. Barfoot proposes to Rhoda that she should honor her radical principles by living with him, as those people who "have thrown away prejudice and superstition" dare to do. Rhoda's initial response is skeptical: "This particular reform doesn't seem very practical. It is trying to bring about an ideal state of things whilst we are struggling with elementary obstacles." Even the most cynical female roué in the novel, a society widow who seems to have come from a Wilde play, regards the free union as a reform to be undertaken only by prominent men and women who are willing to martyr themselves for the sake of others. Furthermore, children are the repressed element in Everard's lofty rhetoric of freedom and trust. Rhoda has good reason to worry whether he will feel a sense of responsibility for a child; there had been a scandal in his past when he had gotten a shopgirl pregnant and then refused to marry her; he calls the baby "her child" and smiles when he tells a friend that it died. In his first long conversation with Rhoda, he tells her that he would never stay in an unhappy marriage for the children's sake; later he decides that he does not want children and assumes that Rhoda shares his attitude, although he never asks her about it. Eventually he decides to keep marriage in reserve, in case, as he thinks in characteristically uninvolved language, Rhoda "became a mother." But the more acute issue Gissing dramatizes is Rhoda's realization that, despite her principles, she is subject to agonizing jealousy and despair, at times so devastating that she thinks "if she could not crush out her love for this man she would poison herself."

A more simplistic but equally controversial fin-de-siècle novel about the free union was Grant Allen's *The Woman Who Did* (1895). Allen was a prolific writer and moralist whose self-righteous social concerns led one critic to dub him "the Darwinian St. Paul."[32] His heroine Hermione Barton is a Girton student who is ideologically opposed to marriage: "I am not and never could be slave to any man." She "can never quite forgive George Eliot—who knew the truth, and found freedom for herself, and practised it in her life—for upholding in her books the conventional lies, the conventional prejudices." Thus she decides to live in a free union with her lover Alan Merrick, but not to marry him, even when she becomes pregnant. However, he dies of typhus and leaves her unprovided; his family rejects her; and she returns to London with her baby, calling herself "Mrs. Barton," to face a hard lifetime struggle doing literary hackwork. Hermione's one dream is that her daughter, Dolores, will be the really free woman, the feminist messiah of the new generation, who will "regenerate humanity." Yet Dolores turns out to be a throwback, a thoroughly conventional girl, ashamed of her mother's position and horrified when she discovers her own illegitimacy. When it becomes clear that her notoriety stands in the way of her daughter's marriage, Hermoine takes prussic acid.

While it became a huge best-seller and affected public stereotypes of the sexually rebellious New Woman, *The Woman Who Did* was never popular with feminists and their supporters. H. G. Wells protested that Allen was attacking the wrong institutions: "He does not propose to emancipate them from the narrowness, the sexual savagery, the want of charity, that are the sole causes of the miseries of the illegitimate and the unfortunate. Instead he wishes to emancipate them from monogamy, which we have hitherto regarded as being more of a fetter upon virile instincts."[33] The suffragist leader Millicent Fawcett denounced Allen as one who had never helped women in any practical sense and who was now "not a friend but an enemy" who "endeavors to link together the claim of women to citizenship and social and industrial independence, with attacks upon marriage and the family."[34] The novelist Sarah Grand believed that the story clearly showed "that women have nothing to gain and everything to lose by renouncing the protection which legal marriage gives."[35] Novelists responded to it in the form of *The Woman Who Didn't* (1895), by Victoria Crosse, and *The Woman Who Wouldn't*, by Lucas Cleeve.

Both men and women were ambivalent about the sexual questions they attempted to discuss in a rational and scientific mode. Like many "New Men" of the 1880s, as Judith Walkowitz points out, Karl Pearson was both critical of patriarchy and frightened by feminism; he might champion "the sexual choices of the advanced New Woman in the abstract," but he was "terrified by and disorientated by any signs of female sexual agency in the flesh."[36] When Pearson himself fell in love, he quickly opted for conventional marriage instead of a free sexual union. And both Allen, in *The Women Who Did*, and Gissing, in *The Odd Women,* acknowledged that the idealistic New Women who tried to live by the rationalist rhetoric of socialist feminism and the free union often found themselves in positions of extraordinary personal risk, overwhelmed by feelings of loss, betrayal, jealousy, or possessiveness they had denied or judged irrational.

Olive Schreiner and Eleanor Marx, the daughter of Karl Marx, were two of the New Women of this transitional generation who made the effort to live by their beliefs. Both were idealists caught up in the most radical political and social transformations of the time, living at the frontiers of socialist, feminist, and anticolonialist struggle. Close friends from the time they first met in 1882, Schreiner and Marx shared a vision of sexual equality, camaraderie, and fidelity between women and men. Marx wrote a purely rationalist discourse on sex, Schreiner a lyrical and utopian one; but both denied and suppressed women's anxieties about sexual pleasure, power, and danger that persisted in spite of socialist and scientific rhetoric. Both suffered most of their lives from crippling psychosomatic diseases and nervous symptoms like those of the hysterical women Freud and Breuer were treating in Vienna; Marx eventually committed suicide. Thus, for all their greatness, both were tragic feminist intellectuals of the *fin de siècle* whose lives revealed the huge gap between socialist-feminist theory and the realities of women's lives.

Eleanor Marx was, of course, the daughter of the revolution, whose "feminism was inseparable from her socialism."[37] In 1886, she delivered a passionate speech commemorating the Paris Commune: "When the revolution comes—and it *must* come—it will be by the workers, without distinction of sex or trade or country, standing and fighting shoulder to shoulder."[38] She had seemed to lead an exemplary political and personal life, acting Nora in *A Doll's House,* translating *Madame Bovary,* and touring the United States in 1886–87 during one of the formative periods of the American labor movement.

Yet Marx also felt the conflict between political ideals, social realities, and sexual desires. In 1881, Dr. Bryan Donkin had treated her for anorexia, trembling and convulsive spells, as well as depression and exhaustion. He had attributed these hysterical symptoms to the strain of nursing her parents and also to sexual repression. In 1882, when Schreiner and Marx met in London and became friends, they shared an interest in discussing female sexuality and had talked, for example, about the influence of the menstrual cycle on sexual excitement.[39] But in 1884, when she was twenty-nine, Marx had joined her life to the critic Edward Aveling in a free union, since his wife would not give him a divorce. "We have both felt that we were justified in setting aside all the false and really immoral bourgeois conventionalities," she wrote to a Marxist friend, "and I am happy to say we have received the only thing we really care about—the approbation of our friends and fellow-socialists." When Donkin invited her to join the Men and Women's Club, Marx declined, viewing herself as more sexually radical than the other women members: "It is a very different matter to advocate certain things in theory, and to have the courage to put one's theories into practice; probably many of the good ladies in the Club would be much shocked at the idea of my becoming a member of it."[40]

Marx and Aveling made their union the model for a future of free men and women, and intellectuals such as Karl Pearson applauded their relationship as a glorious example of "the direction [in which] marriage ought to go."[41] In *The Woman Question,* Marx and Aveling expressed their faith in monogamy: "We believe that the cleaving of one man to one woman will be best for all." They explained their confidence that in a socialist state "the two great curses that . . . ruin the relation between man and woman would have passed": unequal treatment of the sexes and dishonesty. No longer, they proclaimed, "will there be the hideous disguise, the constant lying, that makes the domestic life of almost all our English homes an organised hypocrisy." Indeed, in the socialist future, husband and wife would be able to "look clear through one another's eyes into one another's hearts."[42] Yet Edward Aveling was one of the most notorious liars and philanderers in London, a total hypocrite who secretly married a much younger woman in 1897. In March 1898, having discovered Aveling's infidelity, Marx killed herself by taking prussic acid, dying like Emma Bovary or the Woman Who Did. She was only forty-three. Many believed that she and Aveling had shared a suicide pact which only she had honored.

"It is such a mercy she has escaped from him," Olive Schreiner wrote to a friend upon hearing of Eleanor's death.[43] Schreiner had long intuitively despised Aveling; as she wrote to Havelock Ellis when the couple started living together, "to say I dislike him doesn't express it at all; I have a fear and horror of him when I am near. Every time I see him the shrinking goes stronger."[44] Yet her insights about Marx did not protect her in her own life. For Schreiner was one of those notable women whose failure seems especially representative of her generation. She was never able to bring her great literary talents to mature fruition; the book that was meant to be her major work, *From Man to Man*, was never finished, and for long periods she found it impossible to write at all. Despite all her passionate beliefs, she could not work in movements for political change. A series of self-destructive relationships with men in England, including Havelock Ellis and Karl Pearson, forced her to suppress and deny her own sexuality; and she suffered all her life from a series of devastating psychosomatic illnesses. Ellis had prescribed bromides and *nux vomica* for her dizziness, nausea, and crying spells. Bryan Donkin treated her unsuccessfully for asthma attacks and "nerve-storms" that he attributed to the sexual stresses in her life. After Pearson married another woman in the Men and Women's Club, Schreiner returned to South Africa and married a younger man who took her name. But their infant daughter died within a few days of her birth, and the marriage never met her expectations of an intellectual partnership.

These were terrible disappointments to someone whose theoretical and polemical writing dealt so extensively with sexuality. Schreiner believed that the full expression of female sexuality was essential for the development of women, for "something sexual" lay at the "root of all intellectual and artistic achievement."[45] Often expressing her surprise at male doctors' and scientists' ignorance of the most basic facts of women's physiology, she also felt that men were alienated from their own full sexual and human development by stereotypes of masculinity. In letters to Ellis and Pearson, she argued that the paternal instinct was as strong as the maternal one and that human sexuality, freed of some of the pressures for mere survival, was evolving towards the aesthetic and beautiful. As women found themselves able to enter freely into all lines of work, she predicted, they would meet and marry their fellow workers, for the ties of "common interests and . . . common labours" would invariably attract New Women and New Men to each other in "the perfect mental and physical life-long union of one man with one woman."[46]

Like Eleanor Marx, Schreiner felt that feminist anger towards men was an unhappy symptom of oppression rather than an emotion to be encouraged. "We cannot hate any one," she wrote to Karl Pearson. "Man injures woman and woman injures man. It is not a case for crying out against individuals or against sexes, but simply for changing a whole system."[47] As she wrote to Havelock Ellis, Schreiner opposed "anything that divides the two sexes. My main point is this: human development has now reached a point at which sexual difference has become a thing of altogether minor importance. We make too much of it; we are men and women in the second place, human beings in the first."[48]

In *Woman and Labor* Schreiner attempted to work out her vision of a sexual evolution, rather than a revolution, that would bring men and women closer together. Instead of envisioning feminist *coups d'état* and female dominance, Schreiner hoped that the women's movement could be "called a part of the great movement of the sexes towards each other, a movement towards common occupations, common interests, common ideals, and an emotional tenderness and sympathy between the sexes more deeply founded and more indestructible than any the world has ever seen." In eloquent Darwinian metaphors, she wrote about the sexual utopia that lay beyond the end of prostitution, when both sexes would reach their full evolutionary potential: "Always in our dreams we hear the turn of the key that shall close the door of the last brothel; the clink of the last coin that pays for the body and soul of a woman; the falling of the last wall that encloses artificially the activity of woman and divides her from man; always we picture the love of the sexes as once a dull, slow-creeping worm; then a torpid, earthy chrysalis; at last the full-winged insect, glorious in the sunshine of the future."

Yet despite these large-minded visions, Schreiner came to believe that her generation of feminists had been called upon to sacrifice their sexuality and their opportunities for love in order to secure the future freedom of other women. Until New Men were educated to appreciate the love of free women, the most advanced women would be doomed to celibacy and loneliness. Yet if women had the courage to choose independence and solitude over love, they would help make the way for the future in which women would not have to choose. In her allegory, "Life's Gifts," she summed up the position of the feminist avant-garde: "I saw a woman sleeping. In her sleep she dreamt Life stood before her, and held in each hand a gift—in the one Love, in the other Freedom. And she said to the woman, 'Choose!'

"And the woman waited long; and she said, 'Freedom!'

"And Life said, 'Thou hast well chosen. If thou hadst said, "Love," I would have given thee that thou didst ask for; and I would have gone from thee, and returned to thee no more. Now, the day will come when I shall return. In that day I shall bear both gifts in one hand.'

"I heard the woman laugh in her sleep."

Schreiner's fiction thus expressed the bitterness and disillusionment of New Women with men who were not ready to join them in their evolutionary progress. "The Buddhist Priest's Wife," which she wrote during three months in 1892, was Schreiner's personal favorite among her stories of sexual difference. It is "much the best thing I have ever written," she noted; ". . . the substance of it is that which I have lived all these years to learn, and suffered all that I have suffered to know."[49] Schreiner described the story in an earlier draft to W. T. Stead: "A woman scientific in tendency and habits of thought but intensely emotional loves a brilliant politician; she is going away where she will never see him again, she invites him to see her the last night, they discuss love, the ideal of marriage, prostitution, and the evils of celibacy (which I think are very great, though at the present day for many of the best men and women inevitable)."[50] Based on her own unhappy affair with Karl Pearson, the story, as Schreiner herself reflected upon it, is about "the individual natures of the man and the woman, and their relation to one another, which throws a curious side-light on the whole discussion . . . It ends with the woman asking the man to kiss her, and then she goes suddenly out of the room. For the first time it bursts upon him with a sense of astonishment that she loves him; he waits to hear her return; but she never comes; the next day she leaves for India and they never meet again."[51] Schreiner identifies her characters generically as "the woman" and "the man." Her heroine's New Womanhood is made immediately evident by her London "room of one's own," her silver cigarette case, and her nervous smoking; the man's greater social ease is evident in his evening clothes, his passion for sport, and his "half-amused, half-interested" manner of speaking. The topic of their conversation, the social taboos that prevent women from asserting their feelings and desires, is an ironic counterpart to the subtext of her unexpressed and unrequited love for him. Although he admires her "brilliant parts and attractions" enormously and expects her to be "the most successful woman in London," because of her intellect he cannot love her. And she cannot tell him of her feelings because "the woman who had told a man she loved him would have put between them a barrier once and for ever that could not be crossed."

As in *The Odd Women*, the ending of the story made clear that while the New Man had many choices, the New Woman had only a few. The man goes off cheerfully to seek an American wife who will have the "same aims and tastes" that he has and who will bear him children and support his political career. The woman goes off, as he jokingly predicts, to "marry some old Buddhist Priest, build a little cottage on the top of the Himalayas and live there, discuss philosophy and meditate." But Buddhist priests do not have wives;[52] in reality, she has gone off to work bravely alone and then to die, perhaps even to commit suicide. "Cover her up! How still it lies!" writes the narrator. "She that had travelled so far, in so many lands, and done so much and seen so much, how she must like rest now! Did she ever love anything absolutely?. . . did she ever need a love she could not have? Was she never obliged to unclasp her fingers from anything to which they clung? Was she really so strong as she looked? Did she never wake up in the night crying for that which she could not have?"

In their splendid biography of Schreiner, the English feminist historian Ann Scott and the late South African radical Ruth First, assassinated by a letter bomb during her exile in Mozambique, asserted the necessity for a total understanding of the woman intellectual as the product of both personal and social forces. In their view, Schreiner's predicament was the sum of her experience with the colonial culture of South Africa, her encounters with English socialism, and her need to reconcile her work as a writer with her emotional and sexual needs. Since she had come from a society that had no native literature, being a woman was only part of her problem of creative expression; Nadine Gordimer has recalled that during her own adolescence in South Africa, "the concept 'intellectual,' gathered from reading, belonged as categorically to the Northern hemisphere as a snowy Christmas."[53] Similarly, Doris Lessing, in Rhodesia, and Ruth First (whose tragic story of political activism in South Africa was told in *117 Days*, her memoir of imprisonment and in *A World Apart* [1988], the powerful film her daughter wrote about her life) experienced their sex as only one element in the totality of their political engagements and intellectual aspirations.

Like Eleanor Marx and like other heroic New Women of her generation, Schreiner sometimes derived energy and inspiration from the struggle with her contradictory identities, but more often they interrupted or even paralyzed her creative drives. "In the ideal condition for which we look," Schreiner wrote to Havelock Ellis, "men and women will walk close, hand in hand, but now the fight has oftenest to be fought out alone by both." The day when Life would come to women bearing both freedom and love seemed far in the future.

FOUR

Queen George

*I*f sexual anarchy began with the odd woman and the New Woman, textual anarchy might be traced to the death of George Eliot, who had ruled the Victorian novel as Queen Victoria ruled the nation. On a snowy and windy December 29, 1880, Eliot was buried in a splendid funeral at Highgate Cemetery. Among the crowds of mourners following the coffin covered with wreaths of white flowers were such celebrated men of the age as Robert Browning, Herbert Spencer, John Everett Millais, and T. H. Huxley. Although they were unnamed in newspaper accounts, many of Eliot's women friends also attended the funeral; perhaps the most distraught was the writer and trade unionist Edith Simcox, who had worshiped Eliot with single-minded and unrequited love for many years and had taken her as her "muse and her model."[1] Simcox noted in her journal that not all the bystanders understood exactly whose funeral they were witnessing. "Was it the late George Eliot's wife who was going to be buried?" a child asked Simcox, who, overcome with grief and planning to have her own ashes scattered over Eliot's grave, simply answered "Yes."[2]

The confusion over gender roles at Eliot's funeral reflected her anomalous and crucial position in Victorian letters. George Eliot, whose real name was Marian Evans, had played virtually every role of Victorian gender herself. On the feminine side, as one critic observed, "she had created herself first as a daughter, then as a sister, and finally as a mother figure for countless younger men."[3] Yet the male pseudonym, the masculine authority she commanded as a writer, and the range of her intellectual, philosophical, and scientific interests also placed her in the role of father; in the popular imagination, she might have had, as well as have been, a wife. Eliot thus functioned in the history of the English novel as both man and woman, a hybrid with the mixed attributes the Victorians described as "man's brain and woman's heart." These sexual ambiguities were brought to the foreground in such satirical novels of the period as *George Mandeville's Husband* (1894) by the feminist writer Elizabeth Robins, which mounted a full-blown malicious attack on the pretentious woman novelist usurping the masculine role, the "large uncorseted woman" who "was assured she had a powerful and original mind."

As Eliot's funeral marked out a space between male and female mourners, public and private witnesses, so, too, her death marked a significant moment of literary anarchy for the English novel. After a long reign, this queen of the English novel died, and the heirs began to fight over the estate. Who would inherit Queen George's throne, and what new kingdom would the novel possess? Both literary daughters and literary sons were faced with the need to remake the novel in their own image, to find new roles and voices for themselves as writers.

In dealing with the legacy of George Eliot, then, male and female writers of the *fin de siècle* faced several new situations. First of all, they were each confronted with a powerful literary precursor who was a woman. Therefore, the Oedipal model of wrestling with and slaying the literary father-figure, which Harold Bloom has made so central for contemporary critical theory, could not apply for them. Secondly, daughters and sons have different responses to the powerful mother. Thirdly, as I have shown, Eliot's gender position was ambiguous; she disrupted the comfortable binary structure of sexual identity. As a result, the death and greening of George Eliot over the last century makes a useful case study for the literary battles around sexual anarchy.

What kind of maternal role did Eliot play for her literary daughters? As many feminist critics and psychologists have argued, "women experience the dynamics of maternal literary influence differently from the way men do."[4] The psychologist Nancy Chodorow, in a revision of Freudian theory, argued that separation and individuation may be particularly complex tasks for daughters. Daughters may find it difficult to escape their sense of similarity and closeness to the mother, and unlike sons, do not have the difference of gender to help them establish autonomy.[5] While Eliot was often described by her female contemporaries as a mother, there were difficulties with the maternal metaphor as well. Eliot had no children of her own and discouraged adoring "daughters," like Edith Simcox. Increasingly, she came to be regarded as the virgin mother; her lover, George Henry Lewes, addressed her as "madonna" in his letters, and others accepted the term. This spiritualized maternal figure represented a female creativity without sexuality.

Further, Eliot's unquestioned dominance as a literary realist and moralist had long defined the unattainable boundaries of aspiration for other women writers. They had looked on her as "somehow uncanny,"[6] regarding her from afar with an admiration severely tempered by envy and with a depressing recognition of their artistic inferiority. When the American writer Constance Fenimore Woolson, for example, began publishing short stories in the 1870s, a reviewer for the *Century* praised her by saying that "a fragment, and not an inferior fragment, of the mantle of George Eliot" had fallen on her shoulders. But was George Eliot's mantle, a kind of literary shroud of Turin, big enough to go around? Those writers whose shoulders were unprotected by its sacred fragments were resentful of Eliot's reputation. Elizabeth Robins's venom in *George Mandeville's Husband* can be traced to her admission that Eliot was an impossible act to follow: "To sit down daily to the task of being George Eliot, and to rise up 'the average lady novelist' to the end, must, even if only dimly comprehended, be a soul-tragedy of no mean proportion." In 1883, Charlotte Riddell published *A Struggle for Fame,* an autobiographical novel about her own career as a writer. Her heroine succeeds in writing a serious book—that is, one in which the love story is subordinate. But, as the narrator tells us, even for gifted writers, the market for such fiction was slight, and the pressure to write for the mass market immense: "Where, for example, George Eliot counted her thousands, the *Family Herald* counts its tens of thousands!"

Some saw an unhealthy seclusion in the protectiveness of Eliot's companion George Henry Lewes, who had handled all her business and shielded her from harsh reviews. Margaret Oliphant described Eliot as a woman kept in a "mental greenhouse": "I think she must have been a dull woman with a great genius distinct from herself," Oliphant wrote in her journal after Eliot's death. "She took herself with tremendous seriousness, that is evident, and was always on duty."[7] Others envied the special circumstances that made it possible for Eliot to be so productive. The novelist "Rita" summed these up when she wrote that "as a rule, woman's mental gifts are trammeled by her surroundings—by domesticity, household and social obligations, trials and anxieties of wifehood and maternity. George Eliot was mercifully spared all these."[8]

To a younger generation of college-educated women, moreover, Eliot's solemnity was beginning to seem dated, morbid, and absurd. At Cambridge in 1885, Mollie Hughes recalled, the grimmest blue-stocking was "a stern admirer of George Eliot" and would occasionally "unbend into a hollow kind of laugh" at "the emptiness of life."[9] Henry James's invalid sister Alice, who had channeled her own literary talent into a private diary, was disgusted by the image of Eliot in the biographies published after her death: "What a lifeless, diseased, self-conscious being [George Eliot] must have been! Not one burst of joy, not one ray of humor, not one living breath in her letters or journals. . . . Whether it is that her dank, moaning features haunt and pursue one thro' the book, or not, but she makes upon me the impression, morally and physically, of mildew or some morbid growth—a fungus of a pendulous shape, or as of something damp to the touch."[10]

Rachel DuPlessis describes the literary project of this generation of women as "writing beyond the ending," concerned with "the examination and delegitimization of cultural conventions about male and female, romance and quest, hero and heroine, public and private."[11] The term "delegitimization" carries significant implications. In one sense, delegitimization is a strike against patriarchal poetics, a repudiation of the narrative father, and a refusal to take his name. Women writers of this period rejected the male pseudonym for self-consciously feminist *noms de plume,* such as "Sarah Grand." In another and equally important sense, however, delegitimization is also the struggle not to reproduce the mother's story, to dissent from *her* narrative models. For, as Jane Gallop has noted, "the daughter's obligation to reproduce the mother's story is a more difficult obstacle than even the Father's Law, an obstacle that necessarily intrudes even into the lovely, liberated space of women among themselves."[12]

Indeed, for some intellectual women of the period, the wish not to reproduce the mother's story leads to the repudiation of fiction itself. The social worker and reformer Beatrice Webb was a case of a woman who might have written novels; her mother had written a novel called *Laura Gay,* and even when she was a girl, Herbert Spencer had encouraged her studies and told her that she "reminded him of George Eliot."[13] In many respects, too, Webb identified with Eliot. Reading *Daniel Deronda* in 1881, she was drawn towards "the preference she gives to emotive over purely rational thought." F. R. Leavis was the first of many critics to see Webb as a George Eliot *manquée*. Yet, in her own writing Webb consistently rejected fiction as the emotive and feminine side of herself. She regarded novels as a dangerous incentive to daydreaming rather than action. On one occasion, however, Webb did think about writing a novel, and the fantasy is instructive if we see it as expressive of her own search for new feminist forms. In 1895 she wrote in her diary about her need for a break from the discipline of *The History of Trade Unionism:*

> For the last three months an idea has haunted me that after we have ended our shift work on trade unionism I would try my hand at pure 'fiction' in the form of a novel dated 'Sixty Years Hence.' It should not be an attempt to picture a utopia. It should attempt to foreshadow society as it will be eighty years hence if we go on 'evoluting' in our humdrum way. Two main ideas should run through it. The fully-fledged woman engaged in a great career should be pictured just as we should now picture a man, and collectivism should be the orthodox creed carried out as a matter of course in moulding the instituting of the country.

The problem was that the conventions of women's fiction had not caught up with the realities of women's lives. To Webb, in any case, writing labor history was wrirting the father's story, "stiff work," as she said, in contrast to the soft mother's work of fiction.[14]

Margaret Elise Harkness, a cousin and close friend of Beatrice Webb, solved the conflict between activism and imagination by writing novels about working-class life in East London. Harkness wrote under the pseudonym John Law, a nearly allegorical figure of patriarchal authority. Her first novel, *A City Girl: A Realistic Story* (1887), was published when she was twenty-six. It is openly feminist and socialist in its emphasis on class relationships and female emancipation and adds these ideological positions to the narrative. In a letter to Harkness, Frederick Engels praised the narrative realism of the story and its revision of the standard Victorian plot of the seduction of the working girl by the middle- or upper-class man: "You felt you could afford to tell an old story, becaue you could make it a new one simply by telling it truly."[15]

A second response to George Eliot came through the New Women writers, such as Charlotte Mew, George Egerton, "Graham Tomson," Menie Muriel Dowie, Ethel Sharpe, Ada Leverson, Ella D'Arcy, and Ethel Colburn Mayne, who attempted to redefine the genre of the woman's novel through a fiction that was often sexually suggestive as well as formally experimental and innovative. Many clearly differentiated themselves from Eliot. In 1889, for example, Olive Schreiner noted that "No human creature's feelings could possibly be further removed with regard to artistic work—not of course the scientific—than mine from George Eliot's. Her great desire was to teach, mine to express myself, for myself and to myself alone."[16] The German critic Laura Hansson, who described the literature of the New Women in her essays and books, believed that in contrast to George Eliot, who "wrote from a man's point of view, with the solemnity of a clergyman or the libertinism of a drawing-room hero," the New Women made no attempt to imitate men or to please them.[17]

To the New Women of the 1880s and 1890s, moreover, feminine "difference" was the basis of a developing Female Aesthetic, something to be cherished and nurtured rather than denied or disguised under male identities. New Women writers claimed to be writing "with female readers in mind, and to [be] making a political or moral statement on behalf of their sex."[18] Writing fiction came to be regarded as "a political act of sexual solidarity" in itself. Ella Hepworth Dixon, for example, called for "a kind of moral and social trades-unionism among women," that might have brought these two impulses together for thinkers like Webb.[19]

Yet New Woman fiction did not always please fin-de-siècle suffragists. Insofar as it explored female sexuality, marriage, divorce, and single motherhood, it raised touchy issues activists chose to avoid. Thus, Lisa Tickner argues, "they did the suffragists an unwitting disservice by associating women's emancipation with sexual emancipation."[20] In their novels and stories there was a new emphasis on female subjectivity and on the heroine as the center of narrative consciousness. Women novelists were seeking to create new kinds of narratives of female experience outside the conventional fictional destinies of marriage or death, availing themselves of a profusion of alternative fictional forms: short stories, dream narratives, fantasies, utopias, dramas, allegories, and fragments. In many of their stories, as Martha Vicinus points out, "they invented fantasy interludes, in which a woman will dream of an entirely different world or will cross-dress, experimenting with the freedom available to boys and men. Within the conventional tale of courtship and marriage, we have an effort to explain and analyse other, more inchoate desires and hopes of women."[21]

Yet in more than her pen name and initials, a representative New

Woman writer such as George Egerton (Mary Chavelita Dunne) (1859–1945) is still clearly a daughter of George Eliot. The title page of her first book, *Keynotes* (1893), shows a key made from the initials "G. E." as if they indeed formed the key to her short stories. In 1887, when she was trying to make a living on her own in London, Egerton eloped to Norway with a married man, Henry Higginson. The liaison was a dark version of Eliot's menage with Lewes; Higginson turned out to be a violent drunkard and died two years later. But the experience was formative for Egerton. She learned Norwegian and read widely in Scandinavian literature. In 1890, she went back to London to work in the British Museum and translate the novels of Knut Hamsun. Remarried, she began to write short stories. Egerton's narrative project, in her own words, was to cultivate one "small plot": "the *terra incognita* of [woman] herself, as she knew herself to be, not as man liked to imagine her—in a word, to give herself away, as man had given himself in his writings."[22] Her lyrical short stories in *Keynotes* introduced new forms of narrative representation influenced by the Scandinavian realists, such as Hamsun, Ibsen, Strindberg, and Björnsen. *Punch* parodied her writing in March 1894 as "She Notes," by Borgia Smudgiton, with "Japanese Fan de Siècle" illustrations by Mortarthurio Whiskerly.

The book opens with one of the most interesting examples of Egerton's narrative technique in the short story "A Cross Line." A married woman, restless and only partly satisfied by her husband, meets a strange man fishing near her house; she fantasizes running away with him. But at the end of the story, the woman discovers she is pregnant and feels a sudden kinship with the maid, who has lost a child. She decides to stay with her husband, but he will never really know her. As the title hints, they speak in crossed lines, at cross purposes, because female identity transcends male knowing. Like most of her stories, "A Cross Line" is told in the present tense, with sections separated by ellipses; "she, the small, pale, nervous heroine, has no name, as if to emphasize her enigmatic, essential, and untamable feminine 'nature.' " In another story, "An Empty Frame," Egerton highlights the problem of narrative structure. The empty frame is both the frame that has held the picture of her lover, a genius now rejected for a sensible marriage, and the frame of the storyteller. At the end of the story, the woman has an extraordinary vision of her own power now constrained by the margins of her domestic world, so that she will be forced to live inside her head, inside her imagination: "She falls asleep too and dreams that she is sitting on a fiery globe rolling away into space. That her head is wedged in a huge frame, the top of her head touches its top, the sides its sides, and it keeps growing larger and larger and her head with it, until she seems to be sitting inside her own head, and the inside is one vast hollow." Egerton, too, seemed to outgrow her own frame. As her brief career flowered and faded, her dissatisfaction became bitterness and frustration. Her literary territory had indeed left her a small plot in which to maneuver, and it was soon exhausted.

A third group of post-Eliot fictions by women, however, tried to deal both with the artist or writer heroine and with the feminist movement. Primarily realists, they also incorporated some of the impressionistic and lyrical techniques of the New Women writers. Their commitment to the women's movement was their response both to Eliot's repression of her own experience in creating her heroines and to her marginalization of the feminist cause. In *Daniel Deronda* particularly, this is striking, since Daniel, but not the female characters, is allowed access to "the higher life," in his commitment to Zionism, a "wide-stretching purpose," moreover, in which the aspiring heroine Gwendolen Grandcourt feels herself "reduced to a mere speck." The idea that Gwendolen might similarly find an enlarging higher purpose in a commitment to the emancipation of women, a cause in which she, her husband's discarded mistress, and her mother, among others, could join, is so clearly beyond Eliot's vision as to seem parodical.

In the 1890s, however, a number of English women novelists inspired by Eliot did rewrite her stories to allow for the possibility of such female destinies and denouements. Novels like Mona Caird's *The Daughters of Danaus* (1894), Sarah Grand's *The Beth Book* (1897), or Mary Cholmondeley's *Red Pottage* (1899), explore the dilemma of the feminist and artist. "I'm going to write for women, not for men," Beth Maclure concludes in *The Beth Book*, Grand's story of a woman trapped into a disappointing marriage, who becomes a successful writer and a feminist leader and orator. Critics commented that Sarah Grand's language was "as new as hard study and George Eliot can make it"; and Grand, who believed that *Middlemarch* was the greatest novel ever written, kept a picture of George Eliot in her morning-room.[23] On the whole, however, both the novels and the careers of the novelists ended in defeat and despair.

Mona Caird's *The Daughters of Danaus* (1894) dramatizes the contradictions of motherhood and art, femininity and artistic creativity.

Caird's title alludes to the myth of the fifty daughters of Danaus, forced into marriage and condemned all their lives to carry water in a sieve. Algitha and Hadria Fullerton are bright and gifted women frustrated by the conditions of daughterhood in a large Scottish family. Algitha wants to study social work in London; Hadria longs to become a concert singer. Yet both are subjected to a domestic routine that takes away their time for concentrated work and breaks it into "jagged fragments." Their own house has another legend of female slavery attached to it; here a Highland chief held captive, raped, and starved the daughter of his bitterest enemy. The sisters debate Emerson's dictum that "genius will triumph over circumstances," that "given great artistic power, given also a conscience and a strong will," no combination of adverse circumstances can "prevent the artistic powers" from emerging. But, they point out, Emerson leaves out the question of gender. "Emerson never was a girl! . . . If he had been a girl, he would have known that circumstances DO count hideously in one's life."

Even a feminist writer whom Hadira befriends warns her that "a woman cannot afford to depise the dictates of Nature. She may escape certain troubles in that way; but Nature is not to be cheated, she makes her victim pay her debt in another fashion. There is no escape." Finally, Hadria hears a lecture on Woman's Sphere full of dire warnings and suffocating gentility: "At the end of the lecture, the audience found themselves invited to sympathize cautiously and circumspectly with the advancement of women, but led at the same time, to conclude that good taste and good feeling forbade any really nice woman from moving a little finger to attain, to help others to attain, the smallest fraction more of freedom, or an inch more of spiritual territory, than was now enjoyed by her sex. When, at some future time, wider privileges should have been conquered by exertions of some one else, then the really nice woman could saunter in and enjoy the booty. But till then, let her leave boisterous agitation to others, and endear herself to all around her by her patience and her loving self-sacrifice."

Hadria's tale has a familiar ending. She marries a man who promises to let her develop her art. For a brief period, she takes him at his word, leaving him to care for their children while she studies in Paris. But in the end, guilt overwhelms her; given the choice between motherhood and her career as an artist, she must choose her children. Caird ends with a passionate denunciation of the bonds of motherhood: "Motherhood, in our present social state, is the sign and seal as well as the means and method of a woman's bondage. It forges chains of her own flesh and blood; it weaves cords of her own love and instinct."

One comic version of the New Woman novel was Rhoda Broughton's *A Beginner* (1894). Emma Jocelyn has anonymously published *Miching Mallecho,* a first novel about "hereditary vice" with some purple passages of "virile dealing with the passions." Broughton's account of the disasters that befall a woman trying to write about sexuality is chastening. First, Emma's married cousin Lesbia is entranced with the book and thinks about committing adultery on its recommendation. The *Pudbury Post* is "reminded at every page of the method and manner of George Eliot," while the reviewer for *The Porch* attacks the author as a "puny scribbler." Worst of all, the anonymous *Porch* reviewer turns out to be Emma's suitor. Finally, Emma allows her aunt to buy the whole edition of *Miching Mallecho* back from the publishers and to burn both it and the manuscript. She herself is "withdrawn from circulation," by marrying a paternal older man who "is not very fond of literary society."

Mary Cholmondeley's *Red Pottage* (1899) is another fin-de-siècle woman's meditation on frustration and failure. As a young girl, Cholmondeley had "raised her eyes in humility and fidelity to George Eliot."[24] As an adult, however, having practiced Eliot's credo of renunciation, and embittered by years of useless self-sacrifice, she wrote the darkest feminist revision of Eliot's realism. Set in "Middleshire," near the "River Drone," *Red Pottage* is cynical about the bourgeois world of Middlemarch and St. Ogg's. The heroine, Hester Gresley, has written a successful novel called *An Idyll in East London;* but, as an unmarried lady, she must live at provincial Warpington Rectory with her stupid and jealous brother, a clergyman who burns the manuscript of her second novel, *Husks,* because he finds it immoral. Although a local clergyman who has read *Husks* describes it as a masterpiece, it is lost forever. "They have killed my book," Hester cries. She has a mental breakdown, and it is clear that she will never reconstruct her novel. Thus the century ends with an image of English women's fiction going up in flames and reduced to ashes—another apocalyptic conflagration.

Paradoxically, while the experimentation of the aesthetes won them serious attention, the stylistic and structural innovations of the New Woman novelists only reinforced the perception that their work was ideological or propagandistic. Interventions in the realist narrative, such as allegories, dreams, poems, or fantasy sequences, seemed to detract from the more valued ironic tone of the omniscient narrator, and thus "threw into question the distance between author and character."[25] By the mid-1890s it was widely stated that the New Woman novel was passé. Writing in February 1896, H. G. Wells could announce that "it is now the better part of a year since the collapse of the 'New Woman' fiction began."[26]

By the turn of the century, Eliot's reputation was also in serious decline. But Eliot's revival, resurrection, or greening in the twentieth century has followed an interesting course. Her popular image, once that of an aloof and powerful queen-mother, evolved into one of an imperfect, impulsive, and attractive sister whose conflicts and choices prefigured modern women's emergent selves. Virginia Woolf was one of the first revisionists. "I am reading through the whole of George Eliot, in order to sum her up," she wrote to a friend in January 1919. "So far, I have only made way with her life, which is a book of the greatest fascination, and I can see already that no one else has ever known her as I know her." Woolf had repeated some of Eliot's choices in her own life. Like Eliot, she had chosen a man who devoted himself to her career and to the fulfillment of her genius. Childless, protected, even sybilline, she certainly inherited and redefined the role of the leading woman novelist. To her struggling female contemporaries, Woolf, like Eliot, may have seemed to have been kept in "a mental greenhouse." But she had good reason to understand both the stresses of such a protected existence and the psychological necessities for it. To Lady Robert Cecil, Woolf wrote about Eliot:

"I think she is a highly feminine and attractive character—most impulsive and ill-balanced . . . and I only wish she had lived nowadays, and so been saved all that nonsense. I mean, being so serious, and digging up fossils, and all the rest of it. . . . It was an unfortunate thing to be the first woman of the age. But she comes very well out of it so far."

Responses to Eliot have echoed the transformation of feminism and criticism, so that women readers' preferences among Eliot's novels have changed from decade to decade. At the turn of the century, when modern women writers rediscovered Eliot as a sister, they identified passionately with *The Mill on the Floss*, seeing themselves in the rebellious Maggie Tulliver, decoding the representations of her sexuality, and vowing not to make the sacrifices of love and art that she had done. *The Mill on the Floss* is primarily a novel about female childhood and adolescence. "Haven't we all had pretty little cousins like Lucy Deane, whose hair curled naturally, and who were always neat when we were dirty, and mannerly when we were rude," wrote Willa Cather in 1897, "who never tore their frocks nor dropped their fork at the table, and whose China-blue eyes grew wide with astonishment at our tomboyish proceedings? And haven't we all just ached to push those immaculate cherubs into the mud—just as Maggie did?"[27]

Katherine Mansfield wrote with feminist fervor to John Middleton Murry in 1919, defending Eliot against an obtuse review by Sidney Waterlow in the journal Murry edited: "I don't think S. W. brought it off with George Eliot. He never gets underway. The cart wheels want oiling. I think, too, he is ungenerous. She was a great deal more than that. Her English warm ruddy quality is hardly mentioned. She *was* big, even though she was 'heavy' too. But think of some of her pictures of country life—the breadth, the sense of sun lying on warm barns, great warm kitchens at twilight when the men come home from the fields, the feeling of beasts, horses and cows, the peculiar passion she has for horses. (When Maggie Tulliver's lover walks with her up and down the lane and asks her to marry, he leads his great red horse, and the beast is foaming—it has been hard ridden and there are dark streaks of sweat on its flanks—the *beast is the man,* one feels *she* feels in some queer inarticulate way.) Oh, I think he ought really to have been more generous. . . . Perhaps that's unjust. But I feel I must stand up for my sex." Murry's reply gave some indication of Eliot's reputation among literary men, for he wrote to Katherine explaining his inability to judge Waterlow's fairness to George Eliot, since "I've never read a line of her."[28]

Simone de Beauvoir first read George Eliot's novels as a schoolgirl. In *Memoirs of a Dutiful Daughter,* the first volume of her autobiography, Beauvoir frequently refers to Eliot's formative impact on her intellectual life and on the shape of her future career. Beauvoir read *The Mill on the Floss* at the age of fifteen and found her religious apostasy, "spiritual exile," and intellectual aspirations radiantly named. In Maggie Tulliver she found a heroine who shared both her physical and psychological characteristics:

> Maggie Tulliver, like myself, was torn between others and herself: I recognized myself in her. She too was dark, loved nature and books and life, was too headstrong to be able to observe the conventions of her respectable surroundings, and yet was very sensitive to the criticism of a brother she adored.

Beauvoir had a particularly intense identification with the outcast Maggie, who after giving up Stephen, is determined to win back the estranged esteem of her family and village society:

> It was when she went back to the old mill, when she was misunderstood, calumniated, and abandoned by everyone that I felt my heart blaze with sympathy for her. I wept over her sorry fate for hours. The others condemned her because she was superior to them; I resembled her, and thenceforward I saw my isolation not as a proof of infamy but as a sign of my uniqueness. I couldn't see myself dying of loneliness. Through the heroine, I identified myself with the author: one day other adolescents would bathe with their tears a novel in which I would tell my own sad story.

It is a strikingly recalled moment of vocation, one which Beauvoir places crucially in the shaped narrative of her life. She was never to write a fictional equivalent of *The Mill on the Floss*; but *Memoirs of a Dutiful Daughter* is clearly a structured homage to Eliot's novel. Indeed, throughout her career, Beauvoir sustained the image of Maggie as model young feminist revolutionary. In *The Second Sex*, Maggie figures as the paradigm of the triumphantly sensitive young girl who attacks "official optimism, readymade values, hypocritical and cheerful morality. . . . The heroes—particularly Tom, Maggie's brother—obstinately uphold accepted principles, congeal morality in formal rules; but Maggie tries to put the breath of life into them, she upsets them, she goes to the limit of her solitude and emerges as a genuine free being, beyond the sclerosed universe of the males." And when Beauvoir thought about her career as a writer, Eliot/Maggie were her alter egos: "I passionately wanted the public to like my work; therefore, like George Eliot, who had become identified in my mind with Maggie Tulliver, I would myself become an imaginary character, endowed with beauty, desirability, and a sort of shimmering transparent loveliness . . ."[29]

Eliot was a major precursor for contemporary women novelists as well. While Beauvoir celebrated Maggie's death as her existential freedom, Margaret Drabble viewed it as an emblem of women's "sexual doom." In *The Waterfall* (1969), Jane Gray, who is in love with her cousin Lucy's husband, is haunted by the specter of Maggie Tulliver drowning herself "in an effort to reclaim lost renunciations." Jane, who is a poet, finds herself propelled and overwhelmed by the flood of her own passions; morality and responsibility sink under the force of her submissive desire. Jane Gray's Maggie is a bit of a cow, passive, irrational, and destructive, like herself: "Maggie Tulliver had a cousin called Lucy, as I have, and like me she fell in love with her cousin's man. She drifted off down the river with him, abandoning herself to the water, but in the end she lost him. She let him go. Nobly she regained her ruined honor, and ah, we admire her for it: all that superego gathered together in a last effort to prove that she loved the brother more than the man. . . . Maggie Tulliver never slept with her man: she did all the damage there was to be done, to Lucy, to herself, to the two men who loved her, and then, like a woman of another age, she refrained."

With the beginning of the women's liberation movement, all of this changed. For feminists of the 1970s, both more disillusioned about possibilities of individual freedom and more committed to an analysis of patriarchal constraints, the most central and compelling novel in the Eliot canon was *Middlemarch*. Never one of the popular novels of adolescence, *Middlemarch* is typically read for the first time in college, and its story of Dorothea Brooke, an intellectual and ardent young woman who can only realize her ambitions vicariously by marrying first the dried-up pedant Casaubon and then the handsome young politician Will Ladislaw, came painfully close to the lives of a generation of academic women on the margins of their professions, many of whom had married older and more successful male intellectuals, and who were often eyeing younger male radicals. In the 1970s, references to *Middlemarch* abounded in women's literature and feminist criticism, ambivalent and disturbing allusions both to a fantasy world of salvation through romantic love and to a public world of salvation through social commitment.

At the beginning of the women's liberation movement, feminist attitudes towards Eliot were hostile. As Kate Millett declared in *Sexual Politics*, Eliot was the lost leader who "lived the revolution . . . but did not write of it." "Dorothea's predicament in *Middlemarch*," according to Millett, "is an eloquent plea that a fine mind be allowed an occupation; but it goes no farther than petition. She marries Will Ladislaw and can expect no more of life than the discovery of a good companion whom she can serve as secretary." In 1972 Lee R. Edwards called *Middlemarch* "a kind of talisman for many young women" and "a sacred text," but also felt "angered, puzzled, and finally depressed" by Eliot's contradictory messages. Edwards used herself as a case history in order to "trace the peculiar relationship of George Eliot's work not just to me, but to women in general." Reading *Middlemarch* first as a college student frustrated by novels that celebrated "insipid heroines," she had been thrilled by Dorothea as "an endorsement . . . of energy and social commitment" in women; but rereading the novel as a struggling assistant professor in the dawn of the women's movement, she felt discouraged by the poverty of Dorothea's options: "For *Middlemarch* is finally not an endorsement of this energy, but first an examination and finally a condemnation of it." *Middlemarch*, Edwards concludes, "can no longer be one of the books of my life."

Feminist critics often reacted with such disappointment to Dorothea's vocational and marital mistakes because they had made these mistakes themselves. Florence Howe, for example, confesses her thoughts upon reading *Middlemarch* in her first year of graduate school: "In the novel . . . Dorothea . . . chooses to marry a dusty old professor. She reasons thus: I must marry, that's all a woman can do; but I'd like to do something really useful with my life; so why not marry a man whose work is important and, since I am intelligent, put myself at his service; then I'd be part of something important and useful. . . . When I was twenty-two, I thought Dorothea was a fool; not because of her rationale, however, but because she had made so poor a choice. Her husband was a pathetic drudge, without either common sense or genius. What was wrong with Dorothea, I thought then, was that she hadn't found herself a *bright* and *young* man to serve. I would not make her mistake: I could recognize dullness; I would seek the bright young man. And I did."[30]

Joyce Carol Oates's novel, *Do With Me What You Will* (1973), is a Gothic version of Eliot's triangular plot and a grim endorsement of its archetypal patterns. Her abused heroine Elena moves somnambulantly from one powerful man to another; at the center of the novel, Elena comes close to a breakdown, trying to leave the old lawyer who is her husband for the young lawyer who is her lover. In the library of her rented mansion, she discovers "an old mildewed volume of *Middlemarch*," which she forces herself to read, although "several pages of the novel were missing in one of the early chapters. She had read right through; then the pages leaped from page 106 to 187, and she kept right on reading, though with less interest." Elena thus skips most of Book 2, the analysis of Dorothea's marriage to Casaubon. The gap or discontinuity in her *Middlemarch* is ironically the place where her own moral history might be told. In Susan Cheever's *Looking for Work* (1979), the young heroine Salley is a modern-day Dorothea who reads *Middlemarch* with desperate intensity, looking for ways out of the impasse of her marriage. *Middlemarch* has even surfaced in the detective novel. In P. D. James's *Innocent Blood* (1980), a murderess keeps her sanity in prison by reading two chapters of *Middlemarch* a day and by making herself the prison authority on "three-volume novels about intelligent masochistic women who perversely marry the wrong man." And in Rebecca Goldstein's *The Mind-Body Problem* (1983), the heroine Renée takes *Middlemarch* on her honeymoon to Rome, where Dorothea and Casaubon went. Her husband, a mathematical genius who teaches at Princeton, is not like Casaubon, she insists. "Such errors as Dorothea's don't happen in math, when a proof is a proof whether of a theorem or a genius . . . I, at the very least, had the real thing."

But feminist obsession with George Eliot has not been merely literary. In 1974, after four years of hiding to evade arrest for her part in various bombings, the Weatherwoman Jane Alpert was holed up in a furnished room in Pittsfield, Massachusetts, trying to decide whether to surrender to the FBI. As she explains in her memoir *Growing Up Underground* (1981), she had cut her ties to the radical left, denounced her former lover Sam Melville as a male supremacist after his death in the Attica riots, and joined the women's movement. In this moment of spiritual crisis, Alpert records in a chapter called "Renunciation," she turned for guidance not to feminist or political manifestos, nor to American classics such as *Moby Dick* (which had been written in Pittsfield and in honor of whose author Alpert's lover, born Samuel Grossman, had renamed himself), but to *Daniel Deronda*.

As Alpert writes, "A bit of George Eliot's dialogue kept echoing in my mind. 'If you determine to face these hard ships and still try,' the composer Herr Klesmer says to the heroine, 'you will have the dignity of a high purpose, even though you may have chosen unfortunately.' . . . I decided—and George Eliot had as much to do with my choice as anyone else—that I would take the high road. I would turn myself in." Although the surrender of a fugitive woman bomber may not have been the sort of high purpose George Eliot had in mind, there's something predictable about the fact that Alpert should have chosen Eliot as a model and looked for inspiration to Eliot's stern moralism, making Pittsfield a place of as much allegorical resonance in her narrative as Middlemarch or St. Oggs had been for Eliot's feminist readers a century before.

And as the utopian promises of the radical movements of the 1960s and 1970s have faded into the more complex realities of the *fin de siècle*, young women trying to satisfy their needs for love and work still find Eliot's novels relevant and profound. "I read *Middlemarch* last weekend," reported Marie F. Deer, the secretary of the Yale Class of 1982, in the *Yale Alumni Magazine* in December 1988; "and I was very extremely pleased. Great book. Read it."[31] Yet modern American male novelists, if they mention her at all, still use Eliot as an example of the dreary moralism of a dead era, a writer who has nothing to say to our time. It's easy for a man to get a laugh with a reference to the unreadability of George Eliot. "The mark of a truly sadistic school system," notes John Gregory Dunne, "is one that teaches *The Mill on the Floss*."[32]

Many of the contradictions in Eliot's reputation came to an explosive head during the international conference held at Rutgers University in 1980 in honor of the centennial year of her death. Like a scene from a novel by David Lodge, the conference became a battleground on which the fight for possession of George Eliot was waged between Americans and British, feminists and formalists, Marxists and deconstructionists, historians and literary critics, scholars and writers. Germaine Greer arrived with a large carpet bag full of knitting and loudly clicked her needles, like Madame Defarge, through the men's papers. Alison Lurie and Diane Johnson made disparaging comments about Eliot's influence from their panel of novelists. Old friends quarreled over lunch. After the banquet, held in a student dining hall where mysterious sounds of crashing glass behind the screens suggested that the student waiters were hijacking the wine before it got to the table, there were nearly blows when a bearded young man rose in wrath to call one of the panelists "a miserable little trollop(e)." The academics pondered. Did he mean that she was a whore or a second-rate writer? The panelist began to cry, but before other bearded professors could reach him, the unknown accuser fled into the night. Was Eliot a woman writer, as Nina Auerbach, Sandra Gilbert, and Mary Jacobus maintained, or was she, rather, in the words of the historian Sheldon Rothblatt, a "man of letters"? Was she a great precursor of the modern novel, or a dreary anachronism with little to say to our time? Within the small world of academia, at least, Queen George still has the power to divide daughters and provoke sons.

FIVE

King Romance

While fin-de-siècle women writers had a difficult time coming to terms with the matriarchal legacy of George Eliot, among male writers dissent from the Eliot legend had long been smoldering. "I agree pretty well with all you said about George Eliot," Robert Louis Stevenson wrote to his friend Sidney Colvin in 1877. "A high, but, may we not add?—a rather dry lady." Swinburne blamed Eliot for his literary misfortunes, telling Edmund Gosse that "George Eliot was hounding on her myrmidons to his destruction." To Gosse, meanwhile, Eliot was a figure of absurd solemnity, a "large, thick-set sybil" in a silly hat, surrounded by deluded worshipers, the essence of all that was old-fashioned and Victorian.[1] The twenty-one-year-old William Butler Yeats detested George Eliot, who "understands only the conscious nature of man."[2] Gerard Manley Hopkins, writing in praise of Stevenson to his friend Robert Bridges in 1886, compared the young man to "the overdone reputation of the Evans-Eliot-Lewis-Cross woman (poor creature! one ought not to speak slightingly, I know), half real power, half imposition."[3] W. E. Henley, too, described the male critic's weariness with George Eliot's strenuous moralism: "He read her books in much the same spirit and to much the same purpose that he went to the gymnasium and diverted himself with parallel bars."[4]

Why were male writers so much more violent than their female contemporaries in their responses to Eliot? First of all, there were historical and economic reasons for their hostility. By the time Eliot died, women writers constituted a set of frightening rivals in the literary marketplace. In the 1870s and 1880s, at large English publishing houses like Bentley's, more than 40 percent of the authors were women. In the United States, three-quarters of the novels published during this period were written by women. Irritation with the fecundity of the successful woman novelist, churning out ill-digested but best-selling trash, surfaces in private journals, as well as in critical essays and stories of the period written by men. Trollope's Lady Carbury in *The Way We Live Now* (1875) "had already acquired the knack of spreading all she knew very thin, so that it might cover a vast surface." The excremental metaphor is even more explicit in Henry James's "Greville Fane"; one of many women novelists he caricatured "turned off plots by the hundred . . . With no more prejudices than an old sausage mill, she would give forth again with patient punctuality any poor verbal scrap that had been dropped into her." Mechanically reproductive and regurgative, women writers, some men argued, lacked any autonomous creativity.

Women also dominated the periodical press, as the American physician and novelist Silas Weir Mitchell complained in 1887 when he declared that "the monthly magazines are getting so lady-like that naturally they will soon menstruate."[5] When Oscar Wilde took over editorship of a London women's magazine in 1888, he renamed it *The Woman's World*, as if to suggest that women had indeed taken over the world of journalism. What seemed to many like the feminization of literature created identity problems for male artists; as Rachel Bowlby notes, "If culture, as a spaced marked off from business or working concerns, was also associated with femininity, that meant that being an artist might not sit well with a male identity. In the case of novels . . . women were the main consumers, the main readers. The male artist, then might be in something of an ideological bind: neither pure artist nor fully masculine."[6]

Secondly, there may have been psychological reasons why men, especially young men, needed to express superiority to Eliot and contempt for her work. The son's reaction to the powerful mother is different from that of the daughter. Eliot was not the self-sacrificing and self-effacing mother of masculine legend; as Sandra Gilbert and Susan Gubar point out, "where the male precursor had had an acquiescent mother-muse, his heir now confronted rebellious ancestresses and ambitious female peers, literary women whose very existence called the concept of the willing muse into question."[7] One defense against the mother's reign is to appropriate her power by repressing the maternal role in procreation and creation, and replacing it with a fantasy of self-fathering. Indeed, the replacement of hetero-sexual procreation and maternity by "the asexual reproduction of fa-thers on their own" is part of the European literary tradition from Genesis and *Paradise Lost* to Hawthorne's "The Birthmark" and James Watson's *The Double Helix*.[8]

While fantasies of male self-creation and envy of the feminine aspects of generation were not new, they reemerged with a peculiar virulence in the 1880s. Edward Said has written about the bachelor protagonist of late-nineteenth-century fiction, the new narrative pat-tern which begins with the "rejection of natural paternity" and a "revulsion from the novelist's whole procreative enterprise," and leads to "a special procreative yet celibate enterprise, which in turn leads to death."[9] In the male writing of the *fin de siècle*, celibate male creative generation was valorized, and female powers of creation and repro-duction were denigrated. Gerard Manley Hopkins, for example, wrote in 1886 that "the begetting of one's thoughts on paper" is "a kind of male gift," clearly a gift of begetting that requires no female assistance and avoids contact with the maternal body.[10] In numerous texts, male writers imagined fantastic plots involving alternative forms of male reproduction or self-replication: splitting or cloning, as in *Dr. Jekyll and Mr. Hyde*; reincarnation, as in Rider Haggard's *She*; transfusion, as in *Dracula*; aesthetic duplication, as in *The Picture of Dorian Gray*; or vivisection, as in *The Island of Dr. Moreau*. These enterprises are celibate, yet procreative metaphors for male self-begetting. They reject natural paternity for fantastic versions of fatherhood.

In a further gesture of self-creation, the Muse was transformed from a feminine to a masculine figure. Male writers constructed a new myth of creativity in which the work of art was the product of male mating and male inspiration, totally independent of even metaphorically fem-inine cross-fertilization. Sometimes the male muse was embodied in a fantasy figure, as in John Addington Symonds's recurrent dream of the beautiful face of a young man with large blue eyes and wavy yellow hair emitting "a halo of misty light . . . This vision of ideal beauty under the form of a male genius . . . prepared me to receive many impressions of art and literature."[11] More often, the muse was a male friend or collaborator, whose example inspired the young writer to create.

Finally, male writers needed to find a place for themselves in Eliot's wake, to remake the high Victorian novel in masculine terms, to lead a revolt of man against Queen George. The revival of "romance" in the 1880s was a men's literary revolution intended to reclaim the kingdom of the English novel for male writers, male readers, and men's stories. In a review on "The Present State of the Novel" in 1887, George Saintsbury credited Rider Haggard and Robert Louis Stevenson with the return to "the pure romance," as distinguished from the "more complicated kind of novel" of Eliot and her contemporaries with its "minute manners-painting and refined character analysis."[12] "Fiction is a shield with two sides, the silver and the golden," wrote Andrew Lang; "the study of manners and of character, on one hand; on the other, the description of adventure, the delight of romantic narrative."[13] Thus, in place of the heterosexual romance of courtship, manners, and marriage that had been the specialty of women writers, male critics and novelists extolled the masculine and homosocial "romance" of adventure and quest, descended from Arthurian epic. Conan Doyle called Stevenson "the father of the modern masculine novel."[14] Lang, too, saluted Haggard and Stevenson as the chivalrous knights from South Africa and Scotland who had restored the wounded and exiled King Romance to his throne:

> King Romance was wounded deep,
> All his knights were dead and gone
> All his court was fallen on sleep
> In the vale of Avalon!
>
> Then you came from south and north
> From Tugela, from the Tweed;
> Blazoned his achievements forth,
> King Romance is come indeed!

Now that Queen Realism was dead, King Romance might recover his virility and power. It had been thought "that there were no more stories to be told, that romance was utterly dried up," W. E. Henley recalled; but Stevenson and Haggard, with his "Zulu divinities" and "queens of beauty in the caves of Kôr" has rescued the novel from arid "analysis of character" and made it green again.[15]

While women writers after George Eliot saw themselves as writing especially for other women, the romance novelists determined to write for boys. Upon reading Stevenson's *Treasure Island,* Rider Haggard was persuaded to "try to write a book for boys."[16] In an essay called "About Fiction" (1887), Haggard differentiated himself from the "people who write books for little girls in the school-room." He would direct his fiction, as he said in the dedication to *King Solomon's Mines,* "to all the big and little boys who read." For men, the act of reading masculine romance both bonded and rejuvenated, as Lang notes in his dedication to Haggard of *In the Paradise* (1886): "Dear Rider Haggard,—I have asked you to let me put your name here, that I might have the opportunity of saying how much pleasure I owe to your romances. They make one a boy again while one is reading them . . ." In the epigraph to his story "The Lost World," Sir Arthur Conan Doyle, too, testified to his faith in the creed of eternal boyishness:

> I have wrought my simple plan
> If I give one hour of joy
> To the boy who's half a man
> And the man who's half a boy.

What did it mean to write for boys? For one thing, boys' fiction was the primer of empire. Little boys who read will become big boys who rule, and adventure fiction is thus important training: "Boys' literature of a sound kind ought to build up men . . ." the critic Edward Salmon, himself a fervent imperialist, noted. "In choosing the books that boys shall read it is necessary to remember that we are choosing mental food for the future chiefs of a great race."[17] The popular novels of G. A. Henty, such as *With Clive in India* (1884), *For Name and Fame* (1886), and *Through the Sikh Wars* (1894), were the most direct expression of these political goals. Henty himself owned stock in such colonialist enterprises as the Transvaal Gold Mining and Estates Company.[18] Boys' fiction also conveyed an illusion of eternal masculine youth. As the historian John Boswell points out, "boy" was the euphemistic Victorian terminology for the male lover, as "lad" would be for Housman's generation.[19] Masculine romance, its advocates believed, "tapped universal, deep-rooted, 'primitive' aspects of human nature which the realists could not approach";[20] these included strong if unconscious homoerotic feelings. Boyhood, for these writers, was also an allusion to the "boyish world" of male bonding.

Finally, writing for boys meant *not* writing for girls. Wielding the golden shield of male romance warded off the woman reader, set up by popular journalism as the antagonist of the virile artist. The schoolgirl or maiden client of Mudie's circulating library was the stereotyped puritanical reader who, in George Moore's phrase, kept English literature "at nurse"; to American men of letters she was the "Iron

Maiden" who strangled the American novelist in her fond embrace. Women, moreover, were disqualified from judging the work of masculine romance; as Andrew Lang wrote consolingly to Haggard about the reviews of *King Solomon's Mines*, "the dam[n] reviewers never were boys—most of them the Editor's nieces."[21] Clubland provided a way to exclude those who had never been boys. Male writers' clubs included the Omar Khayham Club, The Athenaeum, the New Vagabonds Club, the Rhymers Club, the Savile Club, and the Rabelais Club, which was organized by Walter Besant in 1880 and included George DuMaurier, Thomas Hardy, Bret Harte, Oliver Wendell Holmes, Henry Irving, Henry James, James Payn, and Robert Louis Stevenson among its members. In these sanctuaries, male writers were safe from the schoolgirl, the Iron Maiden, and most important, the female literary rival.

The literary genre which these writers created is called the male quest romance. In various ways, these stories represent a yearning for escape from a confining society, rigidly structured in terms of gender, class, and race, to a mythologized place elsewhere where men can be freed from the constraints of Victorian morality. In the caves, or jungles, or mountains of this other place, the heroes of romance explore their secret selves in an anarchic space which can be safely called the "primitive." Quest narratives all involve a penetration into the imagined center of an exotic civilization, the core, Kôr, *coeur*, or heart of darkness which is a blank place on the map, a realm of the unexplored and unknown. For fin-de-siècle writers, this free space is usually Africa, the "dark continent," or a mysterious district of the East, a place inhabited by another and darker race.

Images of sex as well as race merged in the mythology of the dark continent and the Orient. "Just as the various colonial possessions . . . were useful as places to send wayward sons, superfluous populations of delinquents, poor people, and other undesirables," Edward Said points out in his important study of Orientalism, "so the Orient was a place where one could look for sexual experience unobtainable in Europe."[22] Such sexual experience might involve a blurring of sexual boundaries. In the "Terminal Essay" to his translation of the *Arabian Nights* (1885–86), for example, Sir Richard Burton delineated the geography of a transgressive space he called the "Sotadic Zone" in which androgyny, pederasty, and perversion held sway. The Sotadic Zone ranged from the Iberian Peninsula to Italy, Greece, North and Central Africa, Asia Minor, Afghanistan, the Punjab, Kashmir,

China, Japan, Turkistan, and the South Sea Islands. Within these latitudes, Burton claimed, "there is a blending of the masculine and feminine temperaments." Here homosexuality ("male *feminisme*") and lesbianism were rife; anal intercourse was routine: "the Vice is popular and endemic, held at the worst to be a mere peccadillo, whilst the races to the North and South of the limits here defined practice it only sporadically amid the opprobrium of their fellows who, as a rule, are physically incapable of performing the operation and look upon it with the liveliest disgust."[23]

Setting these stories in the Sotadic Zone freed the romancers from all conventions of the Victorian three-volume novel. Indeed, "the writer of the quest romance," according to the critic Joseph Boone, "dealt by definition with a world almost totally devoid of women or heterosexual social regulations, a world in which the exploration of sea or desert provided a fresh and alternate subject for one wishing to rebel against the thematic strictures of the literary marriage tradition."[24] If the woman's novel at the end of the nineteenth century is primarily about marriage, these men's novels are about "the flight from marriage."[25] We could go further and suggest that the racial and sexual anxieties displayed in these stories as the vision of the Other mask the desire to evade heterosexuality altogether. Real and fictive colonists, Judith Sensibar brilliantly argues, "may have sought the wilderness as a place where they could more successfully mask homosexual panic . . . taboos on women . . . were also perhaps a way of avoiding the kinds of threatening encounters they felt forced to seek in the 'homophobic' civilized world. In the wilderness they no longer needed to practice compulsory heterosexuality."[26] Structured as stories about men told to men, the romance narrative provided a "safe arena where late-Victorian readers could approach subjects that were ordinarily taboo," including homosexuality.[27] Foreseeing a time when "the ancient mystery of Africa will have vanished," Haggard worried about the fate of the male imagination; "where will the romance writers of future generations find a safe and secret place . . . in which to lay their plots?"[28]

Above all, the quest romances are allegorized journeys into the self. Their psychological complexity is marked for us by their complicated frame structure, in which a male narrator tells the story to an implied male reader or to a male audience. In reading these narratives, we must always ask why *this* man is telling *this* story. What is his stake in the narrative? What is his relationship to the fantasies it represents? Furthermore, the circulation of the quest romance between male speakers/writers and male audiences/readers reinscribes the story of female exclusion so central to the genre and the period. Women are not able to participate in the exchange of storytelling that constitutes fin-de-siècle narrative structure. When the story is retold and adapted in contemporary culture, can it also be told by women? Finally, how does the frame close? What happens when the adventurer returns from the dark continent and sees "home" with different eyes? This aspect of the fiction has been especially challenging and problematic for directors like John Huston and Francis Ford Coppola who have filmed versions of the fin-de-siècle quest romance.

Three masculine quest romances of the *fin de siècle*, H. Rider Haggard's *She* (1886), Rudyard Kipling's *The Man Who Would Be King* (1888), and Joseph Conrad's *Heart of Darkness* (1899), show how themes of the male muse, male bonding, and the exclusion of women came together in a complicated response to female literary dominance, as well as to British imperialism and fears of manly decline in the face of female power. Haggard's *She* was one of the great best sellers of the 1880s. The story of a mysterious African kingdom ruled by an immortal white queen may seem paradoxical because it is about the search for a matriarchal goddess. Yet Haggard's heroes seek this goddess only to destroy her. *She* is about the flight from women and male dread of women's sexual, creative, and reproductive power. Furthermore, as Wayne Koestenbaum notes, "although *She* seems to be founded on a worship of the eternal feminine it is covertly concerned with relations between men."[29] It is a paradigmatic story of the male muse and of masculine self-mothering.

Haggard was in many respects the very model of the fin-de-siècle male romancer. The eighth of ten children, he emigrated to South Africa at the age of nineteen, hoping to make his fortune in the colonies where even younger sons could become great white fathers. By the time he was twenty-one, he had succeeded; he was Master and Registrar of the High Court of the Transvaal, "the youngest head of Department in South Africa," as he proudly wrote his father.[30] While still in Africa, Haggard began to turn out adventure stories and Gothic tales that quickly found an avid readership. Returning to England in 1885 with an English wife he had met in South Africa, Haggard had a period of intense creativity in which he first wrote *King Solomon's*

Mines and then composed *She* in six weeks, "at white heat, almost without rest." "There is what I shall be remembered for," he wrote in his autobiography.[31]

Many critics have seen in *She* a projection of the all-powerful mother; and indeed Haggard's mother Ella had been a writer whose epic poem *Myra, or the Rise of the East* appeared in 1857. Although she had been skeptical of his intellectual gifts, he dedicated much of his work to her and edited some of her poems after her death. In his autobiography Haggard wrote that "no night goes by that I do not think of her and pray that we may meet again to part no more."[32] Another of Haggard's female precursors was Olive Schreiner, whose *Story of an African Farm* had impressed him deeply, although he had advised her to write about more cheerful subjects. But while these women may have seemed like models and rivals, Haggard was most inspired in his literary career by a male muse, his friend and collaborator Andrew Lang, to whom *She* is dedicated, "in token of personal regard and of my sincere admiration for his learning and his works." A major theoretician of male romance, Lang eagerly helped Haggard with passages of Greek and other ancient languages in the novel, as well as commenting on style and content of the manuscript in progress. "I think it is one of the most astonishing romances I have ever read . . . ," he told Haggard enthusiastically. "It seems like a story from the literature of another planet."[33]

Structurally, *She* is a frame narrative introduced by a nameless "editor" and then told in the first person by a Cambridge don named Ludwig Horace Holly. "Branded by Nature" with "abnormal ugliness," Holly is a well-known misogynist, "popularly supposed to be as much afraid of women as most people are of a mad dog." In the Clubland environment of Victorian Cambridge, however, these fears only endow him with intellectual prestige. His closest emotional attachment is to a widowed male friend, Vincy, who dies, entrusting his beautiful infant son Leo to Holly, with directions for his education and a mysterious locked chest, the traditional mythic respository for secrets of birth. Holly thus miraculously achieves virgin fatherhood, paternity without the need for contaminating intercourse with women. In order to reinforce the fantasy of male reproductive autonomy, Holly vows to "do without female assistance" in raising the boy and to avoid Oedipal rivalry with a surrogate mother: "I would have no woman to lord it over me about the child and steal his affections from me."

Instead he hires as a "child-minder" a young working-class man named Job who shares his horror of women.

Leo, who is born in the same year as Haggard, grows up contentedly in this all-male family within the larger male community of Cambridge. Holly's only difficulties about his Apollo-like "son," "the handsomest man in the University," are that "every young woman whom he met . . . insisted on falling in love with him." But Holly successfully protects Leo from these predatory women, and he is educated according to his real father's wishes as a student of Greek, Arabic, and mathematics. When he is twenty-five, Leo opens the chest which is his sole legacy. It contains a parchment with the story of his birth and his family curse; he is not the son of woman, but rather Kallikrates, the reincarnated priest of Isis, formerly the lover of Ayesha or "She," the immortal white goddess who lives in Kôr, in the heart of Africa. She has killed his mother and doomed his father; thus, the father's message is that Leo should "seek out the woman and learn the secret of Life, and thou mayest find a way to slay her." The quest for She is thus both a quest for the Ur-Mother, who holds the secret of life, and the quest to usurp her power. It is not coincidental that the year when this quest begins, 1881, is also the year when women were first admitted to the Cambridge examinations, and when, symbolically, the strongholds of male knowledge begin to fall.

Holly, Leo, and Job decide to set out in quest of Ayesha. As they penetrate the African continent, moving into what would be the single blank space in the center of the map of empire, or the Congo Free State, the three Englishmen are also undertaking a symbolic journey into a body that seems disturbingly sexual, both female and male. The sexual ambiguity of the journey is underscored by the variety of adventures they have along the way. In the first stage of their journey, Holly, Leo, and Job are captured by the Amahagger, the People of the Rocks: tall, "of a magnificent build," "exceedingly handsome," but evil and cruel. The Amahagger live in caves within the crater of an extinct volcano. Their culture seems to be a matriarchy; the women are "exceedingly good-looking" and sexually aggressive; for in this tribe women "live upon conditions of perfect equality with the men . . ." Like the New Women novelists, they have renounced their dependencies on men; "descent is traced only through the line of the mother, and while individuals are as proud of a long and superior female ancestry as we are of our families in Europe, they never pay attention to, or even acknowledge, any men as their father, even when their male parentage is perfectly well known." Officially, the Amahagger worship women as creators: "Without them the world could not go on; they are the source of life." Yet this worship is mere lip service, for every second generation, Amahagger men *slaughter* their mothers: the men "rise and kill the old ones as an example to the young ones, and to show them that we are the strongest." Presumably this killing involves hotpotting, an Amahagger form of execution in which a heated earthenware pot is forced over the victim's head—an image of castration and decapitation Haggard personally invented that fits well with folklore motifs linking the sexual and the culinary. There is even a hint that the Amahagger eat their mothers; and their activities echo Haggard's themes, just as their name seems like an anagram of his.

They proceed through a nightmarish landscape, through swamps and desert, "vaporous marshes and stagnant canals, . . . like a Freudianly female *paysage moralisé.*"[34] They penetrate Kôr, however, as if it were a masculine body, through rear cave entrances into the "bowels of a great mountain." In the centermost cavern of Kôr, "the very womb of the Earth," they encounter Ayesha, "She-Who-Must-Be-Obeyed." Tall, magnificent, veiled, and wound about with a phallic golden snake, her beauty is so dazzling that even Holly is seduced when She unveils herself, "as Eve might have stood before Adam." Ayesha is the ageless and beautiful white queen of the African land of Kôr, whose law is the law of the Mother and whose "empire is of the imagination."

Both female Muse and phallic mother, Ayesha is murderous to her rivals, but irresistible to her lovers. Both Leo and Holly are captivated by her; the Englishmen are tormented by dreams of sexual and psychic portent—Holly that he is being buried alive, Leo that he is being split in half. Thus Holly is buried or engulfed in the female body he has always dreaded, while Leo is split between his sexual loyalties. Ayesha offers Leo eternal life if he will go with her through a roaring pillar of fire which sweeps through the caves. But when She first enters the fire, something goes terribly wrong. Instead of gaining eternal beauty, She ages two thousand years in minutes, before the men's horrified eyes: "the skin had puckered into a million wrinkles, and on her shapeless face was the stamp of unutterable age." As they watch in anguish, She shrivels and yellows; her beautiful hair drops off, and she becomes a tiny wizened monkey-like creature screaming in death-agony.

As several critics pointed out, Ayesha is an incestuous maternal figure, who must die before she consummates her relation with the younger Leo. With the death of this phallic and aggressive mother, the space is cleared for unbroken male bonding and creativity. Holly and Leo go away together to experience their "joint life" somewhere in Tibet, where no women will find or separate them. Eternal life will not come from the mysteries of the female reproductive cycle, but from masculine intellect and spiritualism.

The vast popularity of *She* suggests how powerfully it spoke to a male community. In its first few months of publication, *She* fulfilled Lang's expectations by selling over thirty thousand copies. Edmund Gosse found the novel "simply unsurpassable." Walter Besant congratulated Haggard on having written a work that put him "at the head—a long way ahead—of all contemporary imaginative writers." Henley declared that he had read all night and had been unable to put the book down until he had finished. Among the scores of parodies that followed publication, *She* also engendered a volley of male imitations and reproductions emphasizing the gender ambiguities of the plot. There were poems by Lang and Walter Besant entitled "She," "He," "Twosh," and "Of He and She," published in the private "recreations" volume of the Rabelais Club. Besant's "Of He and She" worried openly about male primacy and self-generation:

> In lonely slumber lay the earliest He,
> While from his rib was framed a lesser She.
> Lo! now the miracle reversed we see:
> From She unconscious springs a lesser He.
> Of He and She doubts fall on me and thee.
> How if the old tale with new agree?
> How if it 'twas She that slumbered and that He
> Was from the first a parody of She?[35]

Lang and Walter Pollock also collaborated on a novel called *He: By the Authors of It,* which appeared in 1887, a book which transposed Haggard's African setting to London's Clubland. Lang's sonnet "She," frequently reprinted in modern editions of the novel, underlines its meaning for a generation of men who read it as a testimonial to an eternal space of male aspiration, adventure, and imagination:

Not in the waste beyond the swamps and sand,
   The fever-haunted forest and lagoon,
Mysterious Kôr thy walls forsaken stand,
   Thy lonely towers beneath the lonely moon—
   Not there doth Ayesha linger, rune by rune
Spelling strange scriptures of a people banned.
   The world is disenchanted; over soon
Shall Europe send her spies through all the land.

Nay, not in Kôr, but in whatever spot,
   In town or field, or by the insatiate sea,
Men brood on buried loves, and unforgot,
   Or break themselves on some Divine decree,
   Or would o'erleap the limits of their lot—
   There, in the tombs and deathless, dwelleth She!

Haggard's circle assumed that women would not be among the novel's band of admirers and devotees. Walter Besant warned Haggard that female readers would not be able to appreciate _She_: "If the critic is a woman she will put down this book with the remark that it is impossible—almost all women have this feeling towards the marvellous."[36] In fact, however, _She_ has interested many women writers, from Willa Cather to Margaret Atwood.[37] Haggard's most passionate female admirer was undoubtedly Elizabeth Bowen, who read _She_ at the age of twelve and believed that it had radically changed her view of life. Bowen "read _She_, dreamed _She_, lived _She_ for a year and a half." The book, she recalled in a BBC broadcast in 1947, stood "for the first totally violent impact I ever received from print. After _She_, print was to fill me with apprehension. I was prepared to handle any book like a bomb." Bowen's attraction to the book, she thought, was _not_ an identification with the power and sexuality of Ayesha:

> Did I then, I must ask, myself aspire to "She's" role? I honestly cannot say so. "She" was _she_—the out-size absolute of the grown-up. The exaltation I wanted was to be had from the looking on. She had entered the fire (the thing of which I was most frightened). She shocked me, as agreeably and profoundly as she shocked Horace Holly. For me, she continued to have no face—I saw her as I preferred her, veiled, veiled; two eyes burning their way through layers of gauze.

Instead, Bowen identified with Holly as the writer, with "the power of the pen . . . the inventive pen."[38] In her story "Mysterious Kôr," published in *Penguin New Writing* in 1944, Bowen rewrote some of Haggard's fantasy themes from a woman's perspective. Her heroine Pepita is out walking with her boyfriend Arthur in the London of the Blitz, an eerie moonlit city that makes a mockery of the blackout: "London looked like the moon's capital—shallow, cratered, extinct." The lovers can find no place to be alone in the city; and Pepita longingly recalls the image of "mysterious Kôr," an eternal city of enchantment and romance. Kôr becomes her symbol of all that has been lost in the war: privacy, intimacy, hope, even desire. It is Pepita's imaginative retreat from the realities of the Blitz, and it figures as a specifically feminine fantasy that Arthur cannot grasp. For Bowen, too, writing in a London under fire, the promise of literary power and immortality in Haggard's story could be a sustaining personal vision.

When the twenty-three-year-old literary prodigy Rudyard Kipling arrived in London in 1889, with the dazzle, as Edmund Gosse remarked, of "a new star out of the East," literary Clubland saw him as a pretender to Haggard's and Stevenson's throne. "We'll tell you all about Rudyard Kipling—your nascent rival," Henry James wrote to Robert Louis Stevenson in 1890; "he has killed one immortal—Rider Haggard . . ."[39] "Kipling is by far the most promising young man who has appeared since—ahem—I appeared," Stevenson answered graciously; and despite the predictions of some that they would be literary rivals, Haggard sponsored him for membership in the Savile Club, and the two men became close friends.[40] They were often linked as writers of male adventure, not only in criticism but also in satire such as J. K. Stephens's verses on contemporary fiction, with its mocking demand for a season when "the Rudyards cease from kipling and the Haggards ride no more." Like Haggard, Kipling was fascinated by the sexual lure of the Orient and the dark continent. During his years in India, he had struggled with an unfinished book called *Mother Maturin*, which expressed his feelings about the castrating seductiveness of Mother India.[41]

At the top of the list of stories Kipling had published that already had defeated Haggard was "The Man Who Would Be King" (1888). Other writers of male romance, from Arthur Conan Doyle and Andrew Lang to H. G. Wells, conceded that "The Man Who Would Be King" was a "masterpiece," "one of the best stories in the world."[42] Like *She*, it can be read as a myth of romantic masculine aspiration, as an allegory of imperialism, as a psychosexual journey, as a fantasy of destructive female sexuality, or as a fantasy of literary power. Most readers, however, including John Huston, who turned it into an epic film, have taken it as simply "one of the greatest adventure stories ever written," the tale of two "likeable rogues who are loyal to each other and to their ideals and beliefs."[43]

Daniel Dravot and Peachey Carnehan, two vagabonds and petty swindlers who are veterans of the British Indian Army, meet a journalist, usually identified with Kipling himself, as they are traveling on trains in India. The journalist narrates the story of their plan to become the kings of Kafiristan, a remote and virtually unknown region of Afghanistan, "one mass of mountains and peaks and glaciers and no Englishman has ever been through it." There Peachey and Dan hope to use their military skill to win the natives over and to help them conquer their enemies. Ultimately, as rulers of Kafiristan, they intend to use British know-how to exploit the country's full economic potential. India, with its rules and laws and hierarchy, is too confining for their ambitions; "we have decided that India isn't big enough for men such as us."

The journalist-narrator becomes drawn into their project initially because they are brother Masons, who greet him with the secret codewords, signs, and grip of the Craft. But his willingness to help them out comes also in part from his tacit sympathy with their rebellion against the laws of class hierarchy. The epigraph to the story, imitating the language of Masonic law, presents male relationships as transcending class: "Brother to a Prince and fellow to a beggar if he be found worthy."[44] In their bold and courageous effort to find a new frontier, "some other place where a man isn't crowded and can come into his own," Dan and Peachey appeal to the side of the journalist that is disillusioned with the triviality and venality of Anglo-Indian life.

Thus the narrator agrees to witness a "Contrack" between the men that binds them to stick together, to stay away from liquor and women: neither to "look at any Liquor, nor any Woman black, white, or brown, so as to get mixed up with one or the other harmful"; and to stand by each other in time of trouble. The source of the contract is Proverbs 31:3: "Give not thy strength unto women, nor thy ways to that which destroyeth kings," especially, as Peachey later notes, "when they've got a new raw Kingdom to work over." Their plan works miraculously well. They survive the dangerous trip across the border to reach Kafiristan, where they teach the men how to fire rifles and lead them triumphantly against all their enemies. By a strange historical twist, the Kafiristani know Masonry, and Dan's direction of Masonic rites persuades them that he is a god who knows all their secrets. He is crowned king as the son of Alexander by Queen Semiramis.

At this point in the story some of the differences between Dan and Peachey begin to emerge, and the contract begins to fray. Peachey is not as qualified for kingship as Dan. He can do the practical work of advising the villagers about farming and drilling them in military formation; but Dan is the one who learns the language and begins both to establish a government and to dream of empire. He sees the villagers as the Lost Tribes of England, and plans to turn them into another body of colonial soldiers to fight and die for the queen. "I won't make a Nation," says he. "I'll make an Empire! These men aren't niggers; they're English! Look at their eyes—look at their mouths. Look at the way they stand up. They sit on chairs in their own houses. They're the Lost Tribes or something like it, and they've grown to be English . . . Two million people—two hundred and fifty thousand fighting men—and all English!" In pretending to be a king, Dan takes on the qualities of enlightened British rule. And Dan himself demands a queen, a wife to help him found a dynasty. Miscegenation is not an issue, for they are "white people . . . not like common, black Mohammedans," and the women are "prettier than English girls and we can take the pick of 'em. Boil 'em once or twice in hot water and they'll come out like chicken and ham."

The marriage upon which Dan insists is his downfall, for a God, as the natives believe him to be, cannot mate with a human being. The girl chosen to be his bride is "crying fit to die," thinking that she will be sacrificed to the god, perhaps eaten as the boiling metaphor suggests. Indeed, Dan licks his lips, "thinking of the wife he was going to get in the morning." When before all the people the terrified bride bites his neck and he bleeds, the Kafiristani realize that he is mortal. Despite a heroic resistance, the former kings are powerless against the enraged natives, who carry out a horrible revenge; they take Dan out on a rope bridge across a ravine, cut the ropes, and then decapitate him. Peachey is crucified, but survives; crazed and lamed, he returns to the city with Dan's dried and withered head, still wearing its gold and turquoise crown, to tell the tale to the journalist. Having told his story, he wanders off into the market and dies; when his body is discovered, the head and crown have disappeared.

The story is certainly Kipling's own sardonic meditation upon kingship—not only political power, but also literary power and ambition. The journalist-narrator identifies strongly with Dan and Peachey's quest for fame. The tale of their doomed adventure is framed by the narrator's more modest efforts in the newspaper office and by his sense of the brevity and fragility of empires. As the narrator tells us, "I greatly fear that my King is dead, and if I want a crown I must go hunt it for myself." Kipling's crown, however, would be made of laurels rather than gold, and he would win it precisely by telling stories of the Indian Hills and of British male daring and bonding. "When I came out of that furious spell of work towards the end of '88 I rearranged myself," he said in his memoirs, explaining why he left India for England, where a young writer could come into his own. Thus, finally, we can read the story as an allegory of writing: The Man Who Would Be King Romance.

John Huston's movie version of *The Man Who Would Be King* (1975), starring Michael Caine and Sean Connery, also stresses the glories of masculine ambition. The film has been described as the high point of the genre of "the colonial film," otherwise called the "English Western" or "Eastern."[45] Huston emphasized the bonding and doubling of Dan and Peachey: "These two men are like the opposite sides of a coin. They are a unit. I wouldn't know how to divide them. One starts a line of dialogue, the other finishes it. They always speak as two and they are identical until the moment when they divide and separate."[46] In explaining his reasons for making the film, Huston made clear that he thought of it as a universal fable of heroism: "The story has a trajectory. There is a wideness and handsomeness to it, and of the men; it echoes some dream that I think is in all our hearts, even as we grow older. That continual longing for great adventure. They confirm something that is in our yearning souls, and there is a bravery there, that kind of courage that we aspire to, and an affirmation that if you are brave enough the Gods will be with you; if you dare enough, you will be aided and abetted; and if you are brought up short (and this is the story), why, it's because once you attain the place you seek there is the danger of becoming high and mighty, of falling victim to the disease of power that most of those who live in a rarefied atmosphere are assailed with, once you begin to believe that you are indeed the supreme being, issuing the orders and making all the decisions. It has that sweep to it, and an underlying deep truth, which I hope and pray audiences will discover."[47]

Huston interpreted the story as a myth of power and doomed ambition, one of a number of interpretations that take the title as a clue. If we assume that the story is about politics, power, and history, and the problems facing the man who would be king, we can also read it as an allegory of European imperialism. Critics have noted that the action of "The Man Who Would Be King" reflects a number of events in recent history. In the 1880s the Indian government and the Russian Empire were fighting over expansion into central Asia and Afghanistan. Kipling had been present in 1885 when the Viceroy of India received the Amir of Afghanistan on a state visit, and had traveled as far as the Khyber Pass. Dan and Peachey think of themselves in terms of Sir James Brooke, the legendary English soldier who pacified Borneo and became Rajah of Sarawak. And the story also evokes the most traumatic Anglo-Indian memory of imperialism, the Indian Mutiny of 1857, when the Bengal Army rebelled against their British officers over an order they perceived as an attack on their religious practices. The Mutiny became notorious because of highly publicized atrocities committed by the Bengal Army, which were avenged in equally vicious and bloody retributions by the British; it became a turning-point in British attitudes towards their Indian colonial subjects and in Indian resistance to that rule.

"This business is our Fifty-Seven," Peachey tells Dan. Dan's hubris in setting himself up as a King and god among the Kafiristani ("by virtue of the authority vested in me by my own right hand"), his insistence on imposing "civilized" British methods on their culture, and his defiance of their religious beliefs, ultimately provokes their mutiny and their violent revenge against the Englishmen. But more generally, Kipling uses Dan and Peachey as figures for British rule in the Punjab and its post-Mutiny feelings of omnipotence and divine right. In the aftermath of the Mutiny, feelings of racial antagonism intensified. The British came to believe that they ruled by racial superiority over an emotional, superstitious, and depraved Indian people. Regarding themselves as "the incarnation of austerity, courage and self-control," they felt almost divinely chosen in their claims to empire. Only the young Englishman, wrote John Strachey in 1888, has the judgment, character, and intellect that "are necessary to the government of men." One Punjabi officer described himself as "very nearly in the position of a benevolent despot" who did "pretty much what I thought right and just." Another extolled "the first sweet taste of unbounded power for good over others, the joy of working out one's own design, the contagious pleasure of influencing hundreds, the new dignity of independence, the novelty of rule and swift obedience." These heady feelings inspired semi-magical thinking and superstitious beliefs in the godlike power of Englishmen ruling their little districts. As Walter Lawrence, Lord Curzon's secretary, recalled in his memoirs, "I had the illusion, wherever I was, that I was infallible and invulnerable in my dealing with Indians."[48] Dan's fantasies of destined kingship are not very far from the real rhetoric of the Anglo-Indian Punjab.

Another way of reading "The Man Who Would Be King" is as a story of male bonding. Symbolically, as the story makes clear, the man who would be king must stay away from women. ("Kings," Havelock Ellis noted in *Sexual Inversion*, "seem peculiarly inclined to homosexuality.")[49] The setting of the story reinforces this theme. The Punjab, like the American West, had a mystique of ruggedness and masculinity; Afghanistan and the Pathan tribes who swept down on raids through the Khyber Pass were mythologized as the most virile of the native hordes, as opposed to the "feminized" Bengalis of the south. But the borderline between hypermasculinity and homoeroticism was as tricky to negotiate here as in London's Clubland. According to one historian, Afghanistan was notorious for its homosexual practices; "In Afghanistan and in the frontier, the shameless proverb runs, 'A woman for business and a boy for pleasure.' "[50]

The representation of women in the story also underlines female power to threaten male bonds, to create rivalries between men, and to sap masculine strength. Women are nameless, divisive, and potentially deadly. In the first Kafiristani village Dan and Peachey reach, a fight is underway over a woman who has been abducted, and eight men have lost their lives. Peachey has had a liaison with a Bengali woman who taught him the lingo, but then ran off with the Stationmaster's servant and half his month's pay. The symbolic wound inflicted on Dan by his bride—"The slut's bitten me!" he cries—leads to his death, linking her with the castrating vampire-woman of other fin-de-siècle stories.

Dan's real crime, then, is not his exploitation of the Kafiristani, but his emotional betrayal of Peachey and his violation of their contract of male marriage. At first equals and partners, Dan and Peachey quickly slip into a hierarchical relationship in which Peachey is the "younger brother," the rejected friend. Peachey recognizes that Dan has gone beyond him intellectually; "Dravot was very kind to me, but . . . I knew he was thinking plans I could not advise about, and

I just waited for orders." Soon Dan is explaining that Peachey cannot "help me . . . in the way I want to be helped." Instead, he needs a wife: "A Queen to breed a King's son for the King. A Queen out of the strongest tribe, that'll make them your blood-brothers, and that'll lie by your side and tell you all the people think about you and their own affairs. That's what I want." The Queen will usurp the role of adviser and companion that Peachey has held; and Dan is punished when he rejects Peachey's help for the sexual lure of the woman. But in death, Dan and Peachey are reconciled. Dan's spirit guides the half-blind Peachey back to India and sustains him until he tells their story. They have achieved a love that endures beyond the grave, and that surpasses the love of women.

Like *She* and "The Man Who Would Be King," *Heart of Darkness* is both an expose of imperialism and an allegory of male bonding and the flight from women. Conrad's story of a journey up the Congo to find the mad Kurtz, who has abandoned his idealistic vision of suppressing savage customs and instead has set himself up as a savage god, is the most famous and influential version of the male quest romance. When *Blackwood's Magazine*, familiarly known as *Maga*, commissioned it, the editors congratulated themselves on bringing out "the most notable book we have published since George Eliot."[51] *Heart of Darkness* both took the genre to its artistic heights and brought out the seductiveness of a regression to the primitive. Although, like Haggard and Kipling, Conrad based his story on his personal experience in Africa and his protest against Leopold's exploitation of the Congolese, his eloquent pessimism, psychological complexity, and symbolic style have made his story the most enduring monument of fin-de-siècle disillusionment.

More insistently than the other quest romances, *Heart of Darkness* highlights the importance of narrative transmission from one man to another, in an interminable process. At the center of the narrative is Kurtz's story, available to us only in fragments. It is told by the seaman Charlie Marlow, who has traveled up the river in quest of Kurtz and in the process has discovered and revealed his own heart of complicity with falsehood, savagery, and greed. Moreover, Marlow's story, too, is contained within a narrative frame and told by someone else: an unnamed ex-seaman who, along with Marlow and three other men, a Lawyer, an Accountant, and a Director of Companies, is on a yacht in the Thames where they have gathered for their weekly reunion. This narrator, too, has his moment of enlightened identifi-cation with the story; and finally, the readers of the story, in recon-structing the case study of Kurtz, form their own relation to darkness, horror, and truth. Conrad had imagined these readers as the masculine audience for *Blackwood's*: "One was in decent company there," he commented, "and had a good sort of public. There isn't a single club and messroom and man-of-war in the British Seas and Dominions which hasn't its copy of Maga."[52]

But while *male* readers in the club, messroom, and cabin can share in the narrative transmission of Conrad's story, it is much more difficult for a woman reader to identify with the process or themes of the quest. As the feminist critic Nina Pelikan Straus observes, "Marlow speaks in *Heart of Darkness* to other men, and although he speaks *about* women, there is no indication that women might be included among his hearers. . . . The peculiar density and inaccessibility of *Heart of Darkness* may be the result of its extremely masculine historical ref-erentiality, its insistence on a male circle of readers."[53]

This is so not only because no women are named or specified in Marlow's audience, but because the terms in which Marlow sees the world exclude women from knowledge of the dark truth. From the very beginning, Marlow's quest is one which women can aid but never understand. Frustrated in his efforts to find a job that will take him to the "place of darkness" in the middle of the map, Marlow becomes so desperate that he uses the influence of his aunt: "I, Charlie Marlow, set the women to work—to get a job. Heavens!" Yet although his aunt can help him, she cannot understand what he is doing, and embarrasses him by babbling religious humbug about "weaning those ignorant millions from their horrid ways." "It's queer how out of touch with the truth women are," Marlow ruminates. "They live in a world of their own, and there had never been anything like it, and never can be. It is too beautiful altogether, and if they were to set it up it would go to pieces before the first sunset."

His attitude towards women is one of many details that have led critics to see Marlow as Kurtz's double, a theme brilliantly emphasized in the plan Orson Welles had in the late 1930s for a film of *Heart of Darkness* in which he would play both Marlow and Kurtz. Marlow has a first glimpse of Kurtz as a kindred spirit when he sees a sketch that Kurtz has painted, "representing a woman, draped and blindfolded, carrying a lighted torch." This image of a woman bearing a light she cannot see strikes Marlow as "sinister," but he responds to it instantly with curiosity and a kind of empathy for Kurtz. As the stationmaster tells Marlow, "The same people who sent him specially also recommended you." In fact, the text holds out hints that Marlow will replace Kurtz, take over his life—either by becoming mad and assuming Kurtz's role as God in the Congo, or by marrying his Intended back in the Old World.

Despite his skepticism and revulsion, Marlow comes to feel that Kurtz is a "remarkable man," a man who dared to "step over the threshold of the invisible." His cry "the horror!" is "an affirmation, a moral victory paid for by innumerable defeats, by abominable terrors, by abominable satisfactions." In order for Marlow to be loyal to Kurtz's victory and to protect his world of empowering but awful knowledge, it must be kept from non-initiates. He does not immediately tell his story when he returns. First he is ill, wrestling with death as Kurtz has done and coming to appreciate the greater defiance with which Kurtz has faced the abyss. The fever is a "passage through some inconceivable world that had no hope in it and no desire"; it is a transition from the heart of darkness back to European "civilization." Returning to Brussels, Marlow feels a sense of election and specialness that distinguishes him from the irritating Belgians "hurrying through the streets to filch a little money from each other, to devour their infamous cookery, to gulp their unwholesome beer, to dream their insignificant and silly dreams." When Company officials and distant cousins of Kurtz appear, he refuses to give up information. But he has some letters and a portrait of Kurtz's fiancée, who strikes him as different from her countrymen; she is beautiful, honest, mature. Yet when Marlow calls on her he feels that he must protect her naive faith in Kurtz by lying about what he has seen and heard. The exchange between Marlow and the Intended, according to Conrad, was the most important part of the story: "The interview of the man and the girl locks in—as it were—the whole 30,000 words of narrative description into one suggestive view of a whole phase of life, and makes of that story something quite on another plane than an anecdote of a man who went mad in the Center of Africa."[54] Their dialogue is intensely ironic; Marlow is drawn repeatedly into colluding with her idealistic view of Kurtz, although all his responses have a double meaning for the reader: " 'His end,' said I, with dull anger stirring in me, 'was in every way worthy of his life.' "

We may take this as a chivalrous white lie, meant to spare her feelings and leave her with her memories intact. But the symbolic dimensions of the story suggest otherwise. In keeping the truth about Kurtz from the Intended, Marlow ensures the continuation of the double worlds of men and women. "They—the women, I mean—are out of it—should be out of it. We must help them stay in that beautiful world of their own, lest ours get worse." Nina Straus interprets Marlow's gesture as his unconscious unwillingness to share his knowledge and love for Kurtz with a woman. "Marlow's protectiveness is no longer seen in the service of woman's deluded desires, but serves the therapeutic end of keeping the woman/intended mute."[55]

In this interview, the Intended reminds Marlow of Kurtz's African mistress, whom he has seen in the jungle: "She walked with measured steps, draped in striped and fringed cloths, treading the earth proudly, with a slight jingle and flash of barbarous ornaments. She carried her head high; her hair was done in the shape of a helmet; she had brass leggings to the knees, brass wire gauntlets to the elbow, a crimson spot on her tawny cheek, innumerable necklaces of glass beads on her neck; bizarre things, charms, gifts of witch-men, that hung about her, glittered and trembled at every step. . . . She was savage and superb, wild-eyed and magnificent; there was something ominous and stately in her deliberate progress." Ian Watt calls this woman "the most affirmative image in the narrative, the embodiment of the confident natural energy of the African wilderness"; but in another Conradian sense, while privileged Europeans are kept in the dark about the brute realities of imperialism, human greed, and cruelty, black women *are* the dark. As in the other tales, *Heart of Darkness* pursues the penetration of a female wilderness, here a place of lassitude, paralysis, darkness, and suffocation. Conrad told an interviewer in 1914 that the sight that had most impressed him in his life was "a certain woman, a Negress. That was in Africa. Hung with bracelets and necklaces, she was walking in front of a railroad station."[56] At the heart of the heart of darkness is this image of the black jungle queen.

Conrad's queen reappears as the "dark exogamous bride" of Levi-Straus's *Tristes Tropiques*, who epitomizes the seductive and threatening Other and who has been allegorically allied with the notion of wilderness itself.[57] Not only modernist novelists but also twentieth-century anthropologists learned their narrative techniques from Conrad. While late-nineteenth-century British anthropologists such as W. H. R. Rivers were influenced by reading male quest romances by Haggard and Kipling, Conrad's dark story of the divided self in the culture of the Other became the model for a younger generation of modern ethnographers. "[W. H. R.] Rivers is the Rider Haggard of Anthropology," Bronislaw Malinowski remarked at the beginning of his career; "I shall be the Conrad!"[58] By this vow Malinowski primarily meant that he would attempt to bring to his analysis of Triobrand people the subtlety, profundity, and wisdom of Conrad the artist. But he also experienced the gap between the serene and enlightened self of his ethnographic persona, and the Kurtz-like hostile and threatened self of his personal diaries.

Orson Welles never made the film he had planned, but Francis Ford Coppola's film revision of *Heart of Darkness* in *Apocalypse Now* (1979) provides a fascinating modern gloss on questions of male bonding, transference, and politics. By using Conrad's story and structures in a film about the American experience in Vietnam, Coppola revised the narrative forms of the male quest romance in contemporary terms. Most Conrad scholars, however, were looking for a reverent imitation and were highly critical of Coppola's free adaptation, in which Captain Willard (played by Martin Sheen), a character based on Marlow, is sent to Cambodia to assassinate Colonel Kurtz (played by Marlon Brando), a renegade Green Beret officer who has set himself up in a Montagnard compound as a god. Conrad specialists were both reluctant to give over the authority of their sacred work to a mere filmmaker and obtuse about the meaning of both film process and a Vietnam experience that might not be representable through modernist techniques. It was a spectacular display of academic snobbery. In a symposium in the journal *Conradiana* in 1981, for example, four scholars denounced the film as "fraudulent and glib" and "altogether confusing." Defending their Conrad against Coppola, the Hollywood hack who had previously made *The Godfather*, the academics compared the film to Disneyland, a "Horrorland" of wretched excess in contrast to Conrad's elegant modernist "restraint." They found the voice-over narration written by Michael Herr, author of the Vietnam memoir *Dispatches*, pedestrian compared to Conrad's impressionistic rhetoric, and cited the first line spoken by Willard—"Saigon. Shit."—as an instance of the way he "grunts in the tense amoral clichés of pulp detective fiction."[59]

But with every year since, the brilliance of Coppola's version has become more apparent—not as an adaptation of *Heart of Darkness*, but rather as a contemporary meditation and interpretation, a new work that alludes to Conrad but that also can be read back into the earlier work. Coppola finds extraordinary visual images for Conrad's impressionistic prose, such as the helicopter, used from the first frames of the film for its whirring blades and strange clicking noise, through its nightmarish end, when crashed helicopters seem like dead prehistoric birds burning in the jungle trees. Surrealistic scenes such as the cold-blooded helicopter attack on the beach, with its mechanized cavalry charge and rousing soundtrack of "The Ride of the Valkyrie," both shock the audience and also marshal all the excitement we have learned to associate with such moments in a lifetime of watching adventure movies. Like Conrad, Coppola engages in a critique of imperialism, but he also ironically affirms the pleasure of the film medium and the spectacle of the epic screen.

Coppola's own political point of view shifted several times during the process of making the film. The original screenplay, written in 1968–69 by John Milius, was a militaristic, right-wing, unabashed celebration of Vietnam heroics. George Lucas, slated to direct it while Coppola produced, called it "the American dream" of the "two-fisted, two-gunned tough killer everyone grows up on."[60] They had imagined a movie for John Wayne. But the final version filmed a decade later was the complete opposite: an anti-war film about the Vietnam experience. Yet, while Coppola's overt political attitudes towards American involvement in Vietnam changed over the decade from a naive celebration of two-fisted male adventure to an ironic understanding of the tragedy and insanity of the war, many elements of the film and of its production reflect the unconscious imperialism and sexism of male quest romance.

The representations of women in the film certainly reproduce the themes of Conrad's story and the flight from women characteristic of male romance. The nameless women back home stand for a fake world of domesticity and illusion, like Marlow's Intended. The gap between their world and the world of the jungle is too vast to be bridged; and in a sense the men have chosen the war as an escape from the world of marriage and family. Willard's first act in the film is to burn his wife's photograph; the defector Colby sends his wife an (intercepted) letter: "Sell the house; sell the kids; find someone else; I'm *never* coming back." Home and the domestic have disappeared; as Willard remarks at the beach party, "I had been back there and it just didn't exist anymore."

On the journey up the river, women, always nameless and speechless, appear as symbolic figures of sexual danger at every stage, from the Vietnamese schoolteacher massacred in the attack on the beach, to the girl who throws a grenade at the helicopter; to the Playboy bunnies at the USO show dancing to "Suzy Q," and finally, most chillingly, to the Vietnamese girl with the puppy shot by Willard on the boat. Women on the set were similarly objectified. At the party to celebrate the 200th day of filming, Coppola's wife noted in her journal, a topless girl with "perfect red stars painted around her nipples" jumped out of a silver box to "hoots and whistles."

In the course of the filming, Coppola became involved in an affair and considered ending his marriage. In the view of his wife, Eleanor, the film became a vehicle for Coppola's personal psychic odyssey, a working out of his own identification and projection with Kurtz's megalomania: "He is struggling with the themes of Willard's journey into self and Kurtz's truths that are in a way themes he has not resolved within himself."[61] She saw many similarities between her husband and Kurtz: "There is the exhilaration of power in the face of losing everything, like the excitement of war when one kills and takes the chance of being killed."[62] At some point she felt he had had "sort of a nervous breakdown. The film he is making is a metaphor for the journey into self. He has made that journey and is still making it."[63]

Coppola felt that making the film had correspondences with the Vietnam experience as well as the Conradian one: "The way we made it was very much like the way the Americans were in Vietnam. We were in the jungle, there were too many of us, we had access to too much money, too much equipment, and little by little, we went insane."[64] Moreover, when Coppola filmed *Apocalypse Now* in the Philippines in 1976, he uncannily reproduced some of the imperialistic issues of the text. As Chown pointed out, "in paying the Marcos government for its use of military equipment, Coppola was supporting a government possibly more repressive than the South Vietnamese government of Diem."[65] The government provided Coppola with personal bodyguards, and there were difficulties with the scenes involving explosives because President Marcos was in the area and "if the explosions went off without warning he might think it was a rebel attack."[66] With hordes of Filipinos to wait on them, the visitors thought they were in "a paradise." During the filming, Eleanor Coppola sat in her air-conditioned cottage watching women washing clothes in the river and peasants farming. While the budget for the film swelled to thirty-one million dollars, Coppola had endless luxuries shipped in. As his wife recalled, "I would tell him what no one else was willing to say, that he was setting up his own Vietnam with his supply lines of wine and steaks and air conditioners. Creating the very situation he went there to expose. That with his staff of hundreds of people carrying out his every request, he was turning into Kurtz— going too far."[67] In a "Saturday Night Live" parody of *Apocalypse Now,* "Martin Sheen was an assassin hired by a film company to go up river and stop the excesses of a film director gone mad."[68]

Just as Conrad had struggled with the last paragraphs of his story, Coppola had the most problems with the ending of the film and both considered and filmed several possible endings. As Jeffrey Chown observed, "to find a truthful ending to the film [Coppola] would have had to confront whatever personal changes he had gone through in the making of the film."[69] In the original script by Milius, Kurtz is dying when Willard arrives and Willard tries to rescue him. Similar to the ending of *Heart of Darkness,* and also echoing the John Huston version of "The Man Who Would Be King," Milius's ending makes Willard a witness to Kurtz's confessions: "He tried to tell me what he'd done—about participating in unspeakable atrocities and how he organized the tribes and executed those who opposed him—He told of raiding the Golden Temple for opium—tens of millions of dollars worth. He had plans—he wanted a kingdom—Kurtz wanted to be king."

Coppola's versions, however, emphasized the ambiguities of Willard's relationship to Kurtz rather than Kurtz's power. Willard's relation to Kurtz is even more explicitly a doubling than Marlow's. "If his story is really a confession," Willard says, "then so is mine." In all the versions of the film, Willard actually kills Kurtz, in a ritual temple execution cross-cut with the slaughtering of a carabao, rather than merely witnessing his death. Furthermore, the use in the film of Sir James Frazer's classic study of primitive myths and rituals, *The Golden Bough,* suggests the strong temptation for Willard to replace Kurtz, to become King himself. The film version that was shown in previews and at the Cannes Film Festival ends as the bloody Willard emerges from the temple and is saluted by Kurtz's people, ready to worship the new god. It is left uncertain whether Willard will leave or take over. The final frames show Kurtz's face, with a reprise of "the horror, the horror." While Coppola claimed to prefer this ending himself, he did not have the artistic confidence to retain it in the face of negative responses from his advisers, who thought the film needed a more positive resolution, and from preview audiences who had been asked to comment on the ending specifically. Later Coppola told an interviewer that in his mind "the film should end with a choice, which was 'Should I be Kurtz? Or should I be Willard?' "[70]

In the second version, which appeared when the film was first released in 70mm and is the one on the available videos, Willard and Lance leave the compound. When they return to the boat, Willard turns off the radio, canceling the airstrike. Along with this quiet ending, there were no credits, and theater patrons were issued credit booklets as they left. The third version, for the 35mm prints, showed the Kurtz Compound blown up in an enormous air strike: the apocalyptic ending by fire, the revolutionary conflagration. Yet what Coppola had really wanted, he told his wife, was still another ending in which, "Willard tells Kurtz's son the wrap-up, the statement of what it's all about," passing on the narrative in an unbroken patriarchal chain of signification, wrapping it all up in a final statement.[71] The desire for this ending, never filmed, echoes the sense in Conrad's story that Marlow is seeking Kurtz in order to find the same kind of finality and answer. But what he learns instead is a sense of complicity and open-endedness.

Ironically, the film has accumulated a number of new endings since its release. One is a feminine ending that breaks the patriarchal chain; the journal kept by Coppola's wife Eleanor of the making of *Apocalypse Now* adds a woman's voice to the narrative chorus. During the filming, Eleanor Coppola had internalized the gender myth of the narrative and had felt that she was merely a detached witness, an "innocent bystander, just recording some snapshots about the making of *Apocalypse*, as if it didn't pertain to me."[72] Back in California, however, she began to realize that she, too, had been part of the trip down the river: "I was watching from the point of view of the observer, not realizing that I was on the journey, too. Now I am at a place, I don't know quite how I got here. It feels strange and foreign. I can't go back to the way it was."[73] The personal apocalypse she had witnessed was the destruction of her myth of marriage: "For me, that big, two-headed stone temple at Kurtz Compound represented marriage. The basic structure of belief that my life was based on. It exploded. I wept and ached and tried to put back the stones, hold up the walls, and patch it together as it crumbled."[74]

Finally, history has provided an ending Coppola did not anticipate. The filming had unexpected effects upon the town of Pagsanjan, north of Manila, where the crew stayed. The economy had a temporary boom, and the high-school principal toured the bars every night urging the workers to save their money rather than throw it away on women and booze. "Our people have lost their sense of values," he said. "Everything I've taught them they've forgotten."[75] The long-range effects of the filming were even worse. When the money stopped, the community maintained its new standard of living through male child prostitution. According to Estafania Aldaba-Lim, a former minister of social welfare in the Philippines, "some gays with the crew fell in love with the young macho boatmen, and then it went to much younger boys, down to nine, ten, eleven years old, and the whole town got in on it." By 1989, a flourishing trade in boy prostitutes, tacitly supported by the community, had brought economic advantages to the children and their families.[76] Conrad could not have imagined a more ironic finale to the masculine quest for King Romance.

SIX

Dr. Jekyll's Closet

In January 1886, the same month that Robert Louis Stevenson published *The Strange Case of Dr. Jekyll and Mr. Hyde*, another strange case of "multiple personality" was introduced to English readers in the pages of *The Journal of Mental Science*. It involved a male hysteric named "Louis V.," a patient at Rochefort Asylum in France whose case of "morbid disintegration" had fascinated French doctors. Louis V.'s hysterical attacks had begun in adolescence, when he underwent a startling metamorphosis. Having been a "quiet, well-behaved, and obedient" street urchin, he abruptly became "violent, greedy, and quarrelsome," a heavy drinker, a political radical, and an atheist. So far his "symptoms" might be those of any teenage boy; but what seems to have upset his doctors particularly was that he tried to caress them. The French physicians attributed his condition to a shock he received from being frightened by a viper, and they cured him through hypnosis so effectively that he could not even remember what he had done.[1]

Stevenson (called "Louis" by his friends), may well have read the case of Louis V.; it had been written up earlier in the *Archives de Neurologie*, and his wife recalled that he had been "deeply impressed" by a "paper he read in a French journal on sub-consciousness" while he was writing *Jekyll* and *Hyde*.[2] He was also a friend of Frederic W. H. Myers, who discussed the case for English specialists. But male hysteria was a topic of considerable scientific interest in 1886. Berjon in France published his book, *La grande hystérie chez l'homme;* and in Austria Freud made his debut at the Vienna Medical Society with a controversial paper about male hysteria. While it was recognized in men, hysteria carried the stigma of being a humiliatingly female affliction. Another scholar of male hysteria, Charcot's disciple Emile Batault, observed that hysterical men in the Sâlpetrière's special ward were "timid and fearful men, whose gaze is neither lively nor piercing, but rather, soft, poetic, and languorous. Coquettish and eccentric, they prefer ribbons and scarves to hard manual labor."[3] Later this view of the hysterical man as effeminate would be carried into psychoanalytic theory, where the male hysteric is seen as expressing his bisexuality or homosexuality through the language of the body.

Homosexuality was also a topic of considerable scientific and legal interest in 1886. In January, just as Stevenson published his novel, the Labouchère Amendment criminalizing homosexual acts went into effect, and Krafft-Ebing's *Psychopathia Sexualis* offered some of the first case studies of homosexual men.[4] By the 1880s, such scholars as Jeffrey Weeks and Richard Dellamora have shown, the Victorian homosexual world had evolved into a secret but active subculture, with its own language, styles, practices, and meeting places. For most middle-class inhabitants of this world, homosexuality represented a double life, in which a respectable daytime world often involving marriage and family, existed alongside a night world of homoeroticism. Indeed, the *fin de siècle* was the golden age of literary and sexual doubles. "Late Victorian duality," writes Karl Miller in *Doubles*, "may be identified with the dilemmas, for males, of a choice between male and female roles, or of a possible union of such opposites. The Nineties School of Duality framed a dialect and a dialectic, for the love that dared not speak its name—for the vexed question of homosexuality and bisexuality."[5] J. A. Symonds wrote poignantly in his journals of "the dual life . . . which had been habitual."[6] In Oscar Wilde's *The Importance of Being Earnest*, leading a double life is called "Bunburying" and represents, as one critic notes, "the 'posing' and 'double lives' to which homosexuals were accustomed."[7]

Stevenson was the fin-de-siècle laureate of the double life. In an essay on dreams, he described his passionate aim to "find a body, a vehicle for that strong sense of man's double being" which he had felt as a student in Edinburgh when he dreamed of leading "a double life— one of the day, one of the night."[8] The double life of the day and the night is also the double life of the writer, the split between reality and the imagination. Nonetheless, biographers have long hinted that Stevenson's own double life was more than the standard round of brothels and nighttime bohemia, and have rattled such skeletons in

Stevenson's closet as "homosexuality, impotence, a passionate feeling for his stepson, submission to a wilful and predatory wife."[9] In particular, Stevenson was the object of extraordinary passion on the part of other men. According to Andrew Lang, he "possessed, more than any man I ever met, the power of making other men fall in love with him."[10] Among the group of friends, both homosexual and heterosexual, in Stevenson's large literary and bohemian circle, "male appreciation of Stevenson was often intensely physical."[11]

Some of this appreciation and sexual ambiguity is vividly conveyed in the portrait, *Robert Louis Stevenson and His Wife* (1885), by one of the artists in Stevenson's circle who led his own double life, John Singer Sargent (Figure 2). In the foreground, a slender and anxious-looking Stevenson stares out at the painter, elongated fingers nervously stroking his droopy mustache. On the right, on the very margins of the painting, her body cut off by the picture frame, is the shadowy figure of his wife Fanny reclining on a velvet sofa, wrapped from head to toe in a gilded veil. Between the two is a door in the background wall, opening into a dark closet. For Stevenson himself, the painting was "too eccentric to be exhibited. I am at one extreme corner; my wife, in this wild dress, and looking like a ghost, is at the extreme other end . . . All this is touched in lovely, with that witty touch of Sargent's; but of course, it looks dam queer as a whole." For Sargent, the painting showed Stevenson trapped by domesticity and femininity; it is, he said, "the caged animal lecturing about the foreign specimen in the corner."[12] In his marriage to Fanny, Stevenson wrote to W. E. Henley, he had come out "as limp as a lady's novel. . . . the embers of the once gay R.L.S."[13]

Stevenson's real sexuality is much less the issue in *Jekyll and Hyde*, however, than his sense of the fantasies beneath the surface of daylight decorum, the shadow of homosexuality that surrounded Clubland and the nearly hysterical terror of revealing forbidden emotions between men that constituted the dark side of patriarchy. In many respects, *The Strange Case of Dr. Jekyll and Mr. Hyde* is a case study of male hysteria, not only that of Henry J., but also of the men in the community around him. It can most persuasively be read as a fable of fin-de-siècle homosexual panic, the discovery and resistance of the homosexual self.[14] In contrast to the way it has been represented in film and popular culture, *Jekyll and Hyde* is a story about communities of men. From the moment of its publication, many critics have remarked on the "maleness," even the monasticism, of the story.[15]

John Singer Sargent,
Robert Louis Stevenson and His Wife, 1885.

The characters are all middle-aged bachelors who have no relationships with women except as servants. Furthermore, they are celibates whose major emotional contacts are with each other and with Henry Jekyll. A female reviewer of the book expressed her surprise that "no woman's name occurs in the book, no romance is even suggested in it." Mr. Stevenson, wrote the critic Alice Brown, "is a boy who has no mind to play with girls."[16] The romance of Jekyll and Hyde is conveyed instead through men's names, men's bodies, and men's psyches.

Henry Jekyll is in a sense the odd man of fin-de-siècle literature.

Unable to pair off with either a woman or another man, Jekyll divides himself, and finds his only mate in his double, Edward Hyde. Jekyll is thus both odd and even, both single and double. "Man is not truly one, but truly two," he observes, and his need to pursue illicit sexual pleasure and yet to live up to the exacting moral standards of his bleak professional community have committed him to "a profound duplicity of life," accompanied by "an almost morbid sense of shame." Coming to acknowledge his unutterable desires, Jekyll longs to separate his mind and his body: "If each, I told myself, could be housed in separable identities, life would be relieved of all that was unbearable."

Not only the personality of Jekyll, but everything else about the book seems divided and split; Stevenson wrote two drafts of the novel, the Notebook Draft and the Printer's Copy; the fragments or "fractions" of the manuscript are scattered among four libraries (two would obviously be more poetically just, but I cannot tell a lie); and Longmans published two Jekyll-and-Hyde-like simultaneous editions, a paperback shilling shocker and a more respectable cloth-bound volume.[17] Stevenson alludes obliquely to the composition process in the novel itself when Dr. Lanyon discovers the notebook in which Jekyll has recorded his experiments: "Here and there a brief remark was appended to a date, usually no more than a single word: 'double' occurring perhaps six times in a total of several hundred entries; and once very early in the list and followed by several marks of exclamation, 'total failure!' " Just as Jekyll searches for the proper dose to fight decomposition, Stevenson hints at his own frustration in composing the narrative of doubles.

Like the stories hysterical women told Freud, full of gaps, inconsistencies, and contradictions, Dr. Jekyll's story is composed of fragments and fractions, told through a series of narratives that the reader must organize into a coherent case history. The central narrator of the story is Gabriel John Utterson, who utters the tale, and eventually inherits Jekyll's estate. More than the others in their social circle, Utterson is a "Jekyll manqué."[18] Like many narrators in late-Victorian fiction, he is a lawyer, a spokesman for the Law of the Father and the social order, and "a lover of the sane and customary sides of life." His demeanor is muted and sober; "scanty and embarrassed in discourse"; "undemonstrative" and "backward in sentiment," austere and self-denying, he spends evenings alone drinking gin "to mortify a taste for vintages," or reading "a volume of some dry divinity"; although he likes the theater, he has not "crossed the doors of one for twenty years." He has almost a dread of the fanciful, a fear of the realm of the anarchic imagination.

Yet like Jekyll, Utterson also has an unconventional side to keep down; indeed, his self-mortification seems like an effort to stay within the boundaries of masculine propriety. Utterson's fantasies take the form of vicarious identification with the high spirits and bad fortune of "down-going men," for whom he is often the last respectable friend. "I incline to Cain's heresy," he is wont to say; "I let my brother go to the devil in his own way." Utterson, too, has a particular male friend, the younger "man about town" Richard Enfield, whom he sees every Sunday for an excursion that is the "chief jewel of every week," although "it was a nut to crack for many, what these two could see in each other." In another scene, he shares an intimate evening with his clerk Mr. Guest, his own confidant; at least "there was no man from whom he kept fewer secrets." Perhaps because his own life is so involved with repression and fantasy, Utterson becomes "enslaved" to the mystery of Hyde: "If he be Mr. Hyde . . . I shall be Mr. Seek." He begins to haunt the "by street" near Jekyll's house and to have rape fantasies of a faceless figure who opens the door to the room where Jekyll lies sleeping, pulls back the curtains of the bed, and forces Jekyll to rise and do his bidding.

Fin-de-siècle images of forced penetration through locked doors into private cabinets, rooms and closets permeate Utterson's narrative; as Stephen Heath notes, "the organising image for this narrative is the breaking down of doors, learning the secret behind them."[19] The narrators of Jekyll's secret attempt to open up the mystery of another man, not by understanding or secret sharing, but by force. "Make a clean breast of this [to me] in confidence," Utterson pleads with Jekyll, who rebuffs him: "it isn't what you fancy; it is not so bad as that." Jekyll cannot open his heart or his breast even to his dearest male friends. Thus they must spy on him to enter his mind, to get to the bottom of his secrets. The first chapter is called "The Story of the Door," and while Hyde, as the text repeatedly draws to our attention, has a key to Jekyll's house, Utterson makes violent entries, finally breaking down the door to Jekyll's private closet with an axe, as if into what Jekyll calls "the very fortress of identity."

One of the secrets behind these doors is that Jekyll has a mirror in his cabinet, a discovery almost as shocking to Utterson and the butler Poole as the existence of Hyde. "This glass has seen some queer doings," Poole exclaims in the manuscript (changed to "strange things" in the text).[20] The mirror testifies not only to Jekyll's scandalously unmanly narcissism, but also to the sense of the mask and the Other that has made the mirror an obsessive symbol in homosexual literature. Behind Jekyll's red baize door, Utterson sees his own mirrored face, the image of the painfully repressed desires that the cane and the axe cannot wholly shatter and destroy.

The agitation and anxiety felt by the bachelor friends of Jekyll's circle reflects their mutual, if tacit and unspoken, understanding of Jekyll's "strange preference" for Edward Hyde. Utterson, Enfield, and Lanyon initially think that Jekyll is keeping Hyde. What they see is that their rich friend Harry Jekyll has willed his very considerable estate to a loutish younger man, who comes and goes as he pleases, has expensive paintings and other gifts from Jekyll in his Soho apartment, gives orders to the servants, and cashes large checks Jekyll has signed. However unsuitable, this young man is Jekyll's "favorite," a term that, as Vladimir Nabokov noted in his lecture on the novel, "sounds almost like *minion.*"[21] Even when Hyde is suspected of a crime, Jekyll attempts to shield him, and begs Utterson to protect him: "I do sincerely take a great, a very great interest in that young man."

Jekyll's apparent infatuation with Hyde reflects the late-nineteenth-century upper-middle-class eroticization of working-class men as the ideal homosexual objects. "The moving across the class barrier," Weeks points out, "on the one hand the search for 'rough trade,' and on the other the reconciling effect of sex across class lines, was an important and recurrent theme in the homosexual world."[22] Edward Carpenter dreamed of being loved by "the thick-thighed hot coarse-fleshed young bricklayer with the strap round his waist," while E. M. Forster fantasized about "a strong young man of the working-class."[23] Furthermore, prostitution was "an indispensable part of the male homosexual life . . . with participants beginning usually in their mid-teens and generally leaving the trade by their mid-twenties." The "kept boy" was as common as the rough trade picked up on the streets; when he is "accosted" by the "aged and beautiful" M. P., Sir Danvers Carew, late at night in the dark streets by the river and beats him to death, Hyde both strikes at a father figure and suggests a male prostitute mugging a client on the docks.

Furthermore, Enfield calls Jekyll's abode "Blackmail House" on "Queer Street" and speculates that Jekyll is "an honest man paying through the nose for some of the capers of his youth." While Enfield explicitly does not want to pursue these implications—"the more it looks like Queer Street, the less I ask"—the butler Poole has also noted "something queer" about Hyde. As a number of scholars have noted, the homosexual significance of "queer" had entered English slang by 1900.[24] " 'Odd,' 'queer,' 'dark,' 'fit,' 'nervous,' " notes Karl Miller, "these are the bricks which had built the house of the double."[25] For contemporary readers of Stevenson's novel, moreover, the term "blackmail" would have immediately suggested homosexual liaisons. Originating in sixteenth-century Scotland, it was generally associated with accusations of buggery.[26] Furthermore, the vision of blackmail as the penalty for homosexual sin was intensified by the Labouchère Amendment. While homosexual men had long been vulnerable to blackmail, the new law, as Edward Carpenter noted, "opened wider than ever before the door to a real, most serious social evil and crime—that of blackmailing."[27] Popularly known as the "Blackmailer's Charter," the Labouchère Amendment put closeted homosexual men like Wilde and J. A. Symonds at particular risk. It made a major contribution to that "blackmailability" that Sedgwick sees as a crucial component of the "leverage of homophobia."[28]

In his original draft of the manuscript, Stevenson was more explicit about the sexual practices that had driven Jekyll to a double life. Jekyll has become "from an early age . . . the slave of certain appetites," vices which are "at once criminal in the sight of the law and abhorrent in themselves. They cut me off from the sympathy of those whom I otherwise respected."[29] While these passages were omitted in the published version, Stevenson retained the sense of abhorrence and dread that surrounds Hyde. The metaphors associated with Hyde are those of abnormality, criminality, disease, contagion, and death. The reaction of the male characters to Hyde is uniformly that of "disgust, loathing, and fear," suggestive of the almost hysterical homophobia of the late nineteenth century. In the most famous code word of Victorian homosexuality, they find something *unspeakable* about Hyde "that gave a man a turn," something "surprising and revolting." Indeed, the language surrounding Hyde is almost uniformly negative, although when Jekyll first takes the drug, he feels "younger, lighter, happier in body." Hyde is represented as apelike, pale, and inexpressibly deformed, echoing the imagery of syphilitic afflictions in nineteenth-century medical texts, and Utterson speculates that Jekyll may have contracted a disease from Hyde, "one of those maladies that both torture and deform the sufferer," for which he is seeking the drug as an antidote. Meditating on Jekyll's possible youthful crime, Utterson fears "the cancer of some concealed disgrace; punishment coming, *pede claudo.*" Along with the imagery of disease and retribution, the Latin phrase (literally "on halting foot") suggests a bilingual pun on "pederasty."

The male homosexual body is also represented in the narrative in a series of images suggestive of anality and anal intercourse. Hyde travels in the "chocolate-brown fog" that beats about the "back-end of the evening"; while the streets he traverses are invariably "muddy" and "dark," Jekyll's house, with its two entrances, is the most vivid representation of the male body. Hyde always enters it through the blistered back door, which, in Stevenson's words, is "equipped with neither bell nor knocker" and which bears the "marks of prolonged and sordid negligence."

Finally, the suicide which ends Jekyll's narrative is the only form of narrative closure thought appropriate to the Gay Gothic, where the protagonist's death is both martyrdom and retribution. To learn Jekyll-Hyde's secret leads to death; it destroys Dr. Lanyon, for example, as later, Dorian Gray also causes the suicides of a number of young men and then kills himself. While Jekyll tries to convince himself that his desire is merely an addiction, a bad habit that he can overcome whenever he wants, he gradually comes to understand that Hyde is indeed part of him. In a final spasm of homophobic guilt, Jekyll slays his other "hated personality." Death is the only solution to the "illness" of homosexuality. As A. E. Housman would write in *A Shropshire Lad*:

> Shot? so quick, so clean an ending?
> Oh that was right, lad, that was brave:
> Yours was not an ill for mending,
> 'Twas best to take it to the grave.

Jekyll is a "self-destroyer," Utterson concludes, not only because he has killed himself, but because it is self-destructive to violate the sexual codes of one's society.[30]

In the multiplication of narrative viewpoints that makes up the story, however, one voice is missing: that of Hyde himself. We never hear his account of the events, his memories of his strange birth, his pleasure and fear. Hyde's story would disturb the sexual economy of the text, the sense of panic at having liberated an uncontrollable desire. Hyde's hysterical narrative comes to us in two ways: in the representation of his feminine behavior, and in the body language of hysterical discourse. As William Veeder points out, "despite all his 'masculine' traits of preternatural strength and animal agility, Hyde is prey to what the nineteenth century associated primarily with women."[31] He is seen "wrestling against the approaches of hysteria," and heard "weeping like a woman." Hyde's reality breaks through Jekyll's body in the shape of his hand, the timbre of his voice, and the quality of his gait.

In representing the effects of splitting upon the male body, Stevenson drew upon the advanced medical science of his day. In the 1860s, the French neuroanatomist Paul Broca had first established the concept of the double brain and of left cerebral dominance. Observing that language disorders resulted from left-brain injuries, he hypothesized that the left frontal brain lobes, which controlled the right side of the body, were the seat of the intellectual and motor skills. Thus the left brain was more important than the right and virtually defined the distinction between the animal and the human. The right frontal brain lobes, which controlled the left side of the body, were subordinate; they were the seat of lesser, non-verbal traits. Individuals in whom the right hemisphere predominated had to be low on the human evolutionary scale. In describing or imagining the operations of the double brain, European scientists were influenced by their cultural assumptions about duality, including gender, race and class. They characterized one side of the brain and body as masculine, rational, civilized, European, and highly evolved, and the other as feminine, irrational, primitive, and backward. Many scientists argued that the intellectual inferiority and social subordination of women and blacks could be attributed to their weak left brains. Furthermore, when mental disturbances occurred, as one physician noted in 1887, there must be a terrible struggle "between the left personality and the right personality, or in other more familiar terms, between the good and the bad side."[32]

These ideas about the brain were strongly related to late-nineteenth-century ideas about handedness, since handedness was usually inversely related to brain dominance; and considerable effort was made to get left-handed children to change. Freud's close friend Wilhelm Fliess, however, argued that all human beings were bisexual, with the dominant side of the brain representing the dominant gender, and the other the repressed gender. Thus Fliess believed that normal, heterosexual people would be right-handed, while "effeminate men and masculine women are entirely or partly left-handed."[33]

The imagery of hands is conspicuous in the text of *Jekyll and Hyde* and has also been dramatically put to use in the various film versions, where Hyde's hands seem almost to have a life of their own. It draws upon ideas of the double brain and hand, as well as upon other social and sexual meanings. As a child, Jekyll recalls, he had "walked with my father's hand," suggesting that he had taken on the bodily symbols of the "right"—or proper—hand of patriarchal respectability and constraint. Hyde seems to be the sinister left hand of Jekyll, the hand of the rebellious and immoral son. Suddenly Jekyll discovers that he cannot control the metamorphosis; he wakes up to find that his own hand, the hand of the father, the "large, firm, white and comely" hand of the successful professional, has turned into the "lean, corded, knuckly," and hairy hand of Hyde. The implied phallic image here also suggests the difference between the properly socialized sexual desires of the dominant society and the twisted, sadistic, and animal desires of the other side. Jekyll's "hand" also means his handwriting and signature, which Hyde can forge, although his own writing looks like Jekyll's with a different slant. As Frederic W. H. Myers wrote to Stevenson, "Hyde's writing might look like Jekyll's, done *with the left hand*."[34] Finally, the image draws upon the Victorian homosexual trope of the left hand of illicit sexuality. Jekyll tells Lanyon that in the days of their Damon and Pythias friendship, he would have sacrificed "my left hand to help you." In his secret memoirs, Symonds, too, uses the figure of the useless hand "clenched in the grip of an unconquerable love" to express his double life and the sublimation of his homosexual desires.[35]

Some men, like Symonds and Wilde, may have read the book as a signing to the male community. "Viewed as an allegory," Symonds wrote to Stevenson, "it touches upon one too closely. Most of us at some epoch of our lives have been upon the verge of developing a Mr. Hyde."[36] Wilde included an anecdote in "The Decay of Lying" about "a friend of mine, called Mr. Hyde" who finds himself eerily reliving the events in Stevenson's story. But most Victorian and modern readers ignored such messages or evaded them. While there have been over seventy films and television versions of *Dr. Jekyll and Mr. Hyde*, for example, not one tells the story as Stevenson wrote it— that is, as a story about men. All of the versions add women to the story and either eliminate the homoerotic elements or suggest them indirectly through imagery and structural elements. When Stevenson's friends Andrew Lang and Rider Haggard claimed to have written a version of the story in their collaborative novel *The World's Desire,* they thought the most improbable part was when "the hero having gone to bed with Mrs. Jekyll wakes up with Mrs. Hyde."[37] Thomas Sullivan's 1887 stage adaptation of the story, starring the American actor Richard Masefield, invented a good girl wooed by Jekyll. Hollywood expanded upon this by giving Hyde a "bad" girl—a barmaid or a woman of the lower classes—although she is never a wholly unsympathetic character.

The John Barrymore film in 1920 created an amalgamation of Stevenson's story and Wilde's *The Picture of Dorian Gray.* The high-minded and idealistic Jekyll is in love with the girlish Millicent, the daughter of a Wildean Sir George Carew. But the rakish Carew taunts Jekyll with his innocence, and, in lines taken from Lord Henry Wotton in Wilde's text, urges him to taste temptation. Carew takes Jekyll to a music hall and introduces him to "Miss Gina," an exotic Italian dancer. Lust then becomes Jekyll's motive for the experiment, and his Hyde embarks on a career of debauchery that first leads him to destroy Gina, then takes him to opium dens and brothels, and ends with his vengeful murder of the tempter Carew. Here most explicitly, the "gentlemen," in their silk hats and capes, move easily from the drawing rooms of Mayfair to the alleys of Soho and the East End, while the women's positions are fixed. Millicent and Miss Gina never meet; and we cannot imagine that Millicent would trade places with the dance-hall girl. By grafting the Wilde plot onto the story of Jekyll and Hyde, moreover, the film suggests the seduction of Jekyll by Carew and constructs the triangle of father, daughter, and suitor as the bisexual rivalry of father and daughter for Jekyll's love. Jekyll kills himself by drinking poison, since at the deeper level of the film he is implicated in the unspeakable.

But in films where the homoerotic has been completely suppressed, Jekyll does not have to commit suicide. The question of Jekyll's motives was given a more Freudian cast in the 1941 MGM version directed by Victor Fleming and starring Spencer Tracy, Lana Turner, and Ingrid Bergman. Turner plays Beatrix Emery, Jekyll's innocent, upper-class, blond fiancée, while Ingrid Bergman plays Ivy, the barmaid. When Bea's father breaks off their engagement because of Jekyll's blasphemous experiments and takes his daughter away for a trip to the Continent, Jekyll's bottled-up sexual frustration, as well as the absence of the father and fiancée, causes Hyde to emerge and drives him toward Ivy. In a decade when Hollywood was fascinated by psychoanalysis, Jekyll's fantasies are represented in heavy-handed Freudian dream-sequences, in which Jekyll becomes a champagne bottle popping its cork and then drives and lashes Bea and Ivy like a team of horses.

Jekyll's sexuality is improper both within the bounds of patriarchal Victorian society and within the bounds of American values of the 1940s. Male sexuality is clearly limited to the spheres of either marriage or prostitution. Jekyll's profession itself is ambiguous in its sexuality. At their first meeting, he saves Ivy from a rapist and then examines her for injuries; since she does not know he is a doctor, the scene is full of double entendre. But the point is that "Jekyll has adopted a professional ethic by which available flesh is divested (as it were) of its erotic potential."[38] Yet Bea and Ivy are not simply "good" and "bad" women; Bea also feels desire for Jekyll, while Ivy feels love; and their moral complexity (complicated by the offscreen media identities of Turner and Bergman) deconstructs the simple dualism of Jekyll and Hyde as well. Moreover, the daylight Victorian world of patriarchy, in which Bea is an accepted object of exchange between her father and Jekyll, corresponds to the nighttime world in which Hyde is a sexual sadist who buys and then tyrannizes a working-class woman, whom he keeps imprisoned and finally kills. Women are property in either case. What is particularly interesting is that Hyde never goes after the virginal, "good" woman; his sexuality is clearly seen as bad and thus must be taken to low haunts and lower-class women.

In this film, then, the complex problems of male identity and male sexuality are translated into stereotypical problems of women, and the bisexual elements the text attributes to its male protagonists are made the exclusive property of the female characters. The Oedipal relationship in which Bea is a substitute for her dead mother and subject to her father's incestuous jealousy substitutes for the text's hints that Jekyll is in rebellion against his own father and the Fathers of society. Ivy, rather than Hyde, is represented as an emotional hysteric. The film even makes Jekyll a kindly psychiatrist, whom Ivy visits by day in search of treatment for *her* nervous illness caused by his visits as Hyde by night. (In Reuben Mamoulian's 1931 film version of the story, with Frederic March, Jekyll voices a keen interest in psycho-analysis.) In short, the *women* are sick rather than the uncontrollably mutating Jekyll, who is seen as only the guiltless victim of his altruistic scientific ambitions. Since his desires are acceptably heterosexual,

Jekyll feels no guilt and does not commit suicide; he is arrested by Lanyon and the police and taken into custody as he mutates into Hyde while insisting "I'm Henry Jekyll. I've done nothing."

A particularly interesting film version of Stevenson's story is *Dr. Jekyll and Sister Hyde* (Hammer Studios, 1971). Here the motive is the classic one of the male scientist trying to find the female secrets of creating life. Searching for a means to prolong life, the woman-hating Dr. Jekyll uses the morgue as the source of female reproductive organs for his elixir. When he takes the potion, he becomes a beautiful woman, his own female double, and ecstatically explores his new breasts. Soon the female personality is taking over, first overwhelming the professional Jekyll with a sudden and irresistible desire to shop, but quickly becoming a murderous rival for the single body. In order to prevent her from taking over, Jekyll has to kill women to keep up his supply of the potion. In a nice twist on the idea of the secret identity, he gets his female persona to become Jack the Ripper, since the police are not looking for a woman. Finally, as he runs from the police after a killing, Jekyll is trapped on a rooftop. In a clever version of the text's transformation scene, Jekyll helplessly becomes Sister Hyde; the camera cuts "to a close-up of those strong, hairy hands; we watch them elongate and become hairless."[39] As the weaker sex, Sister Hyde cannot hold on and drops into the hands of the police. The film's mingling of themes of duality and bisexuality, science and religion, is a closer reading of Stevenson's story than the more celebrated Hollywood versions.

With Jekyll and Hyde in mind, we think of the late nineteenth century as the age of split personalities who solve their social and sexual problems by neatly separating mind and body, good and evil, upstairs and downstairs. But is the divided self of the fin-de-siècle narrative everybody's fantasy? Can women as well as men have double lives? Can there be a woman in Dr. Jekyll's closet?

We could certainly not rewrite Stevenson's novel as the story of Dr. Jekyll's sister, Dr. Henrietta Jekyll (M.D., Zurich 1880), even if she were born, like her brother, with an "impatient gaiety of disposition" that left her "discontented" and unfulfilled. While Victorian gentlemen had the prerogative of moving freely through the zones of the city, Victorian ladies were not permitted to cross urban, class, and sexual boundaries, let alone have access to a nighttime world of bars, clubs, brothels, and illicit sexuality as an alternative to their public life of decorum and restraint. In the 1880s, a "lady was simply not supposed to be seen aimlessly wandering the streets in the evening or eating alone."[40] As Virginia Woolf wrote about the 1880s in her novel *The Pargiters* (later, *The Years*), young women could not visit friends, walk in the park, or go to the theater unaccompanied; "To be seen alone in Piccadilly was equivalent to walking up Abercorn Terrace in a dressing gown carrying a sponge."[41] Indeed, at the universities, women students were not permitted to attend lectures at the men's colleges unchaperoned, and even visits from brothers were carefully supervised.[42]

Nor would an Edie Hyde have fared much better. In 1886, the year that Stevenson wrote his story, Eleanor Marx protested that the effects of Victorian sexual repression were far worse for unmarried women of all social classes than for men. "Society provides [for men] the means of gratifying the sex instinct. In the eyes of that same society an unmarried woman who acts after the fashion habitual to her unmarried brothers and the men who dance with her at balls or work with her in the shop, is a pariah."[43] A working-class Edie Hyde wandering around the docks alone in the early hours of morning would have been taken for a prostitute or killed by Jack the Ripper.

Furthermore, a lesbian double life for women was not part of cultural mythology in the 1880s. While, as Jeffrey Weeks has explained, "by the end of the nineteenth century a recognizably 'modern' male homosexual identity was beginning to emerge, . . . it would be another generation before female homosexuality reached a corresponding level of articulacy. The lesbian identity was much less clearly defined, and the lesbian subculture was minimal in comparison with the male and even more overwhelmingly upper class or literary."[44] In 1920, Vita Sackville-West described herself as a "Dr. Jekyll and Mr. Hyde personality," torn between her love for her husband and her "perverted lesbian" attachment to women;[45] but in 1921, English legislators refused to include women in the Labouchère Amendment because lesbianism was too deeply disturbing even to forbid: "To adopt a clause of this kind," one MP proclaimed, "would harm by introducing into the minds of perfectly innocent people the most revolting thoughts."[46]

But the impossibility of actualized double lives for women did not mean that women were not as divided by fantasies, longings, and unrealized desires as men. Women as well as men were "truly two," as the celebrated Boston physician Morton Prince eloquently explained when he wrote at the turn of the century about the repressed sexuality of women:

"The multiform sides of a woman's nature differ from man's only in form and their conventional expressions. The contrasting sides, however, of the gentler sex are much less conspicuous to the world than men's and are more easily overlooked. In women, as every woman knows—but few men—one or more sides of the character are by the necessity of social customs camouflaged. From childhood she is taught by the conventions of society, by the social taboo, to restrain and repress, often even from herself, many impulses and cravings which are born within her, as well as many thoughts and sentiments which she has acquired by experience, by contact with the world and therefore by riper knowledge. The repression under the social codes of these, the natural expressions of a part of her personality had belied nature which has been confined for centuries in a cafe hung with opaque curtains, like unto the spiritualistic dark cabinets. But within her social cabinet, all sorts of orgies of human nature have been seething."[47]

Moreover, as the new science of psychoanalysis was demonstrating, transgressive desires in women seem to have led to guilt, inner conflict, and neurotic self-punishment, rather than to fantasies or realities of criminal acting out. In "Civilised Sexual Morality and Modern Nervous Illness," Freud named neurosis as the opposite of what he called "perversion." While neurotics, according to Freud, negatively repress their instincts, leading to nervous illness and hysteria, perverts more energetically put their desires into practice. These differences, furthermore, are gendered. As Freud concludes, "the discovery that perversions and neuroses stand in the relation of positive and negative is often unmistakably confirmed by observations made on the members of one generation of a family. Quite frequently a brother is a sexual pervert, while his sister, who, being a woman, possesses a weaker sexual instinct, is a neurotic whose symptoms express the same inclinations as the perversions of her more sexually active brother. And correspondingly, in many families, the men are healthy, but from a social point of view immoral to an undesirable degree, while the women are high-minded and over-refined, but severely neurotic." According to Freud's theory, we cannot recast Jekyll and Hyde with female protagonists, because a female Dr. Jekyll with a repressed Sister Hyde is more likely to be agoraphobic than to be picking up (or beating up) men in the street. The brother acting out his instincts in East London will be Jack the Ripper, while his sister will be Jill the Weeper, home with her migraines, depressions, and breakdowns.

Yet medical literature of the *fin de siècle* reveals that observed clinical cases of multiple personality were predominantly female and that in life rather than art, hysterical self-fragmentation was more likely to be a feminine than a masculine response to social pressures. Putting Stevenson's "strange case" in the contexts of late-Victorian sexual culture and contrasting it to medical narratives of the period which described strange cases of *female* split personality reveals both some of the dualistic fantasies of the *fin de siècle* and the ways that they were constructed in terms of gender, sexuality, homophobia, and patriarchy.

Dr. Morton Prince of Boston was the leading American medical expert on multiple personality at the *fin de siècle* and treated two of the most famous female cases, "Miss Beauchamp" and "B.C.A." in the 1890s. The "multiple personalities" of Miss Beauchamp and B.C.A. were all too clearly facets of female repression and rebellion, attempts to live by a different set of values and norms, particularly those having to do with women's restrictive roles. While Victorian men could get through the week on a mere two personalities, Victorian women seemed to need at least three. In the United States especially, duality always seemed insufficient to accommodate the competitive and contradictory ambitions of an expanding nation and to cope with the conflicts in women's roles that were a major factor in the American phenomenon of multiple personality.

But despite their parallels to Stevenson's strange case, these female cases were much less adventurous than Jekyll and Hyde. "Miss Beauchamp" was really Clara Norton Fowler, a twenty-five-year-old "bibliophile," who was "never so happy as when allowed to delve amongst books." In 1898 she came to Prince with neurasthenic symptoms, which he traced to a traumatic shock at the age of eighteen: a male voyeur had spied on her through a window, and "she saw his excited manner and heard his voice between the peals of thunder."[48] Under hypnosis, she developed three personalities, which he called BII, BIII, and BIV, and thought of as the Saint, the Woman, and the Devil. While BII was anxious, rigid, and neurotic, BIII (who first called herself "She," after Rider Haggard's heroine, but then chose the name "Sally Beauchamp"), was vivacious, high-spirited, and amoral. Sally was also openly and passionately enamored of Dr. Prince: "I love you always, you know *always*, but best when you are strong and splendid, when you are tired and people are not nice to you . . ." she wrote to him. "Please forgive me again . . . and let me stay with you. *Please* please please." Prince's daughter recalled that when Sally "was too obstreperous, odors of ether would emerge from the office," as he attempted to "subjugate this mischievous nature." These multiple personalities were created during the therapy, and on the whole did not appear outside of it. Despite Sally's wishes, Prince would not allow her to become the dominant personality. She went "back to where she came from," "imprisoned" and "squeezed" into the body of a unified "Miss Beauchamp," and after her treatment with Prince, she attended Radcliffe College and married another prominent Boston neurologist. Her story was turned into a Broadway play by David Belasco, *The Case of Becky*, in which the neurologist, renamed "Dr. Emerson," declares, "Dorothy is Dr Jekyll; Becky, her other self, is Mr. Hyde."

The case of B.C.A. is even more compelling and more like the story of Jekyll and Hyde. At Dr. Prince's request, Nellie Bean, or "B.C.A." wrote a fascinating study called "My Life as a Dissociated Personality" (1909), which has two narrative sections, one written by the Hyde personality, "B," and the other by the cured personality, "C," looking back on her experience. "A" was a forty-year-old widow in 1898 when she first came to Prince suffering from depression, insomnia, headaches, and odd behaviors. "A" was morbid, helpless, prudish, and terrified of living without a man. Like Fowler, she was intellectual, literary, and frustrated by the pressures towards domestic submission enjoined by her society. One of her symptoms was the emergence of another self, "B," who was daring and independent. B had named herself "Bertha Amory" after the feminist heroine of a novel by Frances Hodgson Burnett. She wore white instead of widow's weeds, enjoyed "fun and a gay time," smoked, danced, and flirted with men, and allowed one Mr. Hopkins to kiss her. B was alarmed by A's anxiety and by her schemes to remarry: "Why, if she got married I would be married too I suppose, and I won't. I *can't*." She thought that A should sell her house instead, and use the money to start a new life. Among B's interests was the field of psychology, towards which she felt "full of enthusiasm." Like Hyde, B felt youthfully liberated from A: "As B, I was light-hearted and happy and life seemed good to me; I wanted to live; my pulses beat fuller, my blood ran warmer through my veins than it ever had done before. I seemed more alive . . . I felt much younger, and looked so, for the lines of care, anxiety, sorrow and fatigue had faded from my face . . . I neglected my family and friends shamefully . . . my tastes, ideals and points of view were completely changed." Furthermore, B felt no guilt over her new behavior: "The only emotion that I remember to have experienced is one of pleasure and happiness. I know nothing of remorse, reproach, and despair."

Prince called B "a psychological impossibility," and his goal in the therapy was to get rid of her. B, for her part, was bewildered by Prince's preference for the strait-laced and neurotic A: "I cannot see why Dr. Prince would rather have that emotional, hysterical set than to have me! It passes comprehension." In notes left on tables and dressers, B pleaded with A not to tell Dr. Prince everything she was doing, and finally planned to run away: "There are lots of things in the world to do and I am going to do some of them if I have half a chance." As Prince constructed a sober compromise figure, C, under hypnosis, B became increasingly alarmed. She begged Prince to let her be the dominant personality: "I am afraid I am going to be a woman just like A & C. I don't want to, Dr. Prince . . . I want to be just what I have always been—just 'B,' free as the wind, no body, no soul, no heart. I don't want to love people because if one loves one must suffer— that is what it means to be a woman—to love and suffer."

But the wild, Brontëish B, with her longings for exploration and freedom, her lack of guilt, and her independence from men, could not survive in Prince's Boston at the turn of the century. In his terms, she was indeed a monster who had to die. Under hypnotic treatment, Prince finally managed to suppress both the A and B personalities, and the C personality took over. As C, Mrs. Bean spent the remaining years of her life as Prince's devoted research assistant and typist. She did not remarry. It seems a convenient resolution for Prince and a prosaic fate for the rebellious B, who had pleaded not to be cured into feminine "normalcy."

> It's fantastic, she said.
> Since becoming a single I've really
> Gotten into myself.
> (Sandra Gilbert, "Singles")

Even in the late twentieth century, the age of the single, the story of Jekyll and Hyde does not seem to have lost its appeal. In 1989–

1990, Michael Caine, Anthony Perkins, Everett Quinton, and Robert Goulet all appeared in adaptations. And fascination with fin-de-siècle male doubling persists, especially in the work of collaborative artists such as Gilbert and George, McDermott and McGough, and the Starn Twins. David McDermott and Peter McGough, particularly, produce work that alludes to fin-de-siècle homosexual themes, such as *Queer— 1885*, or *Green Carnations—1887*.[49] On the screen, the Jekyll-Hyde story has become the dark-side film (*Something Wild, After Hours*), in which an innocent or upright young man meets a femme fatale who takes him to the dark side of himself: a violent, sadistic, and sexually perverse man. The most successful of these films, David Lynch's *Blue Velvet* (1986), uses Isabella Rossellini in a striking homage to her mother, Ingrid Bergman, while Dennis Hopper is a psychopathic version of Spencer Tracy's sadistic Hyde.

Can we imagine a female Dr. Jekyll today? Susan Sontag's short story *Doctor Jekyll* (1978) is a clever postmodernist version set in contemporary Manhattan. Jekyll is a successful surgeon, Hyde a delinquent addict. Hyde finally persuades Jekyll to try some violence in his own right, and Jekyll goes to prison for the attempted murder of Hyde. But Sontag does not attempt to imagine the story from a woman's perspective. Similarly, Joyce Carol Oates, in the series of novels about twins and doubling she published under the pseudonym "Rosamund Smith," projects the heroine's split psyche onto twinned or doubled male characters.[50] And Fay Weldon, in *Lives and Loves of a She-Devil*, has a Hyde heroine who makes herself over into a beautiful Jekyll.

The Scottish novelist Emma Tennant, however, has written a brilliant feminist version of Stevenson's novel called *Two Women of London: The Strange Case of Ms. Jekyll and Mrs. Hyde* (1989). Tennant has suggested that the double story is particularly meaningful both for women and for Scottish writers who invented it and who grew up within a bilingual and double culture; her earlier novel, *The Bad Sister*, also deals with the theme of the split female psyche.[51] Set in the Notting Hill district of London, *Two Women of London* incorporates the true story of a modern Ripper, the Notting Hill Rapist, with a reimagining of the double theme. The beautiful and fashionable art dealer Eliza Jekyll is really the aging welfare mother Mrs. Hyde, abandoned with her three children by her husband and first tranquilized and then transmogrified by drugs. When she reverts to being Mrs. Hyde, Eliza Jekyll becomes a feminist avenger, murdering the rapist and also the man who has abandoned her. In Eliza Jekyll's statement of the case—in Tennant's modernized version of Stevenson's multiple narrative, a message on her answering machine—she explains: "I am as I am: I was brought up to believe in happiness and my parents and school teachers gave me nothing but love and encouragement. I had no idea of the reality of life, of the pain and suffering which once was considered an integral part of it."

There could obviously be an American version of Tennant's novel, but the American urban narrative that suggests itself to me is far more violent. Henrietta Jekyll, a distinguished woman scientist in her mid-fifties, unmarried, admired by all the other single and successful career women in her social circle, longs for another identity, another body, in which to live out her repressed desires. She takes a potion and is transformed into a young, tough, sexy, streetwise babe with a lot of makeup, tight leather clothes, and no inhibitions. So far, so good. But then the story pulls up short. Where does Edie Hyde go once she's all dressed up? To look for Mr. Goodbar? To walk in Central Park? To the porn shops and sex shows in Times Square? All these roles are dangerous and victimizing for women, rather than empowering as they might be for men. Henrietta Jekyll would soon become a rape or homicide statistic, a gory headline in the *Daily News*, or a lurid cover story in *People* magazine.

The Jekyll-Hyde story, however, has taken a weird realistic turn in the United States where, in the last few decades, there has been an epidemic among women of what is now called Multiple Personality Disorder, or MPD. In the MPD Movement, according to Nicholas Humphrey and Daniel Dennett, "women outnumber men by at least four to one, and there is reason to believe that the vast majority—perhaps 95 percent—have been sexually or physically abused as children."[52] The theory is that the sexually abused child shuts off a part of itself in denial, which then undergoes further splittings. (From this point of view, we might speculate that Jekyll's problem was that he had been abused by a relative, teacher, or servant.) The "host" personality thus generates several "alters," and the number of alters is increasing. While the fin-de-siècle fiction of doubles involves two personalities, and the modern medical literature on split personality, as in the symbolically named *Three Faces of Eve* (1957), usually involves three personae, the median number of alters for patients described in the current medical literature is eleven. We might say that as the roles demanded of American women increase, female personalities do as well: by 1975, for example, when her identity became public, "Eve" 's selves had "multiplied like rabbits," reaching a grand total of twenty-two and beating "Sybil" 's previous record of sixteen.[53]

Furthermore, some of these selves are now masculine; in order for the Jekyll-Hyde fantasy of liberation to be fully imagined for a woman, Henrietta Jekyll has to turn into a man. In a fin-de-siècle post-feminist America where there is so much from which to dissociate oneself, women are going to need both a Sister and a Mister Hyde.

SEVEN

The Woman's Case

If *The Strange Case of Dr. Jekyll and Mr. Hyde* was a fin-de-siècle myth of men's double lives in the city, the strange case of Jack the Ripper in 1888 was a myth of warning to women of the dangers of lives outside the home. The Ripper butchered and mutilated a number of prostitutes in London's East End in 1888, opening the women's bodies and neatly removing the uterus and viscera. It was conjectured that the Ripper might be a doctor, since he performed such efficient operations on his patients. And while there was initially speculation that the Ripper might indeed *be* a woman, perhaps a midwife or a female medical student, the Ripper murders quickly became "a modern myth of male violence against women, a story whose details have become vague and generalized, but whose 'moral' message is clear: the city is a dangerous place for women, when they transgress the narrow boundaries of home and hearth and dare to enter public space."[1] "No Jill the Ripper," Gilbert and Gubar remind us, "would emerge to retaliate for her sex either in fact or fiction at the *fin de siècle*."[2]

While the Ripper murders were an aberrant and horrible event, they eerily echoed other fin-de-siècle themes of the opening up, dissection, or mutilation of women. The image of the dead female body—"Cover her up! How still it lies!"—displayed at the end of "The Buddhist Priest's Wife" suggests that the New Woman will end up as an exhibit or specimen case; and in this sense Schreiner's story is one of many late-Victorian case studies that uses the metaphors of the clinic and the laboratory to represent female dissent. If the rebellious New Woman—the "shrieking sister"—or the prostitute could be turned into a silent body to be observed, measured, and studied, her resistance to convention could be treated as a scientific anomaly or a problem to be solved by medicine. The imagined viewer in Schreiner's story can project his own romantic or conventional interpretations on to the enigmatic "outline under the white." Most important, the woman can be turned into a case, transformed from "she" into "it," so that her individual experience becomes impersonal and statistical, meaningful primarily as experimental material for the scientist. In the imaginative as well as the medical literature of the *fin de siècle*, the woman becomes the case study as well as the case, an object to be incisively opened, analyzed, and reassembled by the male writer.

The image of the young woman whose body is penetrated by the science of medicine already had a long post-Enlightenment tradition by the 1880s. In the eighteenth century, European medical students studied the internal organs with the aid of "Anatomical Venuses," elaborate wax models of women, naturally colored, physically detailed down to the eyebrows and eyelashes, and opened up to display the reproductive organs, sometimes including a fetus. The idea of creating bodies out of wax developed in Bologna and reached its height around 1775 in Florence; purchased by kings and noblemen for their medical faculties, the wax models can be seen in the medical museums of Europe, in London, Bologna, Florence, Rome, Vienna, and Budapest (Figure 3).[3] As Ludmilla Jordanova pointed out, these female figures were very different both from earlier depictions of internal organs and from comparable male figures: "The female figures are recumbent, frequently adorned with pearl necklaces. They have long hair, and occasionally they have hair in the pubic area also. These 'Venuses' . . . lie on velvet or silk cushions, in a passive, almost sexually inviting pose." Displayed in glass cases, the women's bodies are wax cases themselves, whose "lids" are opened up to reveal the insides, the mysterious organs of sexuality and reproduction. As Jordanova argued, the Venuses are both "knowingly erotic" and "invite us to peer into bodily recesses and to find there evidence of reproductive capacities." They simultaneously evoke an abstract femininity, equate knowledge with looking deeply into the body, and emphasize women's reproductive destiny.[4] While men, as Verena Tarrant protests in *The Bostonians*, see the case of female sexuality as "a very comfortable, cosy, convenient box, with nice glass sides, so we can see out," women regard "the box in which we have been kept for centuries" as a prison. And this image of the female body as a case, as Pan-

Anatomical Venus, Budapest, 1789.

dora's box, as an object of exhibition and confinement, carried over to the social world.

For the nineteenth century, eagerness to open up the woman and see deeply into the secrets of her body and of creation was central to the process and method of science itself. This passion for observation and analysis was manifested first in the development of scientific, medical, and gynecological instruments, then in dissection, and finally in sexual surgery. When the French doctor Récamier invented the speculum in the mid–nineteenth century, it became possible for doctors to examine the interior of the female body without surgery. The American gynecologist Marion Sims, who experimented with a speculum in 1845, experienced himself as a "colonizing and conquering hero"; "I saw everything as no man had ever seen before," Sims rejoiced; ". . . I felt like an explorer in medicine who first views a new and important territory."[5] Thus in a metaphor that would become standard in medical discourse, Sims aligned himself with the conquistadors who penetrate an alien land. While male novelists, as we have seen, describe their journeys into Kôr, Kafiristan, or the heart of darkness as sexual expeditions into a primordial female body, doctors describe their invasions of the female body as adventurous quests for treasure and power.

The clitoris was the first stop on the male voyage into the female interior. Discovered by an anatomist appropriately named Columbus in the sixteenth century, the Renaissance clitoris was the brave new world, the marvellous female analogue to the penis. Seventeenth-century writers were untroubled neither by the multiple functions of the clitoris, including its potential for lesbian or tribadic pleasure, nor by its size, for as Nicholas Culpepper observed, "it is agreeable both to reason and authority, that the bigger the clitoris in a woman, the more lustful they are."[6] But by the late nineteenth century, the clitoris seemed like a threatening organ. Lesbians were rumored to have grossly enlarged clitorises, and in addition to homosexuality, other "diseases" of the New Woman, such as masturbation, depression, marital dissatisfaction, and nymphomania, were attributed to clitoral over-development.

Since its sole function was female sexual pleasure, for some doctors the clitoris was expendable. In the 1860s, the English physician Isaac Baker Brown pioneered the operation of clitoridectomy, or surgical excision of the clitoris, for female nervous diseases. A skillful surgeon much admired for the "brilliant dexterity he displayed in the use of his left hand when operating on the female perineum,"[7] Baker Brown performed clitoridectomies in his busy London clinic on scores of clients, including five women whose "madness" consisted of wanting divorces; in each case the woman returned to her husband subdued. He believed that the operation was particularly effective in cases of nymphomania, because he never saw a recurrence of such unbridled female passion after the surgery.

On the other hand, the American gynecologist Robert T. Morris feared that evolution might be doing away with the clitoris in educated white women, leading to lessened sexual desire and therefore more female independence from men. Morris believed that Baker Brown's mistake was removing the clitoris rather than adjusting it and regretted that Baker Brown had been "led astray as so many pioneers are." Race and class obviously played a strong role in Morris's understanding of female sexuality. In his view, "the proportion of white women with normal sexual organs is small," and surgery might be necessary to repair their clitoral adhesions. Among black and Indian women, however, he was sure that the clitoris was "free," leading to their greater sexual responsiveness. Morris hoped to prove his hypothesis by measuring the clitorises of Indian women on reservations, but he was disappointed in his research when "agency physicians to whom I referred state that Indian women would not allow them to collect statistics such as we wanted."[8]

The racism of Morris's assumptions about the sexuality and bodily configuration of black and Indian women and his expectation that they would be willing to cooperate with his research point to the other signification of clitoridectomy: the ritual practice of what is sometimes called "female circumcision" in the Third World, especially the Middle East, as a form of controlling women's sexuality. As Gayatri Spivak argued, the excision, effacement, and symbolic suppression of the clitoris is always an effort to define women in terms of their reproductive function and as objects of sexual exchange, to remove the sign of female sexual autonomy and subjectivity.[9]

Women's vulnerability to the claims of such medical charlatans and their willingness to accept drastic surgical remedies for their sexual and emotional problems plays a significant role in this history. In England, by the 1880s and 1890s, clitoridectomies had been discredited; but they were succeeded by ovariotomies, as eagerly sought by women, doctors maintained, "as though the surgeon's knife were gifted with the power of an enchanter's wand."[10] The English surgeon Lawson Tait performed several hundred ovariotomies; Sir Thomas Spencer Wells had performed a thousand by 1880. "Pelvic operations on women has [sic] become a fad," one doctor commented in 1894. "It is fashionable, and the woman who cannot show an abdominotomy line is looked upon as not in the style."[11] Doctors rationalized that "the deprivation of the sexual glands is less felt by" women whose sexual passions were naturally weak.[12]

Opening up the woman was a useful solution to a wide range of medical problems, and the best way to know women completely and to understand them completely was to dissect them. "Just dissect," the French writer Jules Michelet urged the [male] readers of his treatise on *La Femme*; "In a moment you will understand and feel everything."[13] In Turgenev's *Fathers and Sons*, the scientist-hero Bazarov thinks of dissection when he falls in love: "What a magnificent body!" he exclaims. "Shouldn't I like to see it on the dissecting table!"[14] A popular theme in fin-de-siècle painting, as in medical literature, was the doctor performing an autopsy on the body of a drowned prostitute. As Sander Gilman suggested, these representations make us wonder exactly what the doctors are seeking in their explorations: "What will

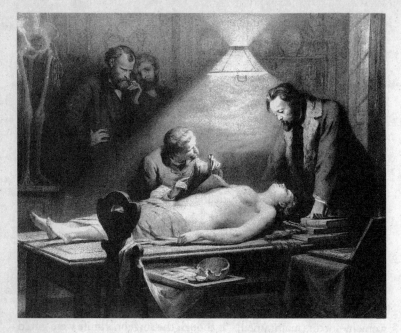

J. H. Hasselhorst, J. C. G. *Lucae and His Assistants*
Dissecting a Female Cadaver, 1864.

be found in the body of these drowned women? Will it be the hidden truths of the nature of the woman, what women want . . . ? The face of the Medusa, with all of its castrating power?"[15] One of the most famous of these paintings, as described by Ludmilla Jordanova, showed the German anatomist J. G. Lucae directing the dissection of the corpse of a drowned young woman as if he were unveiling the secrets of her sexuality: "One of the men has begun the dissection and is working on her thorax. He is holding up a sheet of skin, the part which covers her breast, as if it were a thin article of clothing, so delicate and fine is its texture"[16] (Figure 4). A recent photographic work by the artist Barbara Kruger based on the nineteenth-century dissection paintings, comments on the continuing medical objectification of women; it shows a bearded and bespectacled doctor holding the heart of a young woman whose lightly veiled body is stretched out on the dissecting table; written across the picture are the words "no radio," as if, one art critic suggested, "to equate the surgeon with

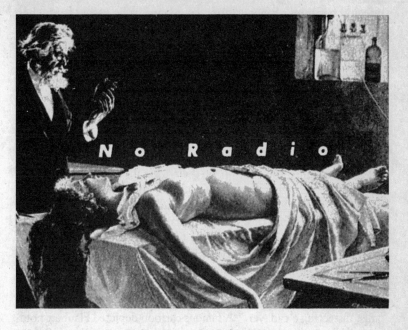

Barbara Kruger, *No Radio*, 1988.

a burglar and the woman with a car that he has just vandalized"[17] (Figure 5).

What, then, about the case of the male body? There were few overt cultural fantasies about the insides of *men's* bodies, and opening up the *man* was not a popular image. One obvious reason is that the penis and testicles are outside the body. They are visible appendages rather than mysterious orifices. Some doctors speculated that the location of male genitalia outside the body reduced their mysterious allure for surgeons: "Happy, thrice happy should man be," wrote one, "because of the simplicity of his genital outfit and its meagre attraction for the operations of surgical science. Had Nature decreed him to wear his genitals within the abdominal cavity, he too might have been compelled to suffer surgical martyrdom for the sake of restoring his reason."[18] Others fantasized role reversal and imagined the horrible carnival of castration if women were the doctors and men the patients. Wells created a vivid nightmare of such a "coterie of Marthas"; "one of them sitting in her consultation chair, with her little stove by her side and her irons all hot, searing every man as he passed before her; another gravely promising to bring on the millennium by snuffing out the reproductive powers of all fools, lunatics, and criminals; a third getting up and declaring that she found, at least, seven or eight or every ten men in her wards with some condition of his appendages which would prove incurable without surgical treatment, and a bevy of younger disciples crowding around the confabulatory table with oblations of soup-bowls of the said appendages . . ."[19]

Similarly, men do not think of themselves as cases to be opened up. Instead, they open up a woman as a substitute for self-knowledge, both maintaining the illusion of their own invulnerability and destroying the terrifying female reminder of their impotence and uncertainty. They gain control over an elusive and threatening femininity by turning the woman into a "case" to be opened or shut. The criminal slashes with his knife. The scientist and doctor open the woman up with the scalpel or pierce her with the stake. The artist or writer penetrates the female case with sharp-honed imagery and the phallic pen.[20] Indeed, as Charles Bernheimer noted, the standard image of the realistic novelist in fin-de-siècle France was the "anatomist dissecting a cadaver." A famous cartoon depicted Flaubert holding up the dripping heart he has ripped from the body of Emma Bovary (Figure 6). Zola, too, viewed his art in clinical terms, describing the writer as one who should "put on the white apron of the anatomist, and dissect, fiber by fiber, the human beast laid out completely naked on the slab of the amphitheatre."[21] The metaphorical naked body represented, such as Nana's, would always be female.

One of the most striking fin-de-siècle stories of an operation on a woman is Arthur Conan Doyle's "The Case of Lady Sannox" (1894), which was also adapted as a play by F. Marriot Watson.[22] Conan Doyle had practiced medicine before he became a writer, and in this story, the hero is a surgeon, Douglas Stone, a "man of steel nerves," who is conducting an adulterous affair with a married ex-actress, "the notorious Lady Sannox." Stone is an exemplary figure of British masculine imperial power. His success as a surgeon has come from qualities of coolness and daring that would have brought him equal fame as a soldier, explorer, or engineer. "His nerve, his judgment, his intuition, were things apart. Again and again his knife cut away death, but grazed the very springs of life in doing it, until his assistants were as white as the patient." Stone's command is thus linked with ideas of racial, class, and sexual hierarchy.

Lemot, *Flaubert Dissecting Emma Bovary*, 1869.

On a winter's evening, as he is about to go out to meet his mistress, Stone receives a call from a rich Turk who offers him a hundred pounds to treat his wife in an emergency. She has cut her lower lip on a poisoned Smyrna dagger and will die from a swift-acting poison unless the lip is cut off. When Stone arrives at the Turk's house, he finds "a woman dressed in the Turkish fashion, with yashmak and veil," lying on a heap of shawls; she has been drugged with opium, and outside the veil all he can see is her dark dilated eyes and her exposed "under lip." While Stone warns that if he performs the operation the "defiguration will be frightful," he is easily persuaded by the Turk's pleas to proceed, not so much because he is greedy as because he has stopped seeing the person in the veil as a human being: "This was no longer a woman to him. It was a case." She has become the Other, the veiled woman who is a possession to be displayed and revealed by the Turk.

Swiftly, Stone cuts a "V-shaped piece" from her lip, and as she jumps up the veil is torn from her face and he recognizes Lady Sannox, who keeps "putting up her hand to the bloody gap, and screaming." The Turk is unmasked, too, and revealed to be Lord Sannox, chuckling over his revenge: "It was really very necessary for Marion, this operation; not physically, but morally, you know, morally." Her beauty destroyed, Lady Sannox disappears from society and "takes the veil" forever. Stone himself goes mad.

At the simplest level of plot, Lord Sannox's revenge on his wife is to destroy her beauty by tricking her lover into mutilating her. Lady Sannox must be punished for her adultery by having her beauty destroyed, her sexuality symbolically mutilated, and finally, her voice taken away—for the excision of the lip is an act against speech as well as against sexuality. We might say that what has got Lady Sannox into trouble is her loose lower lip, her "notorious" sexual exploits, and her labile and indiscreet speech. Therefore she must be silenced and shut up. But obviously a great deal more is at stake. First of all, the operation itself is a displaced clitoridectomy, with the "under lip" a metaphor for the female genitals. When Stone cuts a V-shaped wedge from the lip, he is forced to confront both the horrible operation that he has performed (without an anaesthetic) on his mistress and the fact of female sexual difference itself: the "bloody gap" that paralyzes him with terror or literally turns him to Stone. The steely-nerved surgeon has embodied the manly stiff *upper* lip, the symbol of British fortitude and stoicism. But in opening up the woman, he has inadvertently opened himself and unleashed the repressed emotions that destroy him.

We can see similar illusions of masculine opacity, impregnability, and control in Freud's case studies of female hysterics. In his most famous study, of Ida Bauer, the young Viennese woman whom he named "Dora," Freud used familiar metaphors of opening up the woman. In solving the mystery of Dora's hysterical symptoms, Freud imagined himself as a burglar, picking her locks, breaking and entering into her psyche against her will. As he wrote to his friend Wilhelm Fliess in 1900, "the case has opened smoothly to my collection of picklocks." There's more than a hint in this language of sexual assault, but also of rational penetration. If Dora's "case," like Pandora's box, held the secrets of female sexuality, Freud's key—the new science of psychoanalysis—could unlock it: "No one who disdains the key," Freud wrote, "will ever be able to unlock the door."[23]

Yet in the process of opening Dora up, Freud was unaware that his own unconscious was being exposed as well. Much of what Freud revealed was his own need to be in control, to be certain, coherent, logical, and confident. Freud dated his case study on the very last day of the nineteenth century, claiming that his patient Dora had walked out on him on December 31, 1899. Like Ibsen's Nora, with whom she has many affinities, Dora thus seems to slam the door on Freud on the very threshold of the new century. Yet Dora is herself the door Freud cannot unlock; she is the barrier to Freud's discovery of what women want.

One of Freud's own dreams during the year he treated Dora indeed combines the dread of opening up the male self with fears of mutilation at women's hands and with deeper anxieties about male creativity. In June 1899, during the final stages of his work on *The Interpretation of Dreams,* Freud had a dream of self-dissection. According to one historian, "one of the dream's inciting causes was the annoyance he felt at being reminded by one of his patients that he had not completed the dream book."[24] The patient, Louise N., had asked him to loan her something to read, and Freud had recommended *She:* "a strange book . . . full of hidden meaning . . . the eternal feminine, the immortality of our emotions." But Louise N. interrupted him, commenting, "I know it already. Have you nothing of your own?" Freud interpreted the question to mean that she had read Haggard's book and was taunting him about his uncompleted book on dreams. Thus he replied, "No, my own immortal works have not yet been written."

But Louise N.'s remark might also be taken to mean that she already knew the eternal feminine and its hidden meanings better than he did; didn't he have anything to give her about the hidden meanings of the eternal masculine?

Freud's subsequent dream explores the masculine interior using the imagery of *She*. In the first part of the dream, Freud's ex-teacher Ernst Brücke had set him a strange task that "related to a dissection of the lower part of my own body, my pelvis and legs, which I saw before me as though in the dissecting-room, but without noticing their absence in myself, and also without a trace of any gruesome feeling. Louise N. was standing beside me, and doing the work with me. The pelvis had been eviscerated, and it was visible now in its superior, now in its inferior aspect, the two being mixed together. Thick flesh-coloured protuberances . . . could be seen." In the second half of the dream, Freud was "making a journey through a changing landscape with an Alpine guide who carried me part of the way . . . the ground was boggy; we went round the edge . . . Before this I had been making my own way forward over the slippery ground with a constant feeling of surprise that I was able to do so well after the dissection . . . I really became frightened about my legs and awoke in a mental fright . . ."

Freud's own analysis of the dream interpreted the journeys as metaphors for his self-analysis; and William McGrath sees it as a working through of his fears that he would not live to complete his work, that, like Moses, he would never enter the promised land.[25] Sandra Gilbert, however, sees the dream as a displaced entry into the female body rather than Freud's journey into himself:

> Freud's Haggardesque adventure begins with a pelvic dissection that implies a desexing and . . . his journey ends in feelings of impotence and terror. Like Leo and Holly, who have to be carried on litters into the womb/tomb that is Her land, Freud seems to have been castrated and infantilized early in this dream, so that when he is borne inward over slippery, boggy ground, it is hard, given his own hermeneutics, to avoid seeing his journey not as a classic trip into the self, but as a voyage into the other, and specifically into an other who is horrifyingly female.[26]

I would argue, however, that the mysterious and boggy landscape Freud traverses is his own body and psyche and that the male self, too, can be the site of uncertainty and fear. In presenting his dreams to the public as models for his theory, Freud knew that he was exposing himself even when he was writing about women. Until he has something of his own to give in return, unless he can explain what men want, Freud cannot open up the woman's case.

In the 1980s, well-publicized sex crimes and a proliferation of "slasher" films acted as cautionary tales for contemporary New Women whose sexual and professional expectations and whose freedom to move in the public space of the city seemed to transgress male boundaries and endanger male sanctuaries. The highly successful film *Fatal Attraction* (1987), for example, makes its psychotic villain an elegant woman editor, while the "good" woman is a non-working wife and mother in jeans. In the final minutes of the film, the crazy editor confronts the wife with a knife, but hysterically stabs and slashes her own thighs and pelvis. As one film critic observed, "*Fatal Attraction* confirms the patriarchal fantasy that made clitoridectomy (note against whose body the knife is directed) a 19th century cure for hysteria—that the sexually eager woman is just a gasp away from the castrating Medusa, the murderous phallic mother, and that if sex is not contained by marriage, it will be the end of civilization as we know it."[27]

The Canadian film *Dead Ringers* (1988), directed by David Cronenberg, is the most explicit version to date of the obsession with opening and correcting women's bodies as a form of social order; the crew filming it called it *Fetal Attraction*.[28] Beginning with credits in which ominous surgical and gynecological instruments float against a blood-red background, the film is based on the true story of the 1975 suicide of Cyril and Stewart Marcus, twins who shared a gynecological practice, a New York apartment, and an addiction to barbiturates. The sexually ambiguous identical twin brothers of the film are called Beverley and Elliot Mantle—Bev and Ellie. As children, they play with a Living Woman anatomical doll, a miniature Venus whose body they open and probe; and they gravely meditate on the possibility of "a kind of sex where you wouldn't have to touch each other." While we never see their mother, we do see their rejection by a foul-mouthed little girl, a miniature New Woman who scornfully tells them they don't even know what "fuck" means. As young medical students, they invent a large instrument for gynecological surgery, the Mantle Retractor, which allows them to examine women's bodies without touching them and becomes "a kind of metaphor for the way the twins probe and manipulate the world."[29] Women are both frightening and contaminating and thus must be distanced and mastered.

As adults, the brothers have worked out a life-style that allows them this sense of mastery. They jointly run a clinic for female infertility and share women as patients and as sexual partners. Together they become involved with an actress, Claire Niveau, who cannot bear children because she has a "trifurcated" uterus (Cronenberg's own invention), with three cervixes. But Bev, the more emotional of the twins, falls in love with Claire, and for the first time in his life does not want to share her or his feelings with his brother. The conflict drives him to drugs, and as he deteriorates, he invents a set of bizarre gynecological instruments (resembling instruments of torture or enlarged, silver-plated "parts of insects' bodies")[30] for "operating on mutant women." In a sadistic scene, a drugged Bev attempts to use the Retractor to examine a "Mrs. Bookman," persisting despite her cries of pain. "There's nothing wrong with the instrument," he claims. "It was the woman's body. The woman's body was all wrong." "The patients are getting strange," he later tells Ellie; "Their insides are deformed." Finally he attempts to use his new instruments in surgery, entering an operating room where everyone wears scarlet gowns, like the Inquisition; "I wanted the doctors to be like priests and cardinals," Cronenberg explained.[31]

Such details made it seem to most reviewers and audiences that the film was a horror story about women's fear of gynecology and that it was primarily misogynistic. When he first read the script of *Dead Ringers*, Jeremy Irons had reservations about accepting the part of the twins because his wife and his agent, a woman, were so horrified by the plot; "they found the whole situation of gynecologists taking advantage of their patients very distasteful and very alarming—it's many women's nightmare."[32] Cronenberg helped Irons prepare for the part by giving him a gynecology textbook to study.

Yet by the film's conclusion, it is clear that the twins are seeking within women's bodies the secrets of their own birth and origins. Their androgynous first names are one clue to their bisexuality and displaced femininity, while the name "mantle" suggests their veiled identities. Their doubling is a metaphor for an ultimate homoeroticism and autoeroticism. (Jeremy Irons described their relationship as "fundamentally homosexual, but Platonic.")[33] In a dream sequence, Bev imagines them connected by a pulsating slimy ligament which Claire bites bloodily apart. It's important to the film that we never see their parents, that they share a myth of self-creation, or at least denial that they, too, are born of woman. As one reviewer noted, in their final drugged retreat to the cocoon of their apartment, the twins have a ghastly pallor, "almost as if they'd never been born."[34] In their final drug-dazed suicidal ritual, Bev dissects Ellie with his weird tools, "separates" himself from his twin by opening up the cavity of his chest as if it were a trifurcate womb, and as if Ellie (elle or "she") were the "mutant woman" who cannot give birth but only death.

Cronenberg, who studied literature and science at the University of Toronto, has dealt in all his films with male horror and envy of the reproductive process, pitting the creativity of male scientists and artists against what is seen as the direct and monstrous birthing capacities of women. In *The Fly* he made a cameo appearance as the gynecologist who delivers a mutant, insect-like fetus; in *The Brood,* a father must protect his little girl against the monstrous children extruded by his wife's rage and born from external uterine sacs attached to her body by grotesque umbilical cords. "Every audience wants to see forbidden things," he declares, "things that they wouldn't allow themselves to imagine."[35]

A similar set of media fantasies was released in the late 1970s around the case of the "Yorkshire Ripper," Peter Sutcliffe, who stabbed and eviscerated thirteen women, most of them prostitutes, in the north of England. Like his predecessors, Sutcliffe often visited a wax museum in the seaside town of Morecambe, where he could look at modern versions of the anatomical Venus, lifesize torsos of women with abdomens open to show the stages of fetal development. According to Sutcliffe's biographer Gordon Burns, "Time has eroded definition and basted the developing foetuses and the glistening ropes of intestinal organs to a uniform ox-blood-colour; the impression is of gaping wounds around the umbilicus, growing progressively bigger, gorier, and more congealed."[36] Gazing upon these models gave Sutcliffe a model for his own fantasies and practices; "it is easy," Patricia Highsmith speculated, "to imagine Peter Sutcliffe staring at these female innards . . . and convincing himself that women, prostitutes in particular, were of special danger to menfolk who plunge their private parts into them."[37]

Victorian medical obsessions about women's bodies are also still present in contemporary life. In December 1988, the nineteenth-century case of Isaac Baker Brown seemed uncannily recreated when the Ohio State Medical Board brought formal charges of "grossly unprofessional conduct" against Dr. James C. Burt, who had performed "female circumcisions" on 170 women patients. Dr. Burt believed that "women are structurally inadequate for intercourse," an anatomical problem he could remedy by "removing the hood of a patient's clitoris, repositioning the vagina, moving the urethra, and altering the walls between the rectum and vagina." Burt promised that his "love surgery" would change frigid wives into "horny little mice," but instead his patients suffered "sexual dysfunction, extensive scarring, chronic infections of the kidney, bladder and vagina, and the need for corrective surgery."[38] Charged with over forty-one alleged violations, Burt surrendered his license in January 1989.[39]

Yet the repetition of these images of female powerlessness before male invasion should not lure us into a fatalistic acceptance of the myths of women's case. We have many more resources today both for analyzing and for resisting these myths of "female passivity in the face of male violence." As Judy Walkowitz concluded in her study of the Ripper myth, contemporary women behave quite differently from their nineteenth-century counterparts. When the trial of the Yorkshire Ripper resurrected old stereotypes about good and bad women, there were protests by prostitutes' rights groups and patrols organized for self-protection by women's movement groups.[40] Other strategies have included women's self-defense classes, campaigns against outmoded and inadequate rape legislation, and malpractice suits against doctors like Burt.

Yet what has proved most resistant to analysis is the gender component in the myth, especially the aspect that deals with the fantasies and motivations of men. It is far too simple, on the one hand, to denounce surgical "sexual atrocities" as the evidence, along with pornography and rape, of essential and unchanging misogyny and sadism in men.[41] But the de-gendering of male sexual violence, such as occurred when the gang rapes in New York's Central Park in 1989 were seen as a racial incident committed by economically deprived "youths," is also a simplistic displacement. The sexual anarchy of male violence is a women's problem of the *fin de siècle,* with women taking responsibility for education and self-protection, and limiting their activities in a futile effort to be safe. To be sure, it is a problem for law enforcement, but also, in the form of slasher movies, an *outlet* for aggressive and sexual fantasies even more spectacular than those in the newspapers.

Thus we should not be surprised that *Dead Ringers,* which both aroused and frustrated expectations of the slasher films, was not popular at the box office, horrifying female audiences and disturbing male voyeurs with its unpredictable confrontations and turns. For some reviewers, the film generated castration anxieties. "I think I can state as a general aesthetic rule," wrote the film critic David Denby, "that a man menacing a woman's genitals with steel prongs is not amusing." He found the movie "hell for men as well as women to sit through."[42] Other male reviewers were baffled and perhaps disappointed by the fact that no women are actually mutilated, assaulted, ripped, slashed, or killed in Cronenberg's film. "Why did he create such powerful images—mutant women and surgical instruments—and then use them so lightly?" Andrew Dowler wondered.[43] Yet a few male reviewers of the film understood that men were the subjects being opened up. Cronenberg "shines a bright, cold light on inoperable terrors inside us," Terrence Rafferty concluded, "and then leaves us staring, with blurred comprehension, at the instruments in his clinic's pristine cabinets."[44] Even in 1988, it seemed unthinkable for a director to open up the man's case; but Cronenberg's twins marked a hopeful start.

EIGHT

The Veiled Woman

"The erotic life . . . of women—partly owing to the stunting effect of civilized conditions and partly owing to their conventional secretiveness and insincerity—is still veiled in impenetrable obscurity."
(Sigmund Freud, *Three Essays on the Theory of Sexuality*)

Figures of female sexuality at the *fin de siècle* are frequently represented as both exotic and veiled. After her forced masquerade as the veiled Turkish wife, Lady Sannox "takes the veil absolutely and forever." A statue of a beautiful veiled woman, surrounded by mummified, embalmed, and petrified bodies, guards the entrance to Haggard's Kôr; it is inscribed with the warning words: "Behold! There is no man born of woman who may draw my veil and live." In the African jungle, Kurtz paints a veiled woman: "a small sketch in oils, on a panel, representing a woman, draped and blindfolded, carrying a lighted torch." Even the Bostonian Verena Tarrant, who has always looked "like an Oriental" to Basil Ransom, is finally veiled under the hood of her black velvet cloak, which conceals both her "face and her identity," as he wrenches her away from the lecture hall. Most famously, Oscar Wilde's Jewish princess Salome drops seven veils to reveal the mysteries of sexual difference, creativity, and the psyche.

The veiled woman had many nuances and meanings for fin-de-siècle artists, and one can construct "a poetics or thematics of the veil in the texts of literature, psychoanalysis, and philosophy, as well as in the cinema."[1] She was associated with the mysteries of the Orient, the Sotadic Zone, and the harem or seraglio. Indeed, the Oriental woman behind the veil of purdah stood as a figure of sexual secrecy and inaccessibility for Victorian men in the 1880s and 1890s, much as the nun, another veiled woman, had done for Gothic novelists in the 1780s and 1790s. British civil servants in the Punjab especially were fascinated by the sexual aspects of Indian religion. They took a strong interest in the purdah, in women behind the veil who seemed to embody "what was unknown and inscrutable in Indian life."[2]

Why was the veil linked with femininity? First of all, veiling was associated with female sexuality and with the veil of the hymen. The veil thus represented feminine chastity and modesty; in rituals of the nunnery, marriage, or mourning, it concealed sexuality. Furthermore, science and medicine had traditionally made use of sexual metaphors which represented "Nature" as a woman to be unveiled by the man who seeks her secrets. As Ludmilla Jordanova has shown, these images were embodied in fin-de-siècle allegorical sculpture, such as the statue exhibited in Paris in 1895 by Louis Ernest Barrias. Entitled *La Nature se dévoilant devant la science* (Nature Unveiling Herself Before Science) (Figure 7), it depicts a beautiful young woman, eyes modestly lowered, breasts seductively bared, who lifts her hands to remove the veils that conceal the rest of her body. The statue, identical to one that stood in the hall of the Paris medical faculty during the nineteenth century, suggests the ways that the unveiling of women's bodies became associated with medical and scientific vision.[3] If there had been a companion piece called *Science Looking at Nature,* it would have depicted a fully clothed man, whose gaze was bold, direct, and keen, the penetrating gaze of intellectual and sexual mastery.

The veiled woman who is dangerous to look upon also signifies the quest for the mystery of origins, the truths of birth and death. In one of his shortest but most influential essays, Freud interpreted the myth of Medusa's head as an allegory of the veiled woman, whose unshielded gaze turns men to stone. According to Freud, the decapitated head of Medusa with its snaky looks is a "genitalized head,"[4] an upward displacement of the sexual organs, so that the mouth stands for the *vagina dentata,* and the snakes for pubic hair. For men to unveil the Medusa is to confront the dread of looking at the female sexual organs: "To decapitate: to castrate. The terror of Medusa is thus a terror of castration that is linked to the sight of something. Numerous analyses have made us familiar with the occasion for this: it occurs when a boy, who has hitherto been unwilling to believe the threat of castra-

Louis Ernest Barrias, *La Nature se dévoilant
devant la science*, 1895.

tion, catches sight of the female genitals, probably those of an adult
surrounded by hair, and essentially those of his mother. . . ."

The male gaze is thus both self-empowering and self-endangering,
for what lies behind the veil is the specter of female sexuality, a silent
but terrible mouth that may wound or devour the male spectator. In
seeing that the woman has no penis, the boy, according to Freud,
experiences the fear of his own possible castration. In narrative, too,
the critic Peter Brooks has argued, the unveiling of the female body
leads to the confrontation with absence and castration; "narrative

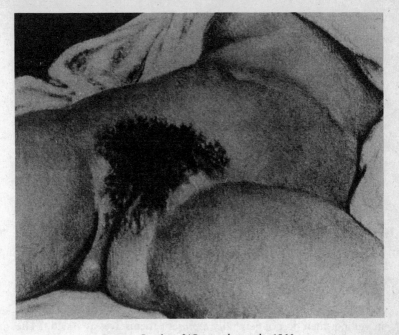

Gustave Courbet, *L'Origine du monde*, 1866.

representations of unveiling the female body . . . must sooner or later reach the problem of unveiling the female sex, which they find to be itself a veil, perhaps from the anxiety that its final unveiling would reveal there is nothing to unveil."[5]

Courbet's scandalous painting of the female sex, *L'Origine du monde* (Figure 8), which had been commissioned by the rich Turkish collector Khalil Bey, was displayed behind a veil. Maxime Du Camp described the shock men felt on viewing the painting: "In the dressing room of this foreign personage one sees a small picture hidden under a green veil. When one draws aside the veil one remains stupefied to perceive a woman, life-size, seen from the front, moved and convulsed, remarkably executed, reproduced *con amore*, as the Italians say, providing the last word in realism. But, by some inconceivable forgetfulness, the artist, who copied his model from nature, had neglected to represent the feet, the legs, the thighs, the stomach, the hips, the chest, the hands, the arms, the shoulders, the neck, and the head."[6]

In this century, the painting was appropriately owned by the psychoanalytic *maître* Jacques Lacan, who may have had it in mind when he remarked in his seminar of February 1975, "Queen Victoria, there's a woman . . . when one encounters a toothed vagina of such exceptional size."

That specter of the *vagina dentata* haunted the dreams of such fin-de-siècle writers as Edmund de Goncourt, who wrote in his journal on Bastille Day, 1883, "I dreamt last night that I was at a party, in white tie. At that party, I saw a woman come in, and recognized her as an actress in a boulevard theatre, but without being able to put a name to her face. She was draped in a scarf, and I noticed only that she was completely naked when she hopped onto the table . . . Then she started to dance, and while she was dancing took steps that showed her private parts armed with the most terrible jaws one could imagine, opening and closing, exposing a set of teeth."[7] The veiled woman hides the guillotine and the man-trap behind her gauzy scarf.

Can men also be allegorically veiled figures? Can we reverse the gender of the image and see the veiled man as a figure of sexual or metaphysical dread? Largely because of the sexual symbolism implied in veiling, men do not generally represent themselves as veiled. "The idea of unveiling men," according to Jordanova, "is comic, implausible and unthreatening, presumably because their bodies are not the symbolic carriers in modern society either of creative or destructive forces." Indeed, she goes on to say, "unveiling men makes no sense, possibly because neither mystery nor modesty are male preserves but are attributes of the other, which is always other to the masculine centre."[8] We have no figures of a boyish Nature unveiling *himself* before Science.

Yet to penetrate the female veil can also be a metaphorical act of self-revelation for men. In *The Madwoman in the Attic*, Sandra Gilbert and Susan Gubar offer a brilliant excursus on the traditional Romantic meanings of the veil. Despite its "uniquely feminine significance," they explain, the veil is a kind of permeable border, an image of confinement and enclosure that is also extremely penetrable; "even when opaque it is highly impermanent, while transparency transforms it into a possible entrance or exit." It suggests the possibility of access to another sphere, another sexuality, another self. In the Gothic novel, the veil "is a necessary concealer of grotesque revelations of sin and guilt, past crimes and future suffering." The Romantic poets seek to lift the veil that separates them from nature, divinity, and vision, while dreading the reality it conceals.

Similarly, there is always a veiled man hiding in fin-de-siècle stories about the veiled woman. She/he reflects the ambiguity and transparency of sexual difference and the sense of guilt, decadence, transgression, and sexual anarchy. Some fin-de-siècle writers, like Goncourt, revealed their identification with the veiled woman in dreams. The English Catholic convert W. G. Ward, for example, dreamed that he found himself at a dinner party next to a charming veiled lady. "At last he exclaimed, 'I have never felt such charm in any conversation since I used to talk with John Henry Newman at Oxford.' 'I am John Henry Newman,' the lady replied and raising her veil showed the well-known face."[9]

The most popular veiled woman of the *fin de siècle* is Salome, the dancing daughter of Herodias. In France, Salome became an obsessive icon of female sexuality for Flaubert, for the artist Gustave Moreau, who did over seventy drawings of her, and for the novelist Joris-Karl Huysmans, who wrote about Moreau's 1876 painting of Salome in *A Rebours* (*Against Nature*) (1884) as "the weird and superhuman" object of his hero's fantasies of feminine evil: "She had become, as it were, the symbolic incarnation of undying Lust, the Goddess of immortal Hysteria, the accursed Beauty exalted above all other beauties by the catalepsy that hardens her flesh and steels her muscles, the monstrous Beast, indifferent, irresponsible, insensible, poisoning, like the Helen of ancient myth, everything that approaches her, everything that sees her, everything that she touches." In his book on fin-de-siècle Vienna, Carl Schorske calls Salome "the *fin de siècle*'s favorite phallic woman."[10] She was painted by Gustave Klimt as a gilded Judith/Salome, an elegant lady of the Belle Epoque who holds the decapitated head casually by her side. Later she appeared as the heroine of Richard Strauss's 1905 opera.

The Salome we remember as the "Goddess of Decadence"[11] was primarily, however, the heroine of Oscar Wilde's play. Influenced by the avant-garde and symbolist theater of Paris, Wilde wrote the play first in French, with the help of Pierre Loüys, Marcel Schwob, and possibly André Gide. Wilde imagined *Salome* from the start as a performance and devoted a great deal of time to discussions of its staging. "I should like everyone on the stage to be in yellow," he told the costume designer Graham Robertson. He imagined Salome in "green, like a curious, poisonous lizard." At one point he decided that she should be naked except for ropes of exotic jewels. With Charles Ricketts, the set designer, he planned a black floor, a backdrop of violet sky, and "in place of an orchestra, braziers of perfume."[12] Indeed, Wilde's ideas for the production were even more powerful and innovative than those of the designers he worked with in the 1890s; as Phillippe Jullian has said, they "went beyond Art Nouveau, and heralded those of the Russian ballet."[13]

However, Wilde never saw the play performed. It was banned by the London Lord Chamberlain's office because it represented a Biblical subject. Wilde's case became a milder fin-de-siècle version of *The Satanic Verses*. He had threatened that if the Censor banned *Salome* he would leave England and take out French citizenship; "I will not consent to call myself a citizen of a country that shows such narrowness in artistic judgement." But few writers, actors, or critics rose to Wilde's defense; in fact he became the butt of jokes from those who had not read *Salome*. "All London is laughing at Oscar Wilde's threat to become a Frenchman," wrote *The New York Times*. Only Bernard Shaw and William Archer spoke out against the censorship. Wilde also had support from a number of French writers, including Mallarmé, Loti, and Maeterlink, to whom he sent the Paris edition of the text. After inadequate attempts at translation by Aubrey Beardsley and Alfred Douglas, he then translated it into English himself and published it in England in 1893 with Beardsley's erotic, sinuous, and bizarre illustrations.

But by the time *Salome* received its first performance in Paris in 1896, Wilde was in prison. While *Salome* was one of the most popular plays on the modern German stage, dating from Max Reinhardt's production in 1903, and was also part of the repertory of the Russian Theatre, it was not officially produced in England until 1931. Even a performance of the opera was banned in 1907. Wilde's notoriety and a counter-decadent reaction created widespread hostility to Strauss's choice of the play for an adaptation. As Romain Rolland wrote to Strauss, "Oscar Wilde's *Salome* is not worthy of you . . . Wilde's Salome and all those who surround her, save only that brute of a Jochanan, are unhealthy, unclean, hysterical or alcoholic, oozing with a perfumed and mundane corruption . . . You surpass your subject, but you cannot make one forget it."[14]

Although Wilde had not intended it, *Salome* thus became a closet drama, both in the sense of a play existing primarily as a text and also, as I shall argue, in the contemporary sense of a heterosexual play by a homosexual writer that has a gay sexual subtext. Such a reading goes against even the most favorable of current critical views, which interpret *Salome* as a play about revolution, New Women, or art. Yet Wilde himself insisted that *Salome* was the most meaningful of his works, the one which allowed him to express himself most fully. In her study of Wilde's theater, Katherine Worth points out that "imagery of veiling and unveiling are frequent in Wilde's prose writings, and is usually associated with some kind of spiritual exploration." Looking at images of the veil and the mask in Wilde's criticism and short stories, Worth concludes that "unveiling was an appropriate image for the activity which Wilde regarded as the artist's prime duty: self-expression and self-revelation. In performing the dance of the seven veils, Salome is then perhaps offering not just a view of the naked body but of the soul or innermost being."[15]

Is the woman behind Salome's veils the innermost being of the male artist? Is Salome's love for Jokanaan a veiled homosexual desire for the male body? For a full understanding of *Salome*, we need to look at its theatrical and cinematic history and at the Beardsley drawings, as well as Wilde's text. It has long been a critical commonplace that the Beardsley illustrations are anachronistic, depict scenes that are not in the text, and are "singularly irrelevant or even at odds with the spirit of Wilde's play."[16] The feminist critic Jane Marcus, for example, flatly declares that "Beardsley was the wrong artist to illustrate *Salome*."[17] Recently, this view has been eloquently contested by Elliot Gilbert, who argues that "the text and pictures of the English Salome are in fact very closely related—commenting on and illuminating one another in a great many ways and achieving a single strong focus." Gilbert sees both Beardsley and Wilde as homosexual artists who "through a notable representation of perverse sexuality in their work, participate in a devastating fin-de-siècle attack on the conventions of patriarchal culture even as they express their horror of the threatening female energy which is the instrument of that attack." Thus what unifies pictures and text is the way that both Wilde and Beardsley, despite their sympathy for Salome's rebellion against patriarchal religion and patriarchal secular authority, recoil "from the full implications of an uncontrolled and murderous female energy."[18]

More could be said to bolster Gilbert's argument. In my view, the Beardsley drawings all depict scenes or moments described in the play. If you take the trouble to look at them closely with the text, their thematic correspondence is clear, even though Beardsley wittily costumes his figures in a variety of exotic styles. Thus the fact that, in Marcus's words, Beardsley's Salome looks like an "eighteenth-century transvestite" does not mean that Beardsley was an arrogant fop who "didn't read the play."[19] In fact, Beardsley's drawings bring out all too powerfully the secret or unspeakable subtext of the play, especially its homoerotic and blasphemous elements. In the edition he presented to Beardsley, Wilde wrote: "For the only artist who, besides myself, knows what the dance of the seven veils is and can see that invisible dance." The dance Beardsley sees is the dance of gender, the delicacy and permeability of the veil separating masculine from feminine, licit from illicit desire. That so many critics have been blind to the meaning of the illustrations shows how cultural unwillingness to look at what is disturbing prevents us from seeing.

Beardsley's first drawing was originally called *The Man in the Moon*, but then changed to *The Woman in the Moon* (Figure 9). In the drawing, Wilde is represented as a huge moon-face, his heavy-lidded eyes gazing languidly at a frightened couple. Marcus praises this illustration as the only "appropriate" one Beardsley did, but describes it as showing a scene that does not appear in the play, "John and Salome . . . cowering in comradely innocence before Herod's face in the moon."[20] Both the tradition of heterosexual readings and the critical truism that Beardsley's drawings had no source in the text encouraged this reading. However, the couple are actually men: Narraboth, the young Syrian with "languorous eyes" who loves Salome and kills himself out of jealousy; and his homosexual admirer, the Page of Herodias, with his "dreamer's look," who urges Narraboth to look at the moon rather than at Salome. Close examination of the drawing shows its deliberate blurring of the line between art and reality, sexuality and gender. The Page is on the right, androgynously dressed in a flowing robe with a triangular dark fan hanging down (the fan he carries for Herodias) that could be either masculine or feminine, phallic or pubic. Narraboth, the naked male figure on the left, holds out one arm in a gesture of protection or prevention, while the line that forms the edge of his drapery merges with the edge of the Page's robe. Wilde is here both a specter of judgment and a gay god of the night who looks down on the lovers. The drawing suggests Adam and Eve covering themselves before Jehovah before they are cast out of paradise; or, in this case, what contemporary slang calls Adam and Steve. It also suggests the drama as Wilde's fantasy, existing in the theater of his imagination.

Karl Beckson, in his edition of *Salome*, describes the flower on the

Aubrey Beardsley,
The Woman in the Moon, 1894.

moon as Wilde's green carnation, an interpretation which misses both
the significance of Beardsley's impeccable black-and-white drawings,
and the consistent flower symbolism he employs. It is in fact a rose,
which appears with its thorns, vines, and briars in several other illustrations. For Beardsley, the rose stands for forbidden passion, the
brevity of love, and especially homosexual love; it is found, "like a
stamp," in many of his drawings. While in the religious and Pre-
Raphaelite art from which Beardsley drew inspiration the full-blown

Aubrey Beardsley,
John and Salome, 1894.

rose is associated with the female body, the rosebud, like the narcissus, represents "both self-eroticism and homosexuality."[21] Female sexuality is far more dangerous and impure; in the drawing of John and Salome, for example, the rosebush seems like a live thing extending its tendrils behind Salome's body to entwine John. It is full of blossoms, while all of its thorns have become giant protuberances wound in Salome's hair like a *vagina dentata* (Figure 10). In the play, the lustful Herod finds that his garland of roses burns him like fire and that "the petals are like stains of blood on the cloth."

Aubrey Beardsley, A *Platonic Lament*, 1894.

The drawing *The Woman in the Moon,* which links Wilde with Salome and places homosexual passion at the center of the play, is linked with A *Platonic Lament* (Figure 11), which shows the Page mourning for the dead Syrian. "He has slain himself who was my friend!" the Page says in the text. "I gave him a little box of perfumes and ear-rings wrought in silver, and now he has killed himself. . . . Well, I knew that the moon was seeking a dead thing, but I knew not that it was he whom she sought. Ah! Why did I not hide him from the moon?" Here the Page is naked and the Syrian draped in a black robe. The figures are arranged to suggest a crucifixion against a cross of roses, an image of religious persecution that is countered in the illustrations by others drawn from magic and the Black Mass. Under the bier, an imp conducts a ritual incantation, with the lines and leaves of Beardsley's artistic signature streaming from the end of his cap. In the sky on the right, the Wildean moon drifts into eclipse, while the rose falls onto the dead Syrian's body.

Beardsley's conflation of Wilde and Salome, of female corrosive desire and male homosexual love, brings to the surface the play's buried and coded messages. There is a mystery here as well. In the late Richard Ellmann's massive biography of Wilde, there is a remarkable photograph taken in Paris in the 1890s of Wilde himself posing as Salome in a wig and jeweled costume, slave bracelets around his arms, kneeling, arms outstretched before the severed head (Figure 12). The picture is credited to the Collection Guillot de Saix, H. Roger Viollet, Paris; but Ellmann does not allude to it in the book nor identify de Saix. When was it taken? At what private theatricals did Wilde decide that "Salomé, ç'est moi"?

What happens when women choose to unveil themselves in defiance or seduction? Female self-unveiling can be a shocking act, for female unveiling substitutes power for castration. From the feminist point of view, the woman behind the veil might not only be splendid but perhaps *normal*. As Hélène Cixous declares, "You only have to look at the Medusa straight on to see her. And she's not deadly. She's beautiful and she's laughing."[22] Jane Marcus's view that the play is "a parable of the woman artist's struggle to break free of being the stereotype of sex object" suggests that *Salome* would be a particularly interesting vehicle for women. When women appropriated the image of Salome in art, however, reinterpreted her on the stage, or sang her role in the opera, public reaction was often hostile. In George Egerton's short story "A Cross-Line," for example, the nameless heroine autoerotically imagines herself in the role of Salome: "She is on the stage of an ancient theatre out in the open air with hundreds of faces upturned towards her. She is gauze-clad in a cobweb garment of wondrous tissue. Her arms are clasped by jeweled snakes, and one with quivering diamond fangs coils round her hips . . . . She bounds forward and dances, bends her lissome waist, and curves her slender arms, and gives to the soul of each man what he craves, be it good or evil." Egerton had vowed to reveal the terra incognita of the female psyche, to "unlock a closed door with a key of my own fashioning."[23] But the

Oscar Wilde in costume as Salome.

effect on male readers was of the scandalously pornographic. Assuming that Egerton must be a man, the journalist T. P. Gill wrote to complain that such stories might put a young man in "such a state that he either goes off and has a woman or it is bad for his health (and possibly worse for his morals) if he doesn't."[24]

Another fin-de-siècle feminist representation of Salome came from the American painter Ella Ferris Pell, whose *Salome* was exhibited at the Paris Salon in 1890 (Figure 13). As Bram Dijkstra describes it,

Ella Ferris Pell, *Salome*, 1890.

Pell's Salome diverged strongly from male fin-de-siècle versions: "She does not gaze at us with a look of crazed sexual hunger; she does not have the wan, vampire features of the serpentine dancer. . . . Instead she is a woman of flesh and blood, not a mythologized flower of evil." Young, healthy, vigorous, and independent, Pell's Salome challenges the dominant male image of the evil temptress and is "a truly revolutionary feminist statement for its period."[25] Yet the painting was largely ignored by critics; and although she worked as a landscape and portrait painter in New York in the 1890s, Pell died in obscurity, disowned by her parents and buried in a pauper's grave.

Only in the operatic tradition have the women who played Salome been seen as separate from the role, perhaps because it demands a powerful singer often physically at odds with the image. Strauss, for example, imagined his Salome as a "sixteen year old princess with the voice of an Isolde." More typically, the operatic soprano, such as Grace Bumbry or Eva Marton, is played as a sexually experienced woman rather than a teasing girl. Furthermore, Strauss wrote the music for the dance last, and few critics have been satisfied with its performance, seeing the singers as too sedate, too heavy, or too old for the suspension of disbelief. Maria Ewing's performance in Peter Hall's staging of 1986 was a signal exception, with its finale of full frontal nudity.

Although Salome is an important figure in the history of dance, women who have performed the part have also had a difficult time, finding themselves conflated with Salome in the public mind and condemned for lasciviousness and perversity. Jane Marcus sees Salome's dance as the New Woman's art form, parallel to the tarantella danced by Nora in *A Doll's House*; both heroines, she writes, "are reluctant to perform their ritual obeisance to their masters, but in the end, choose the degrading act rather than find no means at all of self-expression."[26] Wilde had been impressed by Loie Fuller, "idol of the symbolists," who had "danced the role in her characteristic swirling greens and blues, using mirrors to multiply the image of the dancer."[27] Before the censor's ruling, however, he had rehearsed the play in London with Sarah Bernhardt; but she was nearly fifty and, when questioned about her plans for the dance, had answered enigmatically, "Never you mind!"

One of the first of the feminist Salomes was the young Russian actress Ida Rubenstein, whose 1908 performance precipitated an outburst of Orientalist, anti-Semitic, and misogynist horror. Very tall, thin, and exotically beautiful, a kind of fin-de-siècle Cher, Rubenstein later came to incarnate what Peter Wollen calls "the phallic woman of the Decadence, surrounded by energy, colour, and 'barbarism.' "[28] Her kohl-rimmed eyes and snaky black hair reminded Cecil Beaton of the Medusa; her feathered headdresses, elaborate dresses, and pointed shoes made her a spectacle. Affiliated with the lesbian milieu of Paris, she became an icon of sexual inversion as well, an object of fascination for male homosexual artists like Jean Cocteau and Cecil Beaton.

Initially, Rubenstein, who came from a wealthy Jewish family in St. Petersburg, "was determined to use her large personal fortune to become a star in her own right."[29] Part of a Russian avant-garde steeping itself in forbidden French culture (both Baudelaire and Huysmans were banned in Russia), she had decided to produce her own version of Wilde's *Salome* and had the play translated from French to Russian. Rubenstein was particularly anxious to perform the Dance of the Seven Veils and began to study and practice daily with the choreographer Michel Fokine of the Russian Ballet, while Leon Bakst designed the costumes. As in England, however, the Holy Synod of the Russian Orthodox Church banned the performance because a head of the saint would be used in the production, a sacrilegious image. After negotiation the Synod agreed to allow the play but without reciting the text. Rubenstein and her company decided to perform entirely in mime, circulating copies of the text ahead in St. Petersburg. At the last minute, the Synod confiscated the papier-mâché head of John from the properties room. Even so, Rubenstein's performance was a sensation: "Never before had the St. Petersburg public been treated to the spectacle of a young society woman dancing voluptuously to insinuating oriental music, discarding brilliantly colored veils until only a wisp of green chiffon remained knotted round her loins"; in some accounts it was rumored that she danced naked; although "the director later admitted it had all been a lighting trick."[30]

Rubenstein was disowned by her outraged family and became a notorious figure. In 1909, she appeared as Cleopatra in Diaghilev's first Paris season. Bakst and Fokine transposed the Dance of the Seven Veils to the new ballet; they increased the number of veils to twelve and had Rubenstein reveal herself in a scene described by Cocteau: "Each of the veils unwound itself in a fashion of its own: one demanded a host of subtle touches, another the deliberation required in peeling a walnut, the third the airy detachment of the petals of a rose, and

Maud Allan in *Vision of Salome*, 1916.

the eleventh, most difficult of all, came away in one piece like the bark of the eucalyptus tree." Rubenstein stripped away the last veil herself and "bent forward with something of the movement of an ibis's wings."[31]

In 1907, the Canadian dancer Maud Allan performed her own "Dance of Salome" in European music halls, dressed mainly in large pearls and creating a "Salome craze" that some saw as feminist and subversive. Allan's interpretation of Salome emphasized the visionary as well as the exhibitionist aspects of the story; the second half was called "the Vision of Salome," and "represented the whole episode with the severed head as a kind of phantasm"[32] (Figure 14). In London, however, *The New York Times* reported in 1908, the dance was reputed to have led to public immorality; a society hostess had invited leading ladies of the Court to "a 'Maud Allan' dinner dance, which would be undesecrated by the presence of any man, and at which the guests were bidden to appear in Salome costumes."[33] In her memoirs, Diana Cooper recalled the sensation Maud Allan's daring performance made at the Palace Theatre. Cooper's mother sent her weekly to learn from Allan's ballet techniques, "in spite of the number finishing with Salome's Dance—considered scandalous, for she was all but naked and had St. John's head on a plate and kissed his waxen mouth (a business later forbidden on the Covent Garden stage, where a dish of gravy was substituted)."[34] The American actress Marie Cahill pleaded with Teddy Roosevelt to stop the Salome craze in the United States. When Allan performed again after the war, a right-wing British M.P. named Noel Pemberton-Billing, who believed that the Germans were infiltrating England with thousands of homosexuals, became outraged. In his private journal, *The Vigilante,* he published an essay by his employee Harold Spencer called "The Cult of the Clitoris," which described Allan as a lesbian sadist. When Allan brought a case for libel in 1918, Dr. Serrell Cooke, a witness for Pemberton-Billing, testified that Salome was "quite likely to light up dormant perversion in men who did not even know they possessed it, and in women." Significantly, the fact that Allan recognized the term "clitoris" was used by the defense to prove that she was obviously a degenerate: "Clitoris is an anatomical term," Pemberton-Billing proclaimed, adding tellingly that it was "a *Greek* word [my italics]; understood of the few. I had never heard it in my life before, and I doubt if any member of the Jury had ever heard of it in his life before. The word was calculated to be understood only of those people who in their ordinary common parlance would refer to these things."[35] Allan lost the case.

The 1922 silent film version of *Salome* starring the Russian actress Alla Nazimova had elements of both the Rubenstein and Allan performances and met the same divided and largely hostile response. Nazimova had been a starring actress in Moscow and St. Petersburg before she came to the United States in 1905, and she became a brilliant success in New York in productions of Ibsen and Chekhov. Her movie career was even more dazzling; her house on Sunset Boulevard had a swimming pool in the shape of the Black Sea, and her wild parties were the talk of Hollywood. In her production of *Salome,*

Nazimova adapted the Beardsley drawings for bizarre and fascinating costumes and sets. Although she was forty-four years old, she herself starred as a Salome who was very much an It Girl of the 1920s, appearing in successive styles of movie glamour. Salome first appears as a Mack Sennett bathing beauty in a sequined gym suit and a wig of big bubble-shaped pearls on little antennae, copied from one of the Beardsley drawings of Salome's curls; the pearls quiver erotically like stamens when she first sees Jokannan. In the dance scene, Salome wears a platinum-blond Cleopatra wig and white chiffon; when she kisses the lips of the severed head, she is in a Japanese robe and has her head tightly bound in a satin turban, a snaky phallic look that both echoes Beardsley's drawings and suggests feminine decadence. The supporting male actors, decked out in spangled tights, heavy makeup, and pasties, performed in various styles of high camp; it was rumored that the entire cast was gay.[36]

Critical and box-office responses to this *Salome* were mixed. One reviewer called it "the most extraordinarily beautiful picture that has ever been produced," and found the relationship between the text and the film "weird and wonderful."[37] But audiences hated the film and booed it and Nazimova off the screen. The Dance of the Seven Veils received particular attention; Salome was accompanied by weirdly garbed dwarfs who jumped up and down, copied from the Indonesian lute player in Beardsley's drawing. A review in *The New York Times* suggested that Salome's dance was in fact unrepresentable and that no film version that could pass the censors could be at all commensurate with the audience's imagination of the scene: "This is the climax of the drama. The way is prepared for it by words and actions that unmistakably indicate its character. The spectators know what to expect as well as Herod itself. And when it comes it has the approval of the censors! The moral monitors of New York permit a dance that Herod thinks is worth half a kingdom! Can you imagine it? You cannot." Furthermore, audiences were frustrated and annoyed by the discrepancy between the filmed reactions of the male spectators to Salome's dance and what is actually shown of the dance. As the *Times* critic concluded in disgust, "You see an exceedingly tame and not remarkably graceful performance that Herod wouldn't have given standing room in his kingdom for. Yet on the faces of Herod and the other onlookers you see expressions intended to indicate that such a dance as you have been led to imagine is being performed. . . . But some one may reply that the real dance wouldn't be allowed, and that if it were decent people wouldn't want to look at it. Exactly. The real 'Salome' is impossible on both counts."[38]

There is a similar absurdity in the "madly misconceived" MGM Bible-epic version of *Salome* in 1953 with Rita Hayworth and Stewart Granger.[39] In order to meet the moralistic conventions of the 1950s, this film reverses Wilde's plot and makes its Princess Salome a secret convert to Christianity who dances before a leering Charles Laughton in seven vividly technicolor veils in order to *save* John the Baptist from her evil mother's revenge. Even Rita Hayworth's scream at the end of the dance when she sees the soldiers bear in the head seems anti-climactic; energetically as she dances, nothing she reveals seems adequate to our expectations.

An essay by Roland Barthes on striptease may explain why the women's performances of Salome have seemed so unsatisfying. Barthes maintains that striptease re-veils rather than reveals, "constantly making the unveiled body more remote," in order to protect the spectator from a confrontation with a terrifying female sexual power. The woman's body is covered in rituals, decor, and props "in proportion as she pretends to strip it bare"; these barriers include exoticism; fetishized props such as fans, gloves, and G-strings; and the ritual gestures of the dance itself. Barthes argues that only in the awkwardness of amateur striptease, which denies "the alibi of art" to be "gestures of unveiling," would the "erotic power" of the spectacle be restored.[40] The Mark Morris Dance Company's ballet "Striptease," based on the Barthes essay and part of a sequence called "Mythologies," tries to break through the conventions of staged nudity to recreate the erotic power of awkwardness; at the end of the dance, the naked performers must pick up their discarded clothes and somehow get off stage, exposed and unchoreographed. Morris further subverts the conventions of striptease and the objectification of women's bodies by using men as well as women in his dance. But the incessant commodification of the avant-garde must catch up with all such efforts; in London in the summer of 1988, for example, there was a Soho stripper named Rolanda Barthes who pretended to be doing it for the first time.

Another obvious problem of striptease is the assumption of the male gaze, the objectification of women's bodies, and the difficulty of women performers and dancers controlling the responses of female as well as male viewers. I experienced this first-hand a few years ago when I went on the New York City Porn Tour, organized by the controversial group Women Against Pornography. The tour was offered on weekends, with men admitted every third week. It began at WAP's Fortysecond Street headquarters, next to an abandoned meat market, with a slide show of hard, soft, and commercial porn images of women, and then took groups with a woman guide on to the adult bookstores, film arcades, and sex emporia of Times Square. My group of scholars, sociologists, feminists, and social workers began with the bookstores and novelty shops, where the pornography was carefully categorized and labeled according to perversion, interest, age, and so on. We then moved to the arcades, which featured private video booths where one could watch films of men, women, and animals in various combinations. The tour ended at a kind of sex emporium where there were strippers, closed-channel TV sex shows, and a whole floor of "fetish booths," glassed-in enclosures with a woman on one side and a telephone on the other.

While for me the entire experience of entering this male sexual space was unsettling, sometimes comic (in the very small category of books labeled "professors," for example, all the naked participants were wearing horn-rimmed glasses), and sometimes frightening, the worst moment came at the carousel. The carousel is a porn shop arena of the male gaze, a crude machine of voyeurism. It consists of a raised circular platform, completely surrounded by booths. The customers enter the booths and put in coins to raise the window for a few minutes; they then can look out at the nude women who are dancing and moving about on the platform; they can also see across to other spectators in other windows. (Madonna's music video, "Open Your Heart," is set on a carousel, where she struts, stretches, and preens before the gaze of several excited men and one bored lesbian. I suspect that few female viewers who saw it knew that the carousel really exists outside of MTV, or were in a position to evaluate Madonna's reappropriation of that space.) For what really happens on the carousel is that when a window goes up, the women come over and impersonally thrust parts of their naked bodies inside it—breasts, pelvis, buttocks. I found it almost unbearable to be looking so clinically, so intimately, without desire, at women's bodies. It made them naked in a different way. And when the naked women saw *me* watching them, made eye contact, and saw the faces of other women appearing in the little windows, there was a moment of real mutual embarrassment and shock. Women watching Salome's dance will perhaps always have this sense of identification and discomfort.

The impossibility of Salome's dance when performed as a conventional striptease by women, then, may reside in the cultural mythology of striptease itself. Even in its most extreme, post-structuralist, and parodic forms, striptease is based on the logic of the male gaze. David Lodge's satirical character Professor Morris Zapp takes it to its all too plausible limit in *Small World*: "The classical tradition of striptease . . . which goes back to Salome's dance of the seven veils and beyond . . . offers a valid metaphor for the activity of reading. The dancer teases the audience as the text teases its readers, with the promise of an ultimate revelation that is infinitely postponed. Veil after veil, garment after garment is removed, but it is the *delay* in the stripping that makes it exciting, not the stripping itself, because no sooner has one secret been revealed than we lose interest in it and crave another. . . . Gazing into the womb, we are returned to the mystery of our own origins. Just so in reading. The attempt to peer into the very core of a text, to possess once and for all its meaning, is vain—it is only ourselves that we find there, not the work itself."[41]

Because the imagery of the striptease is so strongly gendered, I think that the most striking modern productions of the play have involved cross-dressing, in the spirit of the Beardsley illustrations and Wilde's own transgressive themes. Theatrical transvestism, the drama critic Laurence Senelick explains, has its roots in the magical and religious origins of theater, through the performance of the shaman whose ritualized sex changes were a sign that "socially-constructed gender roles may be reshuffled, and that no one with the divine spark need be relegated forever to a single sex." Cross-dressing on stage is "a transcendant expression of human potentiality" because of the artificiality of theatrical convention, which "offers not actuality but symbol."[42]

It is true that, traditionally, drag has been the minstrel show of a virulent misogyny, a cruel travesty of the feminine. I found that being a woman spectator at drag shows, from the Black Cap in London to Provincetown, was sometimes a humiliating experience. But even drag can be reframed to speak for women in a ritual of inversion; in contemporary theater and cabaret, as Senelick notes, the "glamour drag found in pubs and clubs deconstructs the illusion of female pulchritude prescribed by our society," while the harsher post-modernist form of "alternative drag tries to deconstruct this deconstruction." Drag artists in South London nightclubs now play for all-female audiences, "hen parties." Dressed in an orange feather boa, Tommy Osborne com-

Lindsay Kemp as Salome, 1977.

mented that "the audience sees drag artists as surrogate women, voicing their hidden feelings." Cross-dressing makes it possible for him to function as a shamanistic figure of release: "Mind, if a man told the jokes I do, they would think it rude. But with a man dressed up as a woman, they scream things back."[43]

Contemporary productions of *Salome*, in which sexual difference and ambiguity rather than the actual female body are emphasized, have been genuinely disruptive and unsettling. In a 1977 all-male production at the London Roundhouse, for example, Lindsay Kemp played Salome as a transvestite (Figure 15), but abandoned "all theatrical aids, glamorous costume, wig, and so on" in the end and performed "the final sequence in his own person."[44] In Maurice Béjart's *Salome* (1983), Salome was danced by the Paris Opera star Patrick Dupond, who, in the finale, was enfolded in a mammoth gown and given a plastic head to kiss that looked like his twin.[45] Most recently, it was interestingly filmed by Ken Russell as *Salome's Last Dance* (1987) as a play within a play; the whole performance is staged as a private theatrical in a homosexual brothel, which in the end is raided by police. Wilde is very much present as a spectator-voyeur, and all the roles are doubled, with Herod played by the brothelkeeper and Salome played by a drab serving-girl who is transformed into a teenage seductress with silver eyeshadow and space opera clothes, who suggestively licks lollypops and admires her own long legs in silver boots. In the Dance of the Seven Veils, however, Salome is revealed to be a boy who flaunts his genitals, slaps his naked buttocks, and shocks the male film viewer into an awareness that he has been sexually titillated by another man.

The threat that the veiled *woman* in *Salome* still represents could also be felt in the extremely stylized production staged by Steven Berkoff in Dublin, Edinburgh, and London; and German director Nikolaus Lehnhoff's controversial production of the opera at the New York Metropolitan Opera in 1989. Arguing that *Salome* "should react to our time and confront us with problems we can understand," the director emphasized the similarities between the previous *fin de siècle* and the 1980s. "In our own time, the Zeitgeist is in many respects similar to that of the late nineteenth century," Lehnhoff explained. "Mankind is closer to the apocalypse now than ever before. But it's not war or atomic bombs that pose the prime threats. Nowadays we are attacked by creeping noisless catastrophes of nature and civilization: the dying of the forests, the AIDS epidemic, Chernobyl." In his harsh post-modernist set, Lehnhoff attempted to create a sense of "terminality" and "catastrophe," with a stage so steeply raked that it looked "as though there must have been an earthquake. And through the entire opera you get the feeling it will fall apart."[46] In the first act, soldiers are lowering limp male corpses into a pit, suggesting the presence of an AIDS-like plague. At the end, when Herod shouts his orders to kill Salome, there is no one left to hear him; everyone is a victim of the sexual anarchy symbolized by Woman. Yet the detour through transvestism finally makes clear that that "womanliness" is the putting on of veils, only "masquerading in a feminine guise."[47] In this sense, the veiled woman, too, is a female impersonator.

NINE

Decadence,
Homosexuality,
and Feminism

S alome, critics have agreed, was both a New Woman and "the icon of the ideology of the Decadents."[1] The decadent or aesthete was the masculine counterpart to the New Woman and, to some Victorian observers, "an invention as terrible as, and in some ways, more shocking" than she.[2] In the conservative mind the two were firmly linked as a couple sharing many attributes. Both were challenging the institution of marriage and blurring the borders between the sexes. Max Beerbohm contended that the amalgamation of the sexes was "one of the chief planks in the decadent platform."[3] In terms of class, too, the New Woman and the decadent seemed to violate proper hierarchies and social organisms. The transgression of class boundaries in their fiction gave rise to great alarm; both celebrated romantic alliances between the classes, with both men and women turning to working-class lovers for a passion and tenderness missing in their own class surroundings.

Decadence is a notoriously difficult term to define. In one sense, it was the pejorative label applied by the bourgeoisie to everything that seemed unnatural, artificial, and perverse, from Art Nouveau to homosexuality, a sickness with symptoms associated with cultural degeneration and decay.[4] In another sense, it was a post-Darwinian aesthetic movement that crossed European boundaries. The decadent aesthetic held that nature was "an unfeeling and pitiless mechanism"; religion, a "nostalgic memory"; and love, a biological instinct for perpetuating the species. Since these traditional consolations were meaningless, the only solution was to live in the experience of the moment, to seek the "new, the rare, the strange, the refined."⁵ In England, Walter Pater became the father of this philosophy, writing in *The Renaissance* (1873) that "our one chance lies in . . . getting as many pulsations as possible into the given time. Great passions give us this quickened sense of life. . . . The love of art for art's sake has most, for art comes to you proposing frankly to give nothing but the highest quality to your moments as they pass, and simply for those moments' sake."

While they were often linked in the press and in popular culture as "twin apostles of social apocalypse,"⁶ New Women and decadent men did not experience themselves as natural allies, and there were many tensions between them that surfaced, especially around the issues of gender and sexuality. The decadent aesthetic rejected all that was natural and biological in favor of the inner life of art, artifice, sensation, and imagination. "My own experience," Wilde remarked in *The Artist as Critic*, "is that the more we study Art, the less we care for Nature. . . . Nature has good intentions, of course, but as Aristotle said, she cannot carry them out." Antinaturalism, as Jean Pierrot explained in *The Decadent Imagination*, inevitably leads to antifeminism; women were seen as closer to "Nature," to the body, and to a crude materialism, while men were aligned with "Art," to the intellect, and to spiritualism. The most brutal and influential version of this misogyny came from Baudelaire, who described woman as a being entirely governed by her biological and physical impulses: "Woman is the opposite of the dandy. Therefore she inspires horror. Woman is hungry so she must eat; thirsty, so she must drink. She is in heat, so she must be fucked. How admirable! Woman is natural, which is to say abominable." The debasement of women's bodies, standard in much French Decadent writing, reached a degree of extraordinary disgust and loathing in Huysmans's *Against Nature*. Women reappear as objects of value in decadent writing only when they are desexualized through maternity or thoroughly aestheticized, stylized, and turned into icons or fetishes.

Moreover, as Fraser Harrison suggested, the English decadents associated with *The Yellow Book* were the most dramatic casualties of the crisis in masculinity: "The threats and demands represented by the ever accelerating movement towards female emancipation on all fronts, seem to have unnerved and unbalanced this group of men and driven them to seek comfort and oblivion in homosexuality, prostitution, addiction to alcohol and opiates, sterile relationships with children, and, in some cases, forlorn celibacy." In this sense, he concluded, they were not rebels but "refugees fleeing in the face of bewildering social evolutions."[7] Harland, Dowson, and Beardsley died young of tuberculosis; Davidson drowned himself, and Symons claimed that he knew twelve men who had killed themselves. Regenia Gagnier see the decadents as a pathetic generation of men who "were either cared for by sisters, intimidated by New Women, or like [Lionel] Johnson, after 'four of five glasses of wine,' denying that 'a gelded man lost anything of intellectual power.' "[8] While the New Women writers were robust and successful, the decadents, invariably portrayed in the *Punch* cartoons as physically feeble specimens, indeed seemed to lead unhappy lives characterized by "a devastating inability to establish and sustain sexual relationships."[9]

"Decadence" was also a fin-de-siècle euphemism for homosexuality, the public or cultural facade that marked out one complex and indeed contradictory position along the axis of English homosexual identity-formation in the late nineteenth century. New Women and homosexual men emerged in the public consciousness at about the same time. The word "homosexual," which had been coined by the Hungarian writer Karoly Benkert in 1869, entered the English vocabulary when Krafft-Ebing's *Psychopathia Sexualis* was translated in the 1890s. By 1894, the New Woman was also a familiar term. Sydney Grundy's play *The New Woman* appeared that year.[10] At the same time, homosexual art and culture in England was at its peak, with Carpenter lecturing on homogenic love in Manchester and the publication of the tragic love story "The Priest and the Acolyte" in the Oxford journal *The Chameleon*.[11]

Wilde's trial for homosexuality in 1895, however, created a moral panic that inaugurated a period of censorship affecting both advanced women and homosexuals. By the mid-1890s it was widely stated that the New Woman novel was passé. Hardy's *Jude the Obscure* (1895), with its hints that the New Woman Sue Bridehead was in some way perverse, began another scandal that marked the labelling of feminists and odd women as deviant. One review called the novel "Jude the Obscene." In its editorial comments on the trial, the *Westminster Gazette* hailed Wilde's conviction as a justification of censorship: "Art, we are told, has nothing to do with morality. Even if this doctrine were true, it has long ago been perverted, under the treatment of the decadents, into a positive preference on the part of 'Art' for the immoral, the morbid, and maniacal. . . . But this terrible case . . . may be the means of inculcating good if it burns its lesson upon the literary and moral conscience of the present generation."[12] In 1898, Havelock Ellis's *Sexual Inversion* was successfully prosecuted by the National Vigilance Association under the Obscene Publications Act, and it was never sold in England during Ellis's lifetime. And while a few of Wilde's friends continued to fight for the repeal of the Labouchère Amendment and to press for Wilde's release, most intellectuals and writers would not stand by him in public. In France a petition was circulated in his defense, but no one—neither Alphonse Daudet, Jules Renard, Anatole France, Edmond de Goncourt, Pierre Loüys, nor Emile Zola—would sign it.

On the other hand, the Wilde trial "crystallized the homosexual emancipation movement"; in Germany the homophile periodical *Der Eigene* began publication in 1896, "to no little degree stimulated by the trials of Wilde."[13] The discourse around homosexuality continued to develop during this period, and two conflicting models of homosexual identity began to emerge, opposing possibilities sometimes held simultaneously by the same individuals, which continue to coexist with powerful consequences today. The first was the paradigmatic fin-de-siècle model of sexual inversion, illustrated by the work of Karl Ulrichs and Magnus Hirschfeld in Germany and Edward Carpenter and John Addington Symonds in England. According to this model of border-crossing and liminality, gay people were an "intermediate sex," "exactly at the threshold between genders."[14] Homosexual men were people born with a high percentage of essential femininity, with a "woman's soul trapped in man's body." Homosexual women were mannish lesbians, women with a high percentage of essential masculinity. Those who held the inversion model could construe it either to defend the idea that homosexuality was innate, essential, congenital, and the "fixed attribute of a closely defined minority,"[15] or to make the case that it was situational, constructed, and a universal human potential.

These identifications also made possible a number of ways for individuals to position themselves, as well as a fluid and diverse set of political and aesthetic alliances between groups. There might be an alliance of homosexuals and lesbians under the heading of inversion; gay men might align themselves with women generally in terms of shared femininity; and gay men, lesbians, and heterosexual feminists might bond on issues of sexual politics, rights and oppression. Alliances might also extend beyond inter-gender bonds to class and race. Carpenter's homosexuality was connected with his commitment to feminism and socialism. In his autobiography *My Days and Dreams*, Carpenter wrote eloquently of the wasted lives of his unmarried sisters: "More than once girls of whom I least expected it told me that their lives were miserable 'with nothing on earth to do.' Multiply this picture by thousands and hundreds of thousands all over the country, and it is easy to see how, when the causes of the misery were understood, it led to the powerful growth of the modern "Women's Movement.' "[16]

The second model, however, saw homosexuality as the "highest, most perfect evolutionary stage of gender differentiation."[17] According to this model, the male-identified man and the woman-identified woman expressed heightened forms of masculinity and femininity and were the most purely "manly" or "womanly" representatives of their sex. Their sexual preference for their own sex was seen as determined by their sexual disgust for the opposite sex rather than by their sharing of its desires. Lesbians were man-haters, gay men were misogynists; each was repelled by the other. Thus, in this model, gay men and lesbians occupied the opposite poles rather than the center or threshold of sexual difference. Male homosexuals would have most in common with heterosexual men who shared their delight in male companionship and, to some degree, their disdain for women. They would see themselves as protecting bastions of patriarchy, male dominance, and male separatism, as anti-feminists rather than supporters of women's rights. Since these attitudes and values of Clubland, the universities, and other institutions were identified with heterosexual men, many Victorian homosexual men saw the "exclusion of women from their intimate lives as virilizing them."[18]

Homosexual discourse itself was full of contradictions about these positions, and the same writers could maintain them both. Carpenter, for example, was repelled by "anything effeminate in a man," and felt "positive repulsion" for women's bodies.[19] Thus his model of homosexuality, in contradiction to his political behavior, was one of gender differentiation; he also found New Women "those in whom the maternal instinct is not especially strong; also . . . those in whom the sexual instinct is not preponderant. Such women do not entirely represent their sex; some are rather mannish in temperament; some are 'homogenic' . . . to others, man's sex-passion is a mere impertinence, which they do not understand, and whose place they consequently misjudge." Carpenter saw normal female sexuality as inextricable from the maternal instinct and thus more physical and at a lower evolutionary level than same-sex love. As he wrote in

Homogenic Love (1894): "In a large number of instances the relation is not distinctly sexual at all . . . in the homosexual love—whether between man and man or between woman and woman—the physical side, from the very nature of the case, can never find expression quite so freely and perfectly as in the ordinary heterosexual love; and therefore . . . there is a tendency for [homosexual] love to run rather more along emotional channels." Indeed, according to Carpenter, homogenic love, in contrast to "ordinary sex-love," which had a "special function in the propagation of the race," was necessary for a society to generate "those children of the mind, the philosophical conceptions and ideals which transform our lives and those of society." As Regenia Gagnier notes, "that good women were no more than the means of reproduction was . . . the source of the anti-feminist thread running through the polemical homosexual literature of the period."[20]

While antinaturalist misogyny did not originate with homosexual men, it nurtured their wish to idealize relationships between men as more spiritual, intellectual, beautiful, and pure than heterosexual love. In the 1890s, Kains-Jackson proselytized for "The New Chivalry" in his journal *The Artist*, arguing that overpopulation made love between men the erotic choice of the future: "Wherefore just as the flower of the early and imperfect civilization was in what we may call the old chivalry, or the exaltation of the youthful feminine ideal, so the flower of the adult and perfect civilization will be found in the New Chivalry or the exaltation of the youthful masculine ideal. The time has arrived when the eternal desire for love which nature has implanted in the breast of man requires to be satisfied without such an increase in population as has characterized the past." The New Chivalry, Kains-Jackson maintained, would have social and athletic advantages as well, for "the joys of the palaestra, of the river, of the hunt and the moor, the evening tent-pitching of campers out, and the exhilaration of the early-morning swim" would all be ten times more satisfying between men.[21] In Frank Harris's biography of Wilde, Wilde took the position that heterosexual love was inferior to homosexuality, arguing that women's bodies were unaesthetic and that the need to produce children deprived women of a more exalted, transcendent, and non-purposeful love.

Predictably, New Women were, at best, ambivalent about alliances with homosexual men. On the one hand, many shared their culture's prejudices against men who were not conventionally "masculine." "The effeminate man and the masculine woman," wrote Eleanor Marx and Edward Aveling, ". . . are two types from which even the average person recoils with a perfectly natural horror of the unnatural."[22] In the Men and Women's Club, Maria Sharpe was shocked by R. L. Parker's defense of boy-love.[23] On the other hand, when homosexual identity-formation depended strongly on misogyny to shore it up, homosexual men could not be dependable allies. As Dora Marsden wrote in the feminist journal *The Freewoman*, "There is an undeniable tendency in many homosexuals to look upon woman as an inferior. . . . It is hardly to be presumed, then, that the men who entertain this instinctive aversion to women are absolutely uninfluenced by it when summoned by women to support their demand for independence."[24]

Olive Schreiner was the most sophisticated and thoughtful of the feminist theorists about homosexuality. In her letters to Karl Pearson, Schreiner explored the aestheticization of sexuality and the ideals of homogenic love. A fully aesthetic sexuality, Schreiner argued, was possible only when sex and reproduction were entirely separate—that is, when the human race could propagate itself by other means, "say by a mixture of human bloods drawn from the arm and treated in a certain manner, a mode analagous to the propagation of the rose tree by cuttings." Then the sexual system might evolve like the cultivated rose, which "having no more need of seed turns all its sexual organs into petals, and doubles, and doubles; it becomes entirely aesthetic. It is only for beauty, not for the continuance of the race; yet it came into existence as all flowers do—simply as a collection of sexual organs." But such a point had not been reached in human sexuality. Instead it had become complex and had both reproductive and aesthetic functions, which kept each other in balance. From Schreiner's feminist point of view, the male sexual aesthetic had two dangers. One one side there was "the prostitution of our large cities, the degradation of the sex functions from child-producing to the moment's sensuous pleasure." On the other was the fear that intellect exercised without the reproductive nature would become sterile and decadent: "Will humanity at last break out into one huge blossom of the brain—and die? Like one of those aloes, which grow for three hundred years, then break out into one large flower at the top of their stem and die!"[25]

The contradictions between the decadent and the feminist position can be seen very clearly in Oscar Wilde's *The Picture of Dorian Gray* (1890). In his personal life, Wilde might have been said to support the cause of the New Woman. As editor of the magazine *The Woman's*

World, he had commissioned articles on feminism and women's suffrage. But Wilde was also one of the leading theorists of decadence, and his novel was the English Bible of decadence, as well as a kind of bible for male homosexuals, inspiring a particular cult of behavior, dress, and speech. Wilde's model of homosexuality is implicitly one of gender differentiation, the most perfected form of male aestheticism, a "romance of art" rather than a romance of the flesh. The picture of Dorian Gray itself is to represent a new Platonic school of art, which will combine Greek romance with Greek "perfection of the spirit." The painter Basil Hallward's love for him, Dorian understands, "had nothing in it that was not noble and intellectual. It was not that mere physical admiration of beauty that is born of the senses and that dies when the senses tire. It was such love as Michael Angelo had known, and Montaigne, and Winckelmann, and Shakespeare himself." Although Dorian's beauty is described as the beauty of "youth," it is clear that only male youth, the "glamour of boyhood," qualifies for the Hellenic and Hedonistic ideal of art. Beginning as a mindless specimen himself, a masculine dumb blond, Dorian begins to believe in his own destiny as the theorist of the alternative New Hedonism: "He sought to elaborate some new scheme of life that would have its reasoned philosophy and its ordered principles, and find in the spiritualizing of the senses its highest realization."

This rationalization of homosexual desire as aesthetic experience has as its subtext an escalating contempt for women, whose bodies seem to stand in the way of philosophical beauty. The aristocratic dandy Lord Henry Wotton speaks the most misogynistic lines in the novel, a series of generalizations about the practicality, materiality, grossness, and immanence of women, who "represent the triumph of matter over mind." Women, as Lord Henry explains to Dorian, are not capable of noble and intellectual love; they are too fleshy and material; they "never know when the curtain has fallen," but hang around, growing "stout and tedious" and old, and going in for reminiscences like Freudian hysterics. Women, in short, "have no sense of art," and their demands interrupt the philosopher at his work: "Women inspire us with the desire to do masterpieces and always prevent us from carrying them out." They can reenter "the sphere of art" only by killing themselves and becoming beautiful objects. Thus the actress Sybil Vane's suicide by taking prussic acid—the drug of choice for abandoned New Women—aestheticizes her death and turns

it into what Lord Henry calls "strange lurid fragment from some Jac-
obean tragedy."

The theorist of decadence in the novel, Lord Henry is also the fin-
de-siècle scientist-figure who enjoys the sadistic power of experimenting on human "cases": "He had always been enthralled by the
methods of natural science, but the ordinary subject matter of that
science had seemed to him trivial and of no import. And so he had
begun by vivisecting himself, as he had ended by vivisecting others."
Thus Dorian's love for Sybil does not make Lord Henry jealous: "he
was pleased by it. It made him a more interesting study." Women and
female reproductive power are irrelevant and even destructive; true
creativity is male, and self-generating. "The lad was his own creation. . . . That was something."

Yet the aestheticization of homosexuality has also to contend with
such harsh realities as aging and venereal disease. Dorian escapes aging
by becoming art, but Wilde also uses the late-nineteenth-century
obsession with visible vice to suggest that the degeneration of the
painting is a sexual disease, the outward sign of Dorian's sexuality in
a repressive culture. As Basil Hallward warns Dorian, "People talk of
secret vices. There are no such things. If a wretched man has a vice,
it shows itself in the lines of his mouth, the droop of his eyelids, and
moulding of his hands even." The changes that take place in the
portrait as the "leprosies of sin" eat it away are like the progressive
pathologies of syphilis: "hideous face," "warped lips," "coarse bloated
hands," a red stain that has "crept like a horrible disease over the
wrinkled fingers," "misshapen body and failing limbs," and a general
air of the bestial, sodden, and unclean. "Was it to become a monstrous
and loathsome thing," Dorian wonders, "to be hidden away in a locked
room?" In Dorian's view, however, "the true nature of the senses"
might be understood if it were not for the "harsh uncomely puritanism"
of a feminized society that has "sought to starve them into submission
or to kill them by pain, instead of aiming at making them elements
of a new spirituality, of which a fine instinct for beauty was to be the
dominant characteristic."

Attended entirely by men, Wilde's trial in 1895, with its revelations
of the gross materiality of homosexual liaisons, from the bad teeth of
Wilde's working-class pick-ups to the stains his landlady found on the
sheets, de-aestheticized homogenic love and brought it back to the
level of the human, mortal, physical, and profane. Nevertheless,

the image of the English male homosexual that prevailed for much of this century was that of the effeminate aesthete or the decadent dandy rather than that of the social democrat, anti-imperialist, or male feminist such as Edward Carpenter. Eve Sedgwick has argued that what she calls "the feminization of the English homosexual" diminished the possibilities for alliances between feminists and gay men. Instead, ironically, it "went with a loss of interest in the political fate of real women. It went with a loss of interest in, or hope for, political struggle in general. Political alliances between gay men and other, comparably oppressed groups were not cultivated."[26] Only in recent years has "Saint Oscar," as Terry Eagleton calls him, been resurrected as a socialist and feminist hero.

In the introduction to his collected works, H. G. Wells claimed that in writing *The Island of Dr. Moreau* in 1895, he had been thinking of Oscar Wilde's trial: "There was a scandalous trial about that time, the graceless and pitiless downfall of a man of genius, and this story was the response of an imaginative mind to the reminder that humanity is but animal, rough-hewn to a reasonable shape and in perpetual internal conflict between instinct and injunction. The story embodies this ideal, but apart from this embodiment it has no allegorical quality. It is written just to give the utmost possible vividness to that conception of men as hewn and confused and tormented beasts."[27] The connections between Wilde and Wells have gone unnoticed by critics, but *The Island of Dr. Moreau,* like all of Wells's stories, has a significant gender subtext. Like Lord Henry, Dr. Moreau is a vivisector, a fin-de-siècle scientist who attempts to separate reproduction from female sexuality, in this case by creating human beings out of animals. Beginning with experiments in the transfusion of blood, Moreau has advanced to tissue transplants and plastic surgery. Moreover, "the possibilities of vivisection do not stop at a mere physical metamorphosis," but involve complete psychic reprogramming. Moreau's decadence is hinted first in his name, with its allusions to the nineteenth-century French scientists Moreau de Tours and Benedict-Augustin Morel, who developed theories of degeneration. He has also developed a scientific aestheticism that makes him indifferent to pain and emotion; his laboratory is a dark version of Huysmans's chamber or Lord Henry's salon, a place where he enjoys the exquisite sensations of science for science's sake: "You cannot imagine the strange colorless delight of these intellectual desires. The thing before you is no longer an animal, a fellow-creature, but a problem. Sympathetic pain—all

I know of it I remember as a thing I used to suffer from years ago."

This attitude towards his surgical patients as merely cases or problems links Moreau with Conan Doyle's Dr. Stone as well as with Dr. Freud. It also suggests a strong element of sexual sadism in the story, most fully realized when Moreau operates in his House of Pain on a powerful female puma, a kind of New Woman figure, or shrieking sister, who indeed reacts to the torture "with a shriek almost like that of an angry virago." Moreau tries to control his Beast People with a new version of the Law of the Father and the Law of the Jungle. But the females are especially resistant to his efforts to civilize them. They do not chant the chorus, "Are we not men?" with equal excitement. The females seem more aligned with the island itself, with organic nature, and the "rich and oozy" ground. They are the first to regress to animality and to "disregard the injunction of decency."[28]. . .

Bram Stoker's *Dracula* (1897) presents another decadent fantasy of reproduction through transfusion that sounds like a macabre version of Schreiner's rose-cuttings. Dracula's offspring are the daughters of his blood born through bites on the neck or arm; in the novel he possesses and transforms both the blond Lucy Westenra and the dark Mina Murray Harker. The novel is also about the thrills and terrors of blurred sexual, psychological, and scientific boundaries. Dracula lives in Transylvania, "on the borders of three states," which we might read as the states of living, dead, and undead, or of masculinity, femininity, and bisexuality. (In the cult film *The Rocky Horror Picture Show* [1975], Tim Curry introduces himself as a "sweet transvestite from Transsexual Transylvania.")

Read in the context of other fin-de-siècle frame narratives, Stoker's novel suggests that the solicitor Jonathan Harker, whose journal introduces the story, is Dracula's double; and in Werner Herzog's film *Nosferatu* Harker indeed does eventually become Dracula, replacing the dying vampire king. Harker's journey to Transylvania is much like Leo and Holly's journey to Kôr or Marlow's journey to the Inner Station—a quest for the heart of darkness. Like these other travelers, he has "queer dreams" as he traverses a strange symbolic landscape, and he hears warnings of the mysterious Count at his destination. We might interpret some of these experiences as Harker's repressed fantasies and anxieties, emerging on the eve of his marriage to the intellectual Mina. In Transylvania, where sexuality is fluid, Dracula desires men as well as women, and men like Harker can also become breathlesssly passive victims of vampire seductresses. At one point, when Harker, safely arrived in Dracula's castle, is shaving, he accidentally cuts himself: "I saw that the cut had bled a little, and the blood was running down my chin. I laid down the razor, turning as I did so half-round to look for some sticking-plaster. When the Count saw my face his eyes blazed with a sort of demoniac fury, and he suddenly made a grab at my throat."

But Dracula does not bite Harker; instead Harker is approached in his slumber in the middle of the night by three beautiful vampire women. While two of the women are dark with aquiline noses like the Count's, the third is blond and strangely familiar: "I seemed somehow to know her face, and to know it in connection with some dreamy fear, but I could not recollect at the moment how or where." As he looks at the woman, who clearly resembles Mina's best friend Lucy, Harker feels "a wicked, burning desire that they would kiss me with those red lips. It is not good to note this down, lest some day it should meet Mina's eyes, and cause her pain; but it is the truth." The blond, her red lips gleaming, bends over him. As he closes his eyes "in a languorous ecstasy and waited—waited with beating heart" to be penetrated by her sharp teeth, Dracula flings her away, exclaiming "This man belongs to me!"

Despite the text's strong hints of homoeroticism, Dracula's victims are all women; his "mission in England," as Christopher Craft observes, is "the creation of a race of monstrous women, feminine demons equipped with masculine devices."[29] Despite their diminutive names, Lucy and Mina exhibit the characteristics of the New Woman and the vampire woman that predict their destiny as Dracula's victims. The female vampire represented the nymphomaniac or oversexed wife who threatened her husband's life with her insatiable erotic demands. According to one gynecologist, "just as the vampire sucks the blood of its victims in their sleep, so does the woman vampire suck the life and exhaust the vitality of her male partner."[30] One theory held that woman's blood lust came from her need to replace lost menstrual blood. Lucy represents the New Woman's sexual daring; sought after by all the men, she girlishly wonders, "why can't they let a girl marry three men, or as many as want her?" The second image of the vampire was the hysteric, the feminist intellectual whose sicknesses drain her family's energies. Mina represents the New Woman's intellectual ambitions; she is a schoolmistress with strong organizational skills and an astonishing memory, who knows shorthand and all the train schedules.

With her "sweet woman's heart," but her "man's brain," Mina is a dangerous hybrid, who must be domesticated through hysteria.

Lucy is the first to be sexually aroused in monstrosity by Dracula's bite, and while the vampire extracts her blood by night, her fiancé Arthur and his friends, the other men who have courted her, replenish it by day through a series of blood transfusions, achieving a kind of blood brotherhood by mingling their fluids in her body. Soon, however, Lucy becomes a vampire: "the sweetness was turned to adamantine, heartless cruelty, and the purity to voluptuous wantonness." At the advice of the vampire expert Dr. Van Helsing, the men set out to invade her tomb, decapitate her, and drive a "round wooden stake, some two and a half or three inches thick and about three feet long," through her heart. They all stand watching as Arthur strikes: "the Thing in the coffin writhed; and a hideous, blood-curdling screech came from the opened red lips. The body shook and quivered and twisted in wild contortions; the sharp white teeth champed together till the lips were cut and the mouth was smeared with a crimson foam. But Arthur never faltered. He looked like a figure of Thor as his untrembling arm rose and fell, driving deeper and deeper the mercy-bearing stake, whilst the blood from the pierced heart welled and spurted up around it." Doctor Van Helsing and Doctor Seward "cut off the head and filled the mouth with garlic," and when the men were through, "there was gladness and mirth and peace everywhere." Lucy has been restored to sweetness and purity.

The sexual implications of the scene are embarrassingly clear. First there is the gang-rape with the impressive phallic instrument. Craft comments that "this enthusiastic correction of Lucy's monstrosity provides the Crew of Light with a double reassurance: it effectively exorcises the threat of a mobile and hungering female sexuality, and it counters the homoeroticism latent in the vampiric threat by rein-scribing . . . The line dividing the male who penetrates and the woman who receives."[31] Then there is decapitation, a remarkably frequent occurrence in male fin-de-siècle writing, from the severed head of Daniel Dravot in "The Man Who Would Be King" to the blackened heads that surround Kurtz's hut in *Heart of Darkness*. It is tempting to see these episodes reflecting the castration anxieties Freud describes in "Medusa's Head"; "To decapitate: to castrate." Indeed, when Dr. Seward sees the vampire Lucy, he observes that her brows "were wrinkled as though the folds of the flesh were the coils of

Medusa's snakes." But the Freudian equation of decapitation and castration is itself a product of fin-de-siècle culture. The severed head also seems to be a way to control the New Woman by separating the mind from the body. Moreover, the imagery of decapitation/castration, as Wendy Doniger O'Flaherty points out, "may symbolize the loss of the power of imagination; psychoanalysis itself may function in this way, as is betrayed by the idiom . . . getting one's head shrunk."[32] Finally, as in the English inn sign "The Silent Woman," which shows a headless female body, decapitation is a Draconian way to shut women up.

The other woman, Mina, is also silenced. "You must no more question," orders the fatherly Dr. Van Helsing. "We shall tell you all in good time. We are men, and are able to bear; but you must be our star." The effects on Mina of "the ceasing of telling things" are immediate. She is unable to sleep, begins to have fits of uncontrollable crying, feels depressed and anxious, and has terrible dreams. While it feels strange to Mina "to be kept in the dark," she supposes "it is one of the lessons we poor women have to learn." In short, when she is no longer taken into their confidence and included in the group, Mina becomes hysterical. Moreover, "the dark" is the place where Dracula lives. Before too long Dracula has her in his grip and is forcing her to drink *his* blood, pressing her mouth to the wound, as she says, "so that I must either suffocate or swallow some of the—Oh, my God, my God!"

Dracula is the most popular of all the fin-de-siècle stories for film; by 1980 over 133 full-length film versions had been recorded. The most influential version, however, was Bela Lugosi's classic performance in the 1932 version directed by Tod Browning. With its Piranesian scale of Gothic space, its effective use of silence and slow movement, and Lugosi's extraordinary pronunciation, the result of his phonetic reading of the English script, the film has set the style for Dracula even for those children of the 1980s who know the story only through Count Duckula TV cartoons. The 1932 film, however, is much more explicit about bisexuality than subsequent films would be. The campy male visitor (not Harker, but Renfield) to Dracula's castle is first photographed through a giant spider web; Dracula drugs him with wine and imperiously waves the three ghostly vampire women away as he himself bends over and envelops his victim.

While most film versions of *Dracula* have been heterosexual, nevertheless, homosexuality is strongly represented in the films, coded into the script and images in indirect ways. *Blacula* (1972), which combines elements of gender and race, is an example of the genre that came from the period of "blaxploitation" cinema in the early 1970s. Like *Shaft* or *Superfly*, which took formula films and placed them in the black urban context, *Blacula* makes the vampire an African prince in modern New York. In the introduction to the film, we learn that Dracula bit the prince in an argument over slavery in 1815 and had him nailed up in a coffin. When the film begins, Blacula is about to be rediscovered by an interracial couple of gay antique dealers, who have come to Transylvania on a shopping trip. They become his first victims, but because a bite on the neck would appear too intimate a gesture, too much like necking for the virile tragic black hero Blacula represents, he gnaws their arms, as if he did not know yet how a vampire behaves.

In *The Lost Boys* (1987), the vampires have become a gang of teenage punks with motorcycles, living in a mythical California boardwalk town full of drifters, runaways, addicts, and assorted weirdos. Merging the story of Dracula with the idea of the lost boys from *Peter Pan*, the film brilliantly portrays vampirism as a metaphor for the kind of mythic male bonding that resists growing up, commitment, especially marriage. The hero, Michael, looks like Jim Morrison, whose blown-up picture adorns the wall of the cavern and whose theme song, "The End," also featured in the opening scene of *Apocalypse Now*, is an important part of the sound track. The king vampire-bat, the Dracula or Captain Hook figure, is courting Michael's mother, but only because he wants to get to the sons. In this contemporary scenario of the vampire myth, then, New Women have been completely eliminated. Women are not vampires; they are either dingbats, like the mother, or remote Muse figures, like the beautiful Star, who seems to be shared by all the lost boys and who is accompanied by a mysterious feral child. The glamorous Lost Boys, with their fabulous peroxide punk haircuts, sensational leather outfits, gorgeous cowboy boots, and telltale sunglasses and single pierced ear, are the real lure. When Kiefer Sutherland, as the leader of the group, comes back bloody-mouthed from an attack on a group of men at a beach party and says to the anguished Michael: "Now you know what we are, and now you know what you are," it's clear that Michael's latent "vampire" tendencies and his homosexual panic are connected. He resists becoming a vampire, even biting his own hand in one scene so as not to give in, in an image that suggests both an animal in a trap and the metamorphosis of *Dr. Jekyll and Mr. Hyde.* As *The Lost Boys* hints, vampirism, like AIDS, is a sexually transmitted disease.

The post-modernist vampire film *The Hunger* casts vampirism in bisexual terms, drawing on the tradition of the lesbian vampire. The well-dressed vampire couple in the film, played by Catherine Deneuve and David Bowie, live in an elegant high-tech apartment and, apart from their taste for blood, could be any dual-career marriage of the decade. Decadence, bisexuality, and consumerism come together in scenes set in a dance club where the punk-rock band sings "Bela Lugosi Is Dead." (Indeed, several post-Dracula films use the urban club as a venue; there are wonderful disco scenes in *Blacula* and in *Love at First Bite,* where George Hamilton plays Dracula as a Transylvanian Fred Astaire.) Contemporary and stylish, *The Hunger* is also disquieting in its suggestion that men and women in the 1980s have the same desires, the same appetites, and the same needs for power, money, and sex.

Many conservatives today would see decadence and sexual anarchy as the products of an alliance between feminists and gay men. As in the nineteenth century, the women's liberation movement and the gay rights movement came into being at about the same time. When the New York City police staged a weekend raid on a gay bar, the Stonewall Inn, on June 27, 1969, gay men, drag queens, and lesbians refused to accept police harassment and fought back. Angry crowds rioted through the night, and in the wake of the Stonewall, the Gay Liberation Front was formed. In contrast to the homophile civil rights organizations of the 1950s and 1960s, which had challenged discriminatory laws and practices, gay liberation saw itself as revolutionary and oppositional. Borrowing from the rhetoric of the New Left, radical feminism, and black militant groups, young Gay Power activists saw their goal as the overthrow of an oppressive system of sex roles and family structure which had made heterosexuality compulsory.

During the 1970s, the gay movement developed alongside the women's movement. Both groups made progress in passing anti-discriminatory legislation, in creating professional caucuses, in forming their own businesses, banks, churches, health clinics, publishing houses, newspapers, journals, and academic programs. Nonetheless, the relationship between feminism and gay liberation took some unexpected turns in the 1970s. The inversion and gender-differentiation models of the *fin de siècle* were still operative: were male-male relationships a kind of masculinity squared, an intensification of patriarchal attitudes of male supremacy and the exclusion of women; or were gay men, by virtue of their oppression and their identification with the "feminine," more sympathetic to feminist issues? While to some women, gay men were more welcome in feminism than straight men because they were assumed to have "feminine" qualities and not to be sexually exploitative or driven by the need for mastery and conquest, to others gay men were hypermasculine and the epitome of phallocentricity. Although lesbians had many conflicts with the women's movement, they were more likely to identify with it than with a male-dominated Gay Liberation movement. As one San Francisco lesbian activist commented, "Gay men were so focused on creating and exploring their own culture, they just didn't want women around."[33] Despite its relative prosperity, moreover, the gay male community was not a strong presence in supporting women's issues. "I don't remember seeing one gay man coming into the NOW office when we were going for the ERA," one activist recalled. "In terms of volunteer recruitment and fundraising for lesbian causes, gay men aren't around."[34]

According to Marilyn Frye, writing in 1983, "gay men generally are in significant ways, perhaps in all important ways, only more loyal to masculinity and male-supremacy than other men." Frye argued that gay men "are more like ardent priests than infidels" in the worship of the phallus and that "the gay rights movement may be the fundamentalism of the global religion which is patriarchy."[35] With regard to cross-dressing and female impersonation, Frye concluded that although "some gay men achieve . . . prodigious mastery of the feminine," mastery of the feminine is always a masculine phenomenon.

On the other hand, according to the feminist critic Alice Jardine in *Men in Feminism,* gay men are better colleagues than straight men in the enterprise of gender studies: "A lot of the women I've talked to realize that it's easier if the man is gay. . . . I guess it's because we don't worry about being penetrated; we worry less about being invaded, fooled, penetrated."[36] Nevertheless, when feminists and gay men seemed to be competing for the limited space and time of the conference, the publishing list, and the gender curriculum, bitter conflicts could arise. The question of men in feminism, Janet Todd warned, suggests "that feminism has had its place in the liberal sun and should move over to leave the victim's space for a greater (male) victim, the homosexual."[37]

Most dramatically, male gay identity after Stonewall was defiantly organized around the concept of a male sexuality freed from the constraints of straight, monogamous, or "feminine" morality. Urban gay men were prime consumers in the erotic marketplace, as patrons of bathhouses, bars, and pornographic movie houses, where anonymous sex with many partners was easily available. Unlimited sex, moreover, became a deeply valued expression of gay identity and community, what Edmund White calls "a force binding familiar atoms into new polymers of affinity."[38] Many women did not share this idealistic view. As Susan Sontag harshly puts it, in the 1970s "many male homosexuals reconstituted themselves as something like an ethnic group, one whose distinctive folkloric custom was sexual voracity, and the institutions of urban homosexual life became a sexual delivery system of unprecedented speed, efficiency, and volume."[39] To some lesbian-feminists, the "take-what-you-want, when-you-want-it, how-you-want-it, anyway-you-want-to-do-it, without-regard-for-the consequences"[40] promiscuity of gay men typified everything that was most brutal and exploitative in male sexuality. To a small minority, however, gay sexuality represented a model for the expansion of female erotic possibilities as well. Gay men, after all, were not the only sexual consumers of the 1970s; women were advertising for partners in the personal columns of newspapers and magazines, going to singles bars, and visiting nightclubs that featured male strippers. But whether or not feminists could support such a fast-track urban sexual lifestyle ideologically, few women could envision it realistically for themselves; the night out with the girls at Chippendale's was not exactly equivalent to the baths or leather bars. At the very least, the debate over sexuality rendered alliances among feminists, lesbians, and gay men problematic.

Much of this conflict, however, is under transformation because of the AIDS crisis. Since the advent of AIDS, gay male sexual behavior and values have changed. One recent study showed that between 1984 and 1987, the percentage of gay urban men in monogamous relationships doubled. Some gay activists even believe that if a cure for AIDS could be found, most gay men would not return to the promiscuity of the pre-AIDS era.[41] For young gay men who were not sexually active before the epidemic, according to David Leavitt, "safe sex has become simply *what sex is.*"[42]

In his comments on the AIDS activist group ACT-UP, Leavitt offers a utopian vision of a new alliance between gay men and other radical groups, including feminists: "In the past being a gay activist seemed to require a pledged loyalty to a mostly white, all-male 'tribe' whose politics of mutual defense took place against a backdrop of relentless consumerism and left little room for a broader view of civil rights. In 1989, by contrast, 'the tribe' has given way to a 'queer nation' which is assertively coed, multi-racial, and anti-consumerist. The closed club has become an open meeting."[43] Indeed, the charged and exhilarating meetings of ACT-UP in New York, chaired by stunningly articulate women and men, seem to offer one model for what Frank Mort calls "radical pluralism, capable of uniting various disparate tendencies—gay, feminist, socialist, libertarian—in a progressive sexual alliance."[44] Whether this alliance is one of the first signs of rebirth out of the crisis, or whether after its utopian moment it, too, will have to go through its own fin-de-siècle cycles of division and fragmentation, will be an important question in the 1990s.

TEN

The Way We Write Now: Syphilis and AIDS

Sexual epidemics are the apocalyptic forms of sexual anarchy, and syphilis and AIDS have occupied similar positions at the ends of the nineteenth and twentieth centuries as diseases that seem to be the result of sexual transgression and that have generated moral panic. Both diseases have provided the occasion for sexual and social purity campaigns and for a retreat from the liberalization of sexual attitudes. Viewing syphilis as divine retribution for the collapse of sexual and marital boundaries, doctors in the 1890s began to publicize the dangers of an epidemic, initiating the period which the French historian Alain Corbin has called "the golden age of venereal peril."[1] Syphilis became an obsessive public crisis at the precise moment when arguments over the future of marriage, discussions of the New Women, and decadent homosexual culture were at their peak. Conservatives were quick to seize upon the disease as a weapon in their fight to restore the values of chastity and monogamy; "continence . . . became the hallmark of all sexual prescription."[2] Medical estimates of the extent of syphilis infection and the rate at which it was spreading at the turn of the century rose alarmingly as the century marker drew near. In the early 1880s, Dr. Charles Mauriac calculated that there were 5,000 new cases a year in Paris; by the turn of the century experts placed the percentage of infected men as high as 20 percent, and in 1902 the director of the Institut Pasteur estimated the number of contagious syphilitics in France at a million.[3] Looking at these projections, doctors predicted the unavoidable "syphilisation" of the Western world.[4]

Themes of crime and punishment, sin and retribution, guilt and innocence, dominated the official discourse about syphilis. Syphilis was "an ideal Protestant disease as well as an ironically Victorian disease. One transgression, a single sexual contact, could lead to a lifetime of suffering. There was no way of knowing for certain if one had been contaminated or not. . . . One was never certain of the cure and, of course, none was deserving of cure. No precautions against it were sufficient, paralleling the Christian notion that no human works could possibly influence divine salvation."[5] Henry Ware Eliot, the father of T. S. Eliot, maintained that syphilis was "God's punishment and . . . hoped a cure would never be found. Otherwise, he said, it might be necessary to emasculate our children to keep them clean."[6] In Old Testament rhetoric, Lady Cook suggested in 1890 that syphilitic men should be branded as a warning to innocent women who might otherwise take them as husbands.[7]

Gender, race, and class were important variables in the discourses surrounding syphilis. As the historian Allan Brandt notes, in the nineteenth century "venereal disease had specifically different meanings for the infected man or woman, meanings that revealed powerful assumptions about the nature of the family and sexuality. These infections served as yet another means of defining the separate spheres of gender identity."[8] By 1900 most of French literature dealing with syphilis was sexist, xenophobic, and racist. In a pattern that became true for other countries as well, they made the foreign-born prostitute the alleged source of venereal contagion and the scapegoat for male sexual anxieties. In Germany and Austria, syphilis became a standard trope of anti-Semitic polemics, a metaphor for racial evil. In the United States, the rising tide of immigration was held responsible for the spread of syphilis; as one gynecologist explained, "The tide [of venereal disease] has been raising [sic] owing to the inpouring of a large foreign population with lower ideals."[9] All of these elements made syphilis a symbolic illness, a significant theme in fin-de-siècle literature and art.

As we live through our own age of venereal peril, the parallels between syphilis and AIDS seem particularly striking. Elizabeth Fee notes that both diseases can be understood as biomedical or moral: "Both diseases, in laboratory terms, are caused by a microorganism— in the case of AIDS, by the HIV retrovirus. Both diseases can be transmitted by sexual contact; both can also be transmitted non-sexually. The social perception of each disease has been heavily influenced by the possibility of sexual transmission and the attendant notions of responsibility, guilt, and blame. In each case, those suffering from the disease have often been regarded as both the cause and embodiment of the disease, and have been feared and blamed by others who define themselves as more virtuous."[10] Coming to public attention at the height of periods of sexual anarchy, both syphilis and AIDS have been interpreted as the inevitable outcome of the violation of "natural" sexual laws. The AIDs pandemic emerged, too, in 1981 after a decade of drastic changes in American sexual and social mores, changes many regarded as leading to deviant and immoral behavior. Among these changes was the acceptance of homosexuality. "AIDS came along," Dennis Altman explains, "just when the old religious, moral, and cultural arguments against homosexuality seemed to be collapsing."[11]

Both are symbolic sexual diseases that have taken on apocalyptic dimensions and have been interpreted as signaling the end of the world. The impact of the AIDS epidemic is all the greater because it coincides with the end of a century. In discussing the impact of AIDS on the visual arts in June 1987, Lisa Philips, a curator for the Whitney Museum, observed that "the kind of art that's being made seems to me to go back to the turn-of-the-century feeling of closure, of impending doom."[12] Physicians describe AIDS in the language of fin-de-siècle catastrophe, constantly updating the estimates of those who will be stricken and the spiraling costs of their medical care. As one American doctor recently commented about AIDS, "We are dealing with a plague with the potential of wiping out our civilization."[13]

Both, too, have been strongly inflected by gender, race, and class, with very different meanings for men and women, heterosexuals and homosexuals, rich and poor, black and white. While the frenzy to place the blame for AIDS on an outsiders' group has led to its construction in the United States as an African or Haitian disease, in the rest of the world, AIDS has been seen as the product of the exportation of American gay lifestyles. Once jokingly called WOGS— the Wrath of God Syndrome—AIDS has been an even more powerful vehicle than syphilis for apocalyptic sermonizing about the wages of sin. In the words of Jerry Falwell, founder of the Moral Majority, "AIDS is God's judgment on a society that does not live by His rules." Not only right-wing politicians and TV evangelists, but also some gay intellectuals, have expressed concern about disease as a punishment for going too far. "I am wise, wiser perhaps than even Jerry Falwell," wrote the composer Ned Rorem, "yet cannot help wondering (I who don't believe in God) if some chastisement is at work."[14] In a notorious parallel to the Victorian calls for the branding of syphilitics, William F. Buckley recommended that "everyone detected with AIDS should be tattooed in the upper fore-arm, to protect common needle-users, and on the buttocks, to prevent the victimization of other homosexuals."[15] With its chilling echoes of Nazi numbers tattooed on the forearms of Jews, homosexuals, and other concentration camp victims, Buckley's statement fueled both fear and outrage.

AIDS, too, has become a symbolic disease in the culture of our *fin de siècle*. In the summer of 1988, the National Film Theatre in London organized a timely series on "Epidemics." In the title film of the series, Elia Kazan's *Panic in the Streets* (1950), an illegal Greek immigrant from a ship called *The Nile Queen* dies of plague on the New Orleans waterfront, and his contacts must be tracked down, quarantined, or killed by the Public Health investigator, an American family man, in order to protect the city. According to the organizers, Mark Finch and Judith Williamson, the film set many of the conventions of "epidemic cinema," such as the sense of the ethnic Other as carrier, the sense of threat to the family, themes of "criminality, contagion, and medical policing," "body horror metaphors," and the "drive for the discovery and control of disease which is presented among society's outcasts."[16] These elements show "that the language and narrative patterns associated with AIDS reportage and fictions were developed long before the illness itself existed"; and that films about AIDS are influenced by "pre-existing dramas of disease."[17]

Yet as a symbolic disease, AIDS is very different from syphilis, and the differences are characteristic of the fundamental changes that have taken place over a century. First and most important, syphilis was an affliction of the anonymous which remained a family secret except in a few cases involving artists. Syphilis had a face, but no voice; while profligates and prostitutes were seen as its risk groups, they did not come forward to speak of the disease. AIDS, however, has become part of the collective history and identity of gay men. According to Paula Treichler, a feminist critic and historian of medical science who has written extensively on AIDS, "AIDS in the United States came to be a story of gay men and a construction of a hypothetical male homosexual body."[18] It cannot be understood apart from a recognition of both the gay culture of the late twentieth century and the homophobia that has always construed homosexuality itself as a disease. As Dennis Altman comments, "it is difficult to speak of the impact of

AIDS without speaking of the changing perceptions of homosexuals, so intertwined are the two in the public imagination."[19]

Secondly, AIDS has engendered a politics of cultural activism. Primarily developed by urban gay men, the activist groups have also developed programs for IV drug users, women, and racial minorities who have not been able to mount organizations on their own. Gay organizations like the Gay Men's Health Crisis in New York, Shanti in San Francisco, the Terence Higgins Trust in England, and ACT-UP (AIDS Coalition to Unleash Power), with its symbol of the pink triangle and its slogan "Silence = Death," have mobilized around the issues of testing, funding, diagnosis, treatment, and patient rights. AIDS activists have taken to the streets to demand that the drug AZT be made available at lower cost to people with HIV infection; they have demonstrated against discriminatory policies and have besieged public health centers and politicians with calls and protests designed to win more funds for research and care. They have called for a new kind of activist art that educates, informs, and mobilizes responses to the health crisis.

Finally, while syphilis was the germ that dared not speak its name, the struggle over the discourse of AIDS has developed alongside the disease itself. Taken up by post-structuralist and post-modernist critics intensely aware of the effects of language and signification, AIDS has become the most self-conscious of all diseases. As Simon Watney has argued, "AIDS is not only a medical crisis on an unparalleled scale, it involves a crisis of representation itself, a crisis over the entire framing of knowledge about the human body and its capacities for sexual pleasure."[20] Jan Zita Grover explains that the cultural situation of AIDS is unprecedented and thus offers an opportunity for symbolic as well as political intervention: "It is not often that we are present at the birth of a cultural phenomenon, in a position to watch the ways it is first woven of words and acts. AIDS is as much a creature of language as it is of the body or of love and fear."[21]

In order to understand how dramatically AIDS has altered behavior and symbolism, we need to look first at the ways that syphilis manifested itself in nineteenth-century culture. The iconography of syphilis was primarily masculine. With its dramatic inscriptions on the male body, the hideous ravages of syphilis, from an enormous and Miltonic list of skin disorders—macules, papules, tubercules, pustules, blebs, tumors, lesions, scales, crusts, ulcers, chancres, gummas, fissures, and scars—to cardiovascular disturbances, locomotor ataxia, tabes, blindness, and dementia, made the disease a powerful deterrent in theological and moral reform campaigns to control male sexuality, seen as one of the main causes of degeneration. Many late-Victorian patriarchs, official and unofficial, regarded syphilis as God's divine judgment on male lust. "The sexual instinct is imperative," one doctor observed, "and will only listen to fear."[22]

In the Victorian home, handbooks of popular medicine made terrifying images of the syphilitic wages of sin readily available for the instruction of the young boy. "Walter," the author of *My Secret Life*, recalled a book about venereal disease shown to him by his godfather when he was a child: "The illustrations in the book, of faces covered with scabs, blotches, and eruptions, took such hold of my mind that for twenty years afterwards the fear was not quite eradicated" (Figure 16). In Blackpool, a wax museum owned by Louis Tussaud displayed graphic models of hideous syphilitic disfigurement to deter sailors "from patronizing the whores along the dock road."[23]

Boys and men were also made constantly aware of the dangers of venereal infection by newspaper advertisements for an exotic catalogue of patent antisyphilis medicines, injections, and ointments: Curtis's Manhood, Sir Samuel Hannay's Specific, Dr. Brodum's Botanical Syrup, Dr. Morse's Invigorating Cordial, Naples Soap, Armenian Pills, Bumstead's Gleet Cure, Red Drops, The Unfortunate's Friend, and Davy's Lac-Elephantis, a popular nostrum that claimed to be the medicated milk of elephants. In France, *syphilographes*, doctors specializing in the study of syphilis, warned that a wide range of ordinary objects might be sources of venereal infection: baths and swimming pools, razors, pipes, cigarette-holders, sheets and towels. Even everyday activities like licking stamps or kissing the crucifix in church held dangers.

But the major source of infection, men were told, was the body of the prostitute. The prostitute was the agent of corruption and contamination, whose putrid body bred stench and disease. Thus the early nineteenth-century French reformer Alexandre Parent-Duchâtelet described the whore as "the woman-sewer"[24] and the brothel as a "seminal drain." The prostitute's body was the vessel in which men discharged and mingled polluting fluids. In the popular novel *Les Mançenilles* (1900) by André Couvreur, syphilis is thus spread by the prostitute Frida "whose bed has become the cesspool of all the people of color of the quartier, bringing their vice and disease from all four corners

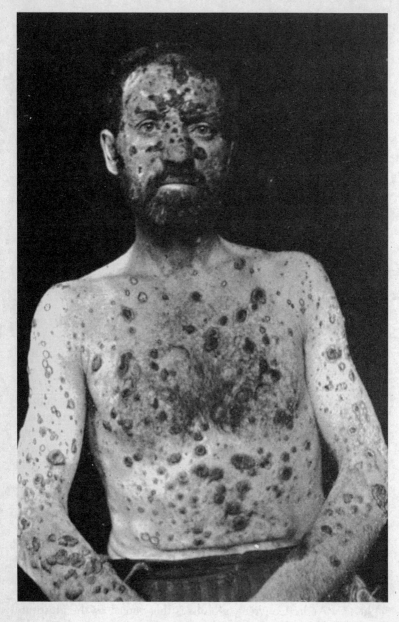

Syphilitic man, 1895.

of the world."[25] This hostility towards the prostitute could be generalized to apply to all women. When the hero of Michel Corday's novel
Vénus (1901) gets syphilis, he responds with a barrage of anti-feminist
naval metaphors: "women appeared to him now across a sad haze, like
enemies; no longer pleasure-craft decked out for a regatta, but a disquieting armada of warships, whose decks bore devastation."[26]

Syphilis was also covertly linked with male homosexuality. Doctors
acknowledge that syphilis could be spread through oral-genital and
anal-genital contact. Lesions on mouth or anus were taken as evidence
of "unnatural acts"; as an American professor of genito-urinary diseases
asserted, these came from "unnatural and beastly methods of indul-
gence between persons of the same and the opposite sex."[27] Social
purity campaigners argued that men spread syphilis through homosexual acts and then infected the prostitute. "Among men," wrote
the feminist activist Josephine Butler, "the disease is almost universal
at one time or another."[28]

In France, doctors used the image of the victimized wife and infected
child to reinforce monogamy against the tradition of male infidelity.
Alfred Fournier, a leader of the French movement to regulate and
control prostitution, was one of the *syphilographes* who "specialized in
the rhetoric of medical terrorism," using the risk of syphilitic infection
as "a perfect excuse to preach marital fidelity and family devotion, to
insist on the importance of the sanitary regulation of prostitution, and
to repress the working class, fantasmatically the ultimate source of all
disease."[29] Fournier demanded that all extra-marital relations should
be made illegal, for if "humankind returned to the golden age of
innocence, the days of syphilis would be numbered." At the international Brussels conference on syphilis in 1902, Professor Burlureaux
declared that "marriage is the most secure shelter against the venereal
peril." These images both endorsed the traditional Victorian view of
male and female sexuality and reinforced normative morality. "Though
their defense of women and the concomitant attack on immoral men
could be mistaken for an incipient feminism," Brandt points out,
". . . in reality, these doctors accepted a common image of women
as innocent, weak, and helpless."[30] And the frenzy over syphilis did
not necessarily mean support for sex education or contraception.
While the commercially manufactured condom had been available
since the invention of the vulcanization of rubber in 1846, the Roman
Catholic Church, amog other institutions, had always opposed its use.
Burlureaux also declared his opposition to condoms or any form of

artificial protection against disease, for reasons of the higher morality, and so as not to provide the manufacturers of contraceptives with any support.[31]

As a result of this publicity and because anxieties about syphilis were so intense, Victorian nerve specialists complained of rampant syphilophobia among their male patients. Dr. William Acton explained that like hysteria, syphilophobia "will assume every form of venereal disease found or described in books . . . every trifling ailment will be exaggerated until the medical man is unable to distinguish what his patient really feels and what he supposes he feels. Did isolated cases only now and then occur, perhaps they might not deserve attention, but so numerous are they in a large capital like London, so anxious are the sufferers to obtain relief by consulting every man who can be supposed to offer them any means of relief, that they spend fortunes in travelling about and visiting every quack."[32] In fin-de-siècle Vienna, Stefan Zweig recalled, every sixth house had a sign advertising a specialist in venereal disease, and all his friends feared infection.[33]

Gender obviously played an important role in the dissemination of this propaganda, for syphilis had very different significance and imagery for women and men. These differences in attitude began in childhood when boys and girls learned about syphilis in different ways. While boys and men were lectured, warned, or even terrorized about venereal disease, well-brought-up girls were not supposed to know that such dangers existed. Girls found out about syphilis accidentally in reading forbidden medical books. Feminists regarded venereal disease as one of the terrible secrets about marriage which women were never told. Cecily Hamilton made the discovery quite young: "By the idle opening of a book . . . I remember the thought which flashed into my mind— we are told we have got to be married, but we are never told that! It was my first revolt against the compulsory nature of the trade of marriage."[34] Ida Bauer—"Dora"—had figured out that her father had syphilis, although Freud would not confirm her suspicions; and Freud had noticed in his practice that "a *strikingly high* percentage" of his neurotic patients had syphilitic fathers.[35] To the dangers of sexuality that women had always known about—rape, unwanted pregnancy, death in childbirth—were added the secret terrors of venereal disease.

For most women, moreover, syphilis was not the product of marital transgression, secret vices, or monstrous desires; it was more likely the wages of ignorance than the wages of sin. Although prostitutes constituted the largest category of female syphilitics, the plight of the diseased wife also attracted medical attention. One popular manual of venerealogy gave instructions to the doctor on breaking the bad news to a syphilitic wife. To most late-Victorian feminists, syphilis was the product of man's viciousness and represented innocent women's entrapment and victimization. The prolonged feminist campaign against the Contagious Diseases Acts educated women to understand that prostitutes were hapless victims of male lust and that the laws gave sanction to "a vast male conspiracy to degrade women."[36] In *The Great Scourge and How to End It,* Christabel Pankhurst called for an end to the sexual double standard that was leading to "physical, mental, and moral degeneracy." Declaring that 75 to 80 percent of Victorian men were infected with gonorrhea, and "a considerable percentage" with syphilis, Pankhurst insisted that men had to change their sexual practices and habits: "Votes for women and chastity for men!"[37]

Most important, feminists viewed syphilis as scientific evidence that the sins of the fathers were visited upon the children. It was well known that the worst physical as well as mental effects of syphilis were hereditary. Congenital syphilis, which the Victorians called "syphilis of the innocents," is even more devastating than the acquired form of the disease, because it has already entered the secondary phase and begun to attack the nervous system. During the nineteenth century, the infant mortality rate for children of syphilitics was exceptionally high; from 60 percent to 90 percent died in their first year. Often described as a "small, wizened, atrophied, weakly, sickly creature," resembling a "monkey or a little old man," suffering, apish, shriveled, and prematurely aged, these syphilitic children appeared to feminists as living symbols of the devolutionary force of male vice.[38]

The literary mythology of syphilis at the *fin de siècle* was very differently expressed by male and female writers. For fin-de-siècle women writers, lust was the most unforgivable of the sins of the fathers, and sexual disease was its punishment, a punishment unjustly shared by innocent women and children. In their stories, sexual disease is male and has nothing to do with the female self. Taking to heart Darwinian arguments about women's self-sacrifice for the good of the species and religious arguments about women's passionlessness, women envisaged themselves as chaste yet maternal heralds of a higher race, who protect mankind by saying no to syphilitic men. In Charlotte Perkins Gilman's short story "The Crux," a girl who hopes to reform her syphilitic fiancé is shocked out of her illusions by a blunt woman doctor: "You may have any number of still-born children, year after year. And every little marred dead face would remind you that you allowed it! And they may be deformed and twisted, have all manner of terrible and loathsome afflictions, they and their children after them, if they have any. . . . Beware of a biological sin, my dear; for it there is no forgiveness." The syphilitic male became an arch-villain of feminist protest fiction, a carrier of contamination and madness, and a threat to the spiritual evolution of the human race. In Sarah Grand's *The Heavenly Twins* (1893), for example, he has "small, peery eyes" and a head that "shelved backwards like an ape's," while his infant son is "old, old already and exhausted with suffering." As Grand warns her readers, "the same thing may happen now to any mother—to any daughter— and will happen so long as we refuse to know and resist." Women's fantasies about syphilis thus centered on the fear of marital penetration and contamination and on anxieties about hereditary transmission of the disease to children.

Men's fantasies of syphilis took very different forms, and there were also distinct national literary traditions in writing about the disease. In France, particularly, male writers had become obsessed with the idea of syphilis and madness as the proud badges of the *poète maudit.* The French physician Joseph Moreau argued that genius itself was a hereditary abnormality, a pathological condition linked to neurosis; and such French writers as Baudelaire, the Goncourt brothers, Flaubert, Maupassant, and Daudet celebrated their syphilis, hallucinations, ennuis, depressions, seizures, and tremors in the confidence that their "horror of life," their embrace of *le mal,* their sense that health was "plebeian and contemptible" made them superior to the bourgeoisie and representative of a more advanced, if less hardy, creative humanity.[39]

But unlike their French brothers, the English were always skeptical of this romantic rationalization of insanity and disease. Havelock Ellis conducted a statistical study of British genius and concluded that it was not significantly correlated with madness. Others expressed a detached and urbane view of French excesses. "The Frenchmen are passing away," Henry James wrote to Robert Louis Stevenson in 1893, "Maupassant dying of locomotor paralysis, the fruit of fabulous habits, I am told. Je n'en sais rien, but I shall miss him." Although there were persistent rumors that various English writers, such as Stevenson himself, Wilde, Bram Stoker, and later James Joyce, were paying for their own fabulous habits with syphilitic infections, for the English, syphilitic insanity was never a beautiful *fleur du mal.*[40]

Most literature about syphilis was cautionary, or antisyphilitic. In an essay on "Puritanism and the Arts," D. H. Lawrence diagnosed the "paralysis of fear" in late-Victorian English art as a terror of sexual disease that became a view of sexuality *as* disease. "The great shock of syphilis," Lawrence wrote, created a rupture in human consciousness. In the nineteenth century, from having been a "pox," a comic, manly disease, syphilis became a secret horror which alienated men from their physical selves. Thus, he thought, the Romantics were all "post-mortem poets." Although he had never had syphilis, Lawrence confessed "how profound is my fear of the disease, and more than fear, my horror. . . . The appearance of syphilis in our midst gave a fearful blow to our sexual life . . . The very sexual act of procreation might bring as one of its consequences a foul disease, and the unborn might be tainted from the moment of conception. . . . The fearful thought of the consequences of syphilis . . . gives a shock to the impetus of fatherhood in any man, even the cleanest."[41] In an example of Lawrence's view, the hero of Arthur Conan Doyle's "The Third Generation" discovers just before his wedding that he has a "hereditary taint," acquired from his grandfather, a "foul old dandy." Told that he must give up his marriage, the young man throws himself in front of a bus. A famous antisyphilitic play, Eugene Brieux's *Damaged Goods,* shows what happens when the man with a hereditary or sexual taint persists in his plans to marry; the hero George Dupont is warned by his doctor, but disregards the warning and gives the disease to his wife and child.

For the male literary avant-garde, however, syphilis was the excrescence of a sexually diseased society, one that systematically suppressed desire and so produced anxious fathers and divided and disfigured sons. In the work of such writers as Ibsen, Stevenson, Hardy, Wells, and Joyce, the sins of the fathers are not lust and vice, but ignorance, guilt, shame, and fear. In Ibsen's *Ghosts,* the most celebrated of the fin-de-siècle problem plays about syphilis, the young artist-hero Oswald Alving goes mad in the final stages of cerebral syphilis inherited from his promiscuous father. Ibsen's ghosts are not the invisible spirochetes of syphilis but the virulent prohibitions of religion and bourgeois morality. Mistaken ideas about sexuality constitute the true hereditary taint: "It is not only what we have inherited from our fathers and mothers that exists again in us, but all sorts of old dead ideas and all kinds of old dead beliefs . . . They are dormant, and we can never be rid of them. Whenever I take up a newspaper and read it, I fancy I see ghosts creeping between the lines. There must be ghosts all over the world."

Produced in London in March 1891, however, *Ghosts* provoked an outburst of horror, outrage, and disgust unprecedented in the history of English criticism. In one typical review, the critic's language unconsciously confused the play with the disease and vilified it in the traditional rhetoric used for prostitution: "an open drain; a loathsome sore unbandaged; a dirty act done publicly." The hysteria over *Ghosts*— over five hundred articles about it were published in England during the following year—suggested how threatened conventional readers felt by Ibsen's intimations that the principles of conjugal obligation, feminine purity, and religious inhibition were not the forces of spiritual evolution but of aesthetic and sexual degeneration.[42]

Some English writers, too, were able to break from the moral strangleholds of Victorian sexual anxiety. In Hubert Wales's *The Yoke* (1907), the forty-year-old unmarried Angelica, who is the guardian of the dashing young hero Maurice, decides that she will sleep with him regularly until he gets married, in order to save him from prostitutes and venereal disease. The book created such a scandal, however, that action was brought against the publisher for obscenity, and in England the book was withdrawn and destroyed. These texts were as close as fin-de-siècle literature came to a defense of sexuality in the face of syphilitic infection. But it is significant that in very few of these texts is the word *syphilis* even used. The disease was unnameable and unspeakable. It was not until one of Siegfried Sassoon's angry poems from the trenches that (he later boasted) the word "syphilitic" was first brought into the sacred and pristine realm of English verse.[43]

Syphilis lost its mystery in medicine by 1913 with the discovery of the spirochete, Salvarsan, and the Wassermann blood test; and its mystery in literature with the Great War in which it numbered among many scourges. But Ibsen's ghosts of old dead ideas have come back to haunt us in the age of AIDS. The response to AIDS has been shaped less by medical knowledge than by "its association with a threatening sexuality, and with the gay movement that emerged around that threatening sexuality, and with other despised and marginalized groups in our culture."[44]

Like syphilis, AIDS has become inextricably intertwined with questions of literature, art, and culture. In 1982, the poet Richard Howard, speaking on a panel during Gay and Lesbian Awareness (GLAD) week at Yale, stunned the young audience when he predicted that "this newly named disease, AIDS, . . . was going to change gay literature utterly, inexorably."[45] For the first few years of the epidemic, little appeared. As Michael Denneny of St. Martin's Press explained, "Only a few gay writers would touch AIDS. . . . It was too shocking and mysterious and people just refused to put it in their art."[46] But then the situation changed so drastically that it seemed for a while like a cultural breakthrough. The first literary impact of AIDS was in the theater, through the plays of William Hoffman, Harvey Feierstein, and Larry Kramer. By 1984, the first novel with AIDS as its central theme appeared, Paul Reed's *Facing It.*[47] By 1987, publishers were rushing to get non-fiction about AIDS onto the market, books dealing with prevention, legal and social issues, alternative healing therapies, and autobiographical accounts of those who had contracted the disease or cared for spouses or lovers. And by 1990, it was no longer possible to keep track of the literature of AIDS. Indeed, what one noticed was the now-ironic absense of the disease in pre-AIDS writing.

Through the late 1980s, there were many comments on the inspiring, consoling, and transcendent role art was playing as a product of the AIDS crisis. "We're on the verge of getting a literature out of this that will be a renaissance," Michael Denneny proudly announced.[48] On a television program on "AIDS in the Arts" in 1987, the *Village Voice* writer Richard Goldstein suggested that "in an ironic sense, . . . AIDS is good for art. I think it will produce great works that will outlast and transcend the epidemic."[49] In an essay the same year on "The Artist and AIDS," the novelist Edmund White described both collective and individual aesthetic responses of gay artists to the epidemic, seeing a return within the gay artistic community to the "solitary 'high' arts." For individual gay writers and artists, there were new priorities. "The prospect of ill health and death inspires a sense of urgency," a questioning of the self. The subject of AIDS is unavoidable, even if unmentioned: "If Yeats was right in thinking sex and death were the only two topics worthy of adult consideration, then AIDS wins hands down as subject matter."[50]

However, these traditional invocations of art as a remedy and even a justification for human suffering have met with a fierce response from AIDS activists. "We don't need a cultural renaissance," Douglas Crimp protested. "We need cultural practices actively participating in the struggle against AIDS. We don't need to transcend the epi-

demic; we need to end it."[51] Susan Sontag's *AIDS and Its Metaphors*
(1989), which turns to the monuments of high culture for consolation
during the crisis, was widely criticized as insensitive, mandarin, or
opportunistic. "Consolation for whom?" D.A. Miller scathingly responded to Sontag. "For people with AIDS, many of whom cannot
even get treatment, whose disease has just been demeaned as one more
sign to the well and well off of their cultural competence? for those
who, in exchange for their dead, have just received a reading list of
plague classics?"[52]

Those living with AIDS and caring for the sick are doubly sickened
by the pieties, bromides, or clichés that seem to trivialize the disease.
Mourning for his dead lover, the poet Paul Monette reacted with fury
to people who told him to "turn the page":

> is this shit from
> the Bible the sayings of Dr. Kübler-Ross
> has Donahue done a show on it maybe
> a ring of widows all walks of life neatly
> combining real estate aerobics and young
> blue-collar bowling dates spare me the pop
> coping skills this page is all that's left of time.[53]

Writers themselves are aware of the inadequacy of art in the face
of death. "What can literature do?" the French novelist Dominique
Fernandez asked in a discussion of literature and AIDS. "Have the
plagues of the Middle Ages ever found a writer commensurate to the
event? When famine devastated Africa, what book of fiction could
have rendered the extent of the disaster?"[54] Future critics may be able
to evaluate the literature of AIDS, but in the midst of the crisis the
texts which seem most meaningful are those which do not too loudly
assert their claims to greatness and significance. Fernandez's novel *La
Gloire de Paria* (1987), which has been described as the French novel
that first brought "le SIDA en littérature,"[55] is one of these books.
Fernandez writes about AIDS within the traditions of fin-de-siècle
decadence, seeing the homosexual as a glorious pariah whose creativity
comes from his marginality. His novel combines apocalyptic views of
decadence and destruction with an ecstatic sense of homosexual election to revolt and martyrdom.

Fernandez's heroes are a gay couple living in Paris. Marc, twenty-
five, is a member of the post-1968 gay generation who views his
sexuality as natural and easy. Bernard, a forty-five-year-old writer, has

grown up as a member of a generation of closeted men and "keeps from his youth devoted to secrecy and shadow, a romantic nostalgia for dangerous and forbidden situations."[56] Prosperous and popular, they live like any other bourgeois couple in Paris; and Marc scoffs at Bernard's arguments about homosexuality as a condition outside the law. Yet, first as their neighbors learn about AIDS from the media, and then as Bernard himself develops the disease, their lives change and they become pariahs.

For Bernard, the advent of AIDS returns him abruptly to the ambiance of his adolescence, the sense of being both cursed and chosen. "Those close to him little by little abandoned him; a gulf formed itself around him; excluded from the community, isolated in the black halo of abjection, there he was returned to his glorious condition of pariahdom." Bernard believes that "a society can only continue to develop and expand by sacrificing some of its members at regular intervals in a ritual ceremony"; gay men have been chosen as the sacrificial victims of the sexual anarchy of the *fin de siècle*. Marc, too, comes to share Bernard's obsessions. When a friend gives Marc the news that Bernard's infection is the result of a contaminated blood transfusion rather than the product of his risky sexual escapades, Marc refuses to tell Bernard: "He needs to tell himself that he is abandoned by everyone, that the world is hostile to him and that he dies as a pariah. If you lift that conviction, you take away all the meaning of his disease, and he will die truly in despair."[57] To Bernard and Marc, their sense of being abandoned by everyone gives death both dignity and glory. In a ritual black mass lovingly arranged by Marc, the lovers die together in an affirmation of their marriage outside the law.

The novel echoes many motifs of fin-de-siècle sensibility, and in his critical study of homosexual culture, *Le Rapt de Ganymede* (1989), Fernandez traced in his own writing the motif of identification with the outlaw and outcast: "Sex is what is least interesting, least important in a homosexual culture. Homosexuality only plays a role in the general history of culture in terms of its symbolic function: as the refusal of normality (but not only of sexual normality), as the choice of marginality (but not only of sexual marginality). The homosexual is not only someone who sleeps with boys, instead of sleeping with girls; he (or at least the homosexual who thinks about his destiny, who contributes to 'homosexual culture') is also someone who feels and thinks differently from the mass of his fellows, someone who holds back, who does not admit the current values, someone who cuts himself off from his time, his country; who seeks outside the beaten paths of opinion, who is not satisfied with the system in place, and who aspires ceaselessly to another world, an unknown elsewhere."[58]

This romantic vision of the homosexual as artist and *l'étranger* is very much part of Fernandez's personal mythology. From adolescence on he identified with those homosexual men who had died a violent death or sought martyrdom: the archeologist Winckelmann, Wilde, the director Pier-Paolo Pasolini. "The true elect," he argues, "are . . . those who are willing to put their head on the block for the public executioner, whether the executioner be called public oppro-brium, Reading Gaol, the queer-baiters of the docks, railroad station gigolos,—or AIDS. To answer the call of an exceptional destiny is not an indication of weakness but of strength." Homosexuality was both a source of endless suffering and "the sign of a secret and mar-vellous election," "the password of a clandestine minority."[59]

Thus AIDS, for Fernandez, becomes the affirmation of the existen-tial risk of gay identity, the inevitable price of revolt. Bernard, in the novel, wishes to deny the existence, or at least the importance, of other risk groups, since dying for his sexuality preserves him from the loss of specialness. For Fernandez as a writer, the homosexual must be in some sense singled out, accursed, a pariah, in order to afford him the motive for his art. "If we reach the point where society makes no distinction any more between homo- and heterosexuality (as a man, needless to say, that's the goal I seek), if homosexuality dis-appears as a sign of election . . . it ceases being for me a literary stimulus."[60]

AIDS is represented very differently in Susan Sontag's short story, "The Way We Live Now" (1986).[61] The title, in a phrase which has now become proverbial, alludes to Trollope's late-nineteenth-century novel of a loss of community and ethical value. But in contrast to Fernandez's insistence on the alienation and loneliness of the homo-sexual martyr, Sontag emphasizes the human community of AIDS, the chain of life and death that links us all. The sick man, who is neither named nor specifically described as having AIDS, has had many lovers, both women and men. He is not abandoned by his friends; the story is told as a continual chorus of twenty-six voices, friends whose names cover all the letters of the alphabet, as they visit, care for, and obsessively discuss the man and his disease. The narrative is complicated because these different people both hear different kinds of information and have different responses to it. While we learn that the sick man is an art dealer, thirty-eight, comes from Mississippi, and travels frequently, the absence of his name and his diagnosis signifies the distance between the sick and the well, between suffering and compassion. The voice of the person with AIDS can only be mediated for us by the twenty-six narrators who form the story's "utopia of friendship."

In many respects, Sontag's story is a compendium of the anxieties, contradictions, superstitions, self-criticism, and social theater generated around the experience of AIDS. The shape of the disease is traced through this accumulation of mundane detail—flowers, gifts, visits, the AIDS establishment of medical advice, the AIDS counterculture of macrobiotic diets and visualization therapy—as well as in the accumulation of ever more urgent questions of contagion, sexuality, fear, and death.

While she scrupulously avoids making illness a metaphor, towards the end of the story Sontag does introduce an allegorical image: an eighteenth-century Guatemalan wooden statue of St. Sebastian brought to the hospital as a gift by Xavier. "And when Tanya said, what's that, a tribute to eros past, Xavier said where I come from Sebastian is venerated as a protection against pestilence. Pestilence symbolized by arrows? Symbolized by arrows." The image of St. Sebastian is both a talisman and a representation of gay art, a sign that in some way the literature and community created around AIDS may survive the pestilence and death. As Richard Ellmann noted in his biography of Oscar Wilde, "Sebastian, always iconographically attractive, is the favorite saint among homosexuals."[62] The image of St. Sebastian is a standard one in the gay literary and artistic tradition, represented in statues, paintings, poems, and novels by Bernini, Domenichino, Titian, Frederick Rolfe, T. S. Eliot, Jean Cocteau, Yukio Mishima, James Merrill, and Pablo Neruda. Oscar Wilde called himself "Sebastian Melmoth" during his Paris years, and in World War I, the "theme of sacrificial martyrdom of lads . . . prompted hundreds of verses on St. Sebastian."[63]

Yet in Sontag's story, the myth of St. Sebastian becomes a fable of hope: "All people remember is the body of a beautiful youth bound to a tree, pierced by arrows . . . people forget that the story continues, Xavier continued, that when the Christian women came to bury the martyr, they found him still alive and nursed him back to health." In part, this open ending derives from Sontag's fierce personal insistence that AIDS must not be represented as fatal: "It is simply too early to conclude, of a disease identified only seven years ago, that infection will always produce something to die from, or even that someone who has what is identified as AIDS will die of it."[64] Sontag's story thus ends not with death, but with a suspended state: "He's still alive, Stephen said."

Sontag's story can be easily misread as detached or cynical social satire. Anatole Broyard, for example, commented that "The Way We Live Now" is "about our latest, most desperate form of sophistication, our new ironical frontier. It is about a man who has AIDS. He is an art dealer and his friends visit him as if he were offering a show of life and death."[65] For David Leavitt, however, "The Way We Live Now" marked a turning-point in the literature of AIDS. Whereas reading previous fiction had been terrifying and hopeless, reading this made him feel "less alone in my dread, and therefore brave enough to read more." Sontag's story "transcended horror and grief, and . . . was therefore redemptive, if not of AIDS itself, then at least of the processes by which people cope with it. . . . It offered a possibility of catharsis, and at that point catharsis was something we all badly needed."[66]

Sontag's message of hope and community may have seemed glib or foolish to some AIDS activists and patients grappling with the enormity of the disease. Edmund White has argued that "if art is to confront AIDS more honestly than the media have done, it must begin in tact, avoid humor and end in anger." Humor must be avoided because it "domesticates terror," and because, like melodrama, it asserts "bourgeois values" that "falsely suggest AIDS is all in the family." Anger must be chosen because "it is only sane to rage against the dying of the light, because strategically anger is a political response, because psychologically anger replaces despondency, and because existentially anger lightens the solitude of frightened individuals."[67]

Yet anger is a cruel muse; rage must find enemies to blame; and since the virus doesn't care what we say about it, anger finds more vulnerable and accessible human beings.[68] Some of these targets are politicians and health officials; others are white middle-class women with AIDS, who seem to be regarded as the undeserving sick. Up until recently, what Paula Treichler calls "female roles in the AIDS story" were the traditional supporting parts of "loving mother, loyal spouse, wronged lover, philanthropic celebrity."[69] But there are signs that as the dangers for women increase, and women figure more prominently in the statistical picture of the disease, they are viewed with more ambivalence, even hostility. David Leavitt comments on the anger he felt when *The New York Times*, which now runs almost daily stories about men, women, and children with AIDS, featured the case of "a young, white, rich heterosexual woman who said she had contracted AIDS after one night of sex with a bisexual man."[70] Such women apparently are not entitled to our attention, although gay men who contract the disease in similar circumstances can be forgiven if they too are young, white, and rich. Leo Bersani describes TV sex education ads as "a nauseating procession of yuppie women announcing to the world that they will no longer put out for their yuppie boyfriends unless these boyfriends agree to use a condom. Thus hundreds of thousands of gay men and IV drug users . . . are asked to sympathize with all those yuppettes agonizing over whether they're going to risk losing a good fuck by taking the 'unfeminine' initiative of interrupting the invading male in order to insist that he practice safe sex."[71] This sort of venom offers little hope that the AIDS crisis will encourage charity and tolerance, let alone that it may be a moment in which sexual hatred is overcome.

These may seem like trivial comments in the midst of a devastating epidemic. Yet if the history of syphilis is any model for the history of AIDS, we know that the epidemic will end, and we will inherit, along with our grief, the legacy of how we behaved. If we can fight against the disease and not each other, AIDS, as Lynne Segal has eloquently summed it up, "could serve as a spur, not for more of the same evasion and hypocrisy around sex, but for more equal sexual relations between women and men and the recognition of sexual diversity . . . And then the sexual revolution can begin in earnest."[72]

The Génitron flashing its electric numbers in the courtyard of the Pompidou Center cannot be stopped or turned back; nor can we legislate or intimidate men and women into the shame and repression of the past. We must not allow fear to push us into a cruel homophobia, make us abandon our commitment to women's sexual autonomy, or lead us to repudiate the fin-de-siècle vision of a future in which sexuality is a source of pleasure, comfort, and joy. A century ago Olive Schreiner dreamed of the day when life would come to women bearing the gifts of both love and freedom. In the final pages of her visionary book, *Woman and Labor*, Schreiner imagined the coming age: "To those of us who, at the beginning of a new century, stand with shaded eyes, gazing into the future, striving to descry the outlines of the shadowy figures which loom before us in the distance, nothing seems of so gracious a promise as the outline we seem to discern of a condition of human life in which a closer union than the world has yet seen shall exist between the man and the woman."[73] What seems today like the apocalyptic warnings of a frightening sexual anarchy may be really the birth throes of a new sexual equality.

$\mathcal{N}otes$

CHAPTER ONE

1 Max Nordau, *Degeneration* (New York: Appleton, 1895), p. 1.
2 Susan Sontag, *AIDS and Its Metaphors* (New York: Farrar Strauss, 1989), p. 88.
3 See James Atlas, "What Is Fukuyama Saying?" *New York Times Magazine*, 22 October 1989, p. 38.
4 See Eugen Weber, *France, Fin de Siècle* (Cambridge: Harvard University Press, 1986).
5 See Atlas, "What is Fukuyama Saying?" p. 38.
6 Frank Kermode, *The Sense of an Ending* (New York and Oxford: Oxford University Press, 1967), p. 97.
7 Karl Miller, *Doubles: Studies in Literary History* (London: Oxford University Press, 1987), p. 209.
8 Richard Dellamora, *Masculine Desire* (Chapel Hill: University of North Carolina Press, 1990), p. 133.
9 "The Political Value of Social Purity," *The Sentinel*, September 1885, p. 480; quoted in Jeffrey Weeks, *Coming Out: Homosexual Politics in Britain from the Nineteenth Century to the Present* (London: Quartet Books, 1977), p. 18.
10 Weeks, *Coming Out*, p. 18.
11 Nancy Stepan, "Biological Degeneration: Races and Proper Places," in *Degeneration: The Dark Side of Progress*, eds. Sander L. Gilman and J. Edward Chamberlin (New York: Columbia University Press, 1985), p. 98.
12 H. M. Hyndman, "English Workers as They Are," *Contemporary Review* 52 (July 1887); quoted in Gareth Stedman-Jones, *Outcast London: A*

Study in the Relationship between Classes in Victorian Society (Harmondsworth: Penguin, 1976), p. 29.

13 William Booth, *In Darkest England and the Way Out*, in *Into Unknown England, 1866–1913*, ed. Peter Keating (London: Fontana, 1976), p. 145.

14 Deborah E. Nord, "The Social Explorer as Anthropologist: Victorian Travellers among the Urban Poor," in *Visions of the Modern City*, eds. William Sharpe and Leonard Wallock (New York: Columbia University Press, 1983), p. 119.

15 Charles Booth, *Life and Labour of the People of London* (1902), I:213, quoted in Stedman-Jones, *Outcast London*, pp. 295–6.

16 *Commonweal*, 12 November 1887, quoted in Stedman-Jones, *Outcast London*, p. 296.

17 Sandra M. Gilbert and Susan Gubar, *Sexchanges* (New Haven: Yale University Press, 1989), p. 37.

18 Karl Pearson, "Woman and Labour," *Fortnightly Review* 129 (May 1894): 561.

19 Peter Gay, *The Bourgeois Experience: Victoria to Freud* (New York: Oxford University Press, 1984), 1:175.

20 Gilbert and Gubar, *No Man's Land* (New Haven: Yale University Press, 1986) 1:4.

21 Carole Pateman, quoted in Susan Aiken, et al., "Trying Transformations: Curriculum Legislation and the Problem of Resistance," *Signs* 12 (1987): 261.

22 Toril Moi, *Sexual/Textual Politics* (London and New York: Methuen, 1985), p. 167.

23 Thomas Laqueur, "Orgasm, Generation, and the Politics of Reproductive Biology," *Representations* 14 (Spring 1986) :14.

24 Claire Kahane, "Hysteria, Feminism, and the Case of *The Bostonians*," in *Feminism and Psychoanalysis*, ed. Richard Feldstein and Judith Roof (Ithaca: Cornell University Press, 1989), p. 287. See also Cynthia Eagle Russett, *Sexual Science: The Victorian Construction of Womanhood* (Cambridge: Harvard University Press, 1989).

25 See Daniel Farson, *The Man Who Wrote Dracula: A Biography of Bram Stoker* (London: Michael Joseph, Ltd., 1975), p. 215. Thanks to Marjorie Howes for this reference.

26 Havelock Ellis, *The Psychology of Sex* (New York: Ray Long and Richard R. Smith, 1933), p. 225, quoted in Gilbert and Gubar, *Sexchanges* vii.

27 Regenia Gagnier, *Idylls of the Marketplace: Oscar Wilde and the Victorian Public* (Stanford: Stanford University Press, 1986), p. 98.

28 Michelle Perrot, "The New Eve and the Old Adam: Changes in French Women's Condition at the Turn of the Century," trans. Helen Harden-Chenut, in *Behind the Lines: Gender and the Two World Wars*, eds. Mar-

garet Higonnet et al. (New Haven: Yale University Press, 1987), pp. 57–58.

29 Michael S. Kimmel, "The Contemporary 'Crisis' of Masculinity," in *The Making of Masculinities,* ed. Harry Brod (New York: Allen & Unwin, 1987), p. 143.

30 See Michelle Perrot, "The New Eve and the Old Adam," p. 59; and Annelise Maugue, *L'Identité Masculine en crise au Tournant du Siècle* (Paris: Rivages, 1987).

31 See Bram Dijkstra, *Idols of Perversity: Fantasies of Feminine Evil in Fin-de-Siècle Culture* (New York: Oxford University Press, 1986).

32 Quoted in Kimmell, "The Contemporary 'Crisis' of Masculinity," p. 143.

33 Perrot, "The New Eve and the Old Adam," p. 59.

34 Maugue, *L'Identité Masculine,* p. 73.

35 Andrew Wynter, *The Borderlands of Insanity* (London: Robert Hardwicke, 1877), pp. 239, 271, 276.

36 Judith Walkowitz, "Science, Feminism, and Romance: The Men and Women's Club, 1885–1889," *History Workshop Journal* 21 (1986):39.

37 Brian Harrison, *Separate Spheres: The Opposition to Women's Suffrage in Britain* (London: Croom Helm, 1978), p. 97.

38 Gay, *The Bourgeois Experience,* p. 288.

39 Harrison, *Separate Spheres,* p. 98.

40 Harrison, *Separate Spheres,* pp. 101, 102, 103.

41 Harrison, *Separate Spheres,* p. 98.

42 Michael Meyer, *Ibsen* (New York: Doubleday, 1971), p. 449; see also Joan Templeton, "The Doll House Backlash: Criticism, Feminism, and Ibsen," *PMLA* 104 (January 1989): 37.

43 Quoted in Sandra M. Gilbert and Susan Gubar, *No Man's Land,* 1:49. On the Pioneer Club, see David Rubenstein, *Before the Suffragettes: Women's Emancipation in the 1890s* (London: Harvester, 1986), pp. 222–25.

44 Amy Levy, "Women and Club Life," *The Woman's World* (London: Cassell and Co., 1888), p. 366.

45 Lewis Lapham, "La Différence," *New York Times,* 4 March 1983.

46 Gay, *The Bourgeois Experience,* p. 288.

47 Eve Kosofsky Sedgwick, *Between Men: English Literature and Male Homosocial Desire* (New York: Columbia University Press, 1985), p. 89.

48 Michel Foucault, *The History of Sexuality,* trans. Robert Hurley (New York: Vintage, 1980), 1:43.

49 Weeks, *Coming Out,* p. 21.

50 Weeks, *Sex, Politics, and Society* (New York and London: Longman, 1981), p. 103.

51 Jonathan Dollimore, "Homophobia and Sexual Difference," *Oxford Literary Review* 8 (1986): 7.

52 Nancy Armstrong, *Desire and Domestic Fiction* (New York and London: Oxford University Press), 1987, p. 9.

53 Nigel Cross, *The Common Writer* (Cambridge: Cambridge University Press, 1985), pp. 204–205.

54 Cross, *The Common Writer*, p. 207.

55 Letter to Algernon Gissing, August 1885, in *Letters from George Gissing to Members of his Family*, eds. Algernon and Ellen Gissing (London: Constable and Co., 1927), p. 166.

56 Rhoda Broughton, *A Beginner* (London: Richard Bentley and Sons, 1894), p. 232.

57 W. R. Greg, "Why Are Women Redundant?" in *Literary and Social Judgments* (Boston: James Osgood & Co., 1873), p. 306.

58 Havelock Ellis, "Thomas Hardy's Novels," *Westminster Review* 129 (April 1883): 334–64.

59 Patricia Stubbs, *Women and Fiction: Feminism and the Novel 1880–1920* (New York: Barnes and Noble, 1979), p. 120.

60 Kahane, "Bostonians," p. 287.

61 Henry James, *The Next Time* (1895), p. 190.

CHAPTER TWO

1 Greg, "Why Are Women Redundant?" p. 306.

2 Arthur C. Young, ed., *The Letters of George Gissing to Eduard Bertz 1887–1903* (New Brunswick: Rutgers University Press, 1961), p. 166. Thanks to David LaMotte for this reference.

3 Jessie Boucherett, in Josephine Butler, ed., *Women's World and Women's Culture* (London: Macmillan, 1869).

4 In Lee Holcombe, *Victorian Ladies at Work* (Hamden, Conn.: Archon, 1973), p. 117.

5 Susan K. Kent, *Sex and Suffrage in Britain, 1860–1914* (Princeton: Princeton University Press, 1987), p. 13.

6 Sheila Jeffreys, *The Spinster and Her Enemies: Feminism and Sexuality 1880–1930* (London: Pandora, 1985), p. 48.

7 *American Journal of Obstetrics*, 15, 1882; quoted in Carl N. Degler, "What Ought to Be and What Was: Women's Sexuality in the Nineteenth Century," in *Women and Health in America*, ed. Judith Walzer Leavitt (Madison: University of Wisconsin Press, 1984), p. 41.

8 Frank Mort, *Dangerous Sexualities: Medico-Moral Politics in England since 1830* (London, Routledge Kegan Paul, 1987), pp. 94–95.

9 Christabel Pankhurst, *The Great Scourge and How to End It* (London: David Nutt, 1913), p. 98.

10 E. Noel Morgan, *Freewoman*, 8 August 1912; in Jeffreys, *The Spinster and Her Enemies*, p. 93.

11 Margaret Hill, *Freewoman*, 5 August 1912; in Jeffreys, *The Spinster and Her Enemies*, p. 96.

12 On Frances Swiney, see Jeffreys, *The Spinster and Her Enemies*, pp. 35–39.

13 Beatrice Webb, *My Apprenticeship* (Harmondsworth: Penguin, 1971), p. 223.

14 Deborah Nord, " 'Neither Pairs nor Odd': Beatrice Webb, Margaret Harkness, Amy Levy, and the Problems of Female Community," *SIGNS*, forthcoming.

15 On single women in England, see Martha Vicinus, *Independent Women: Work and Community for Single Women, 1850–1920* (London: Virago, 1985).

16 Edward Carpenter, *Love's Coming of Age*, in *Selected Writings*, ed. Noel Grieg (London: GMP, 1984), vol. 1.

17 Mary Jeune, "English Women in Political Life," *North American Review*, 161 (1895): 453.

18 E. Lynn Linton, *The Girl of the Period* (London, Bentley, 1883), 2:64–72.

19 Quoted in Lisa Tickner, *The Spectacle of Women: Imagery of the Suffrage Campaign 1907–14* (Chicago: University of Chicago Press, 1988), p. 194.

20 Tickner, *Spectacle of Women*, p. 200.

21 Beresford Hope, House of Commons, *Hansard Parliamentary Debates*, 3 May 1871, in Patricia Hollis, ed., *Women in Public: The Women's Movement 1850–1900* (London: Allen & Unwin, 1979), p. 306.

22 "One of Us," "Why We Men Do Not Marry," *Temple Bar*, 84 (1888), p. 220.

23 Sarah Grand, "The New Aspect of the Woman Question," *North American Review* 158 (1894): 270–71.

24 Olive Schreiner, *Letters*, vol. 1, 1871–1899, ed. Richard Rive (Oxford: Oxford University Press, 1988), p. 106.

25 Rubenstein, *Before the Suffragettes*, p. 202.

26 Beatrice Webb, Diary, 8 March 1889. The woman Marshall eventually married was an economist who taught at Newnham, but she "systematically effaced herself" before her husband. (Rubenstein, p. 192).

27 Grant Allen, "Plain Words on the Woman Question," *Fortnightly Review* 52 (1889): 454–55.

28 "One of Us," "Why We Men Do Not Marry," p. 220.

29 Quoted in Nord, " 'Neither Pairs nor Odd' ".

30 Terry Lovell, *Consuming Fictions* (London: Verso, 1987), p. 106.

31 W. T. Stead, "The Novel of the Modern Woman," *Review of Reviews* 10 (1894): 64.

32 F. O. Matthiessen and Kenneth Murdock, eds., *The Notebooks of Henry James* (New York: Oxford University Press, 1947), pp. 46–47.

33 *Letters of Henry James*, ed. Percy Lubbock (London: Macmillan, 1920), 1:118, 136.

34 See Leon Edel, ed., *Henry James: Letters* (Cambridge: Harvard University Press, 1980), 3:121.

35 Sallie Hall, "Satire and Morality in *The Bostonians*," *Aeolian Harps: Essays in Literature* (1976), quoted in Charles Anderson, Introduction, *The Bostonians* (Harmondsworth: Penguin, 1986), p. 27.

36 Phyllis F. Mannocchi, "Vernon Lee and Kit Anstruther-Thompson: A Study of Love and Collaboration between Romantic Friends," *Women's Studies* 12 (1986): 129–48.

37 Tickner, *Spectacle of Women*, p. 209.

38 Tickner, *Spectacle of Women*, p. 211. See also Marina Warner, *Joan of Arc: The Image of Female Heroism* (London: Weidenfeld, Nicolson, 1987). On the "border case," see Mary Poovey, *Uneven Developments: The Ideological Work of Gender in Mid-Victorian England* (Chicago: University of Chicago Press), 1988, p. 9.

39 Josephine Hendin, Introduction to *The Bostonians* (New York: Bantam, 1984), p. xv.

40 David Grylls, *The Paradox of Gissing* (London: Allen & Unwin, 1986), p. 141.

41 Jo Manton, *Mary Carpenter and the Children of the Streets* (London: Heinemann, 1976), p. 147.

42 Martha Vicinus, *Independent Women: Work and Community for Single Women 1850–1920* (London: Virago, 1985), p. 44.

43 See Judith Wilt, "Desperately Seeking Verena: A Resistant Reading of *The Bostonians*," *Feminist Studies* 13 (Summer 1987): 316.

44 "Too Late for Prince Charming," *Newsweek*, 2 June 1986, p. 56.

45 *New York Times*, 12 April 1987.

46 Cynthia Harrison, "Encore, Encore," *New York Times*, 30 April 1987.

47 Deborah Rosenfelt and Judith Stacey, "Second Thoughts on the Second Wave," *Feminist Studies* 13 (Summer 1987): 346–47.

48 Trip Gabriel, "Why Wed? The Ambivalent American Bachelor," *New York Times Magazine*, 15 November 1987, pp. 24, 34.

49 Judith Walkowitz and Judith Newton, "Preface," *Feminist Studies* 9 (Spring 1983): 4.

50 Andrea Dworkin, *Intercourse* (New York: Free Press, 1987), p. 138.

51 Linda Gordon and Ellen Dubois, "Seeking Ecstasy on the Battlefield," *Feminist Studies* 9 (Spring 1989): 20.

52 Lynne Segal, "Lessons from the Past: Feminism, Sexual Politics, and the

Challenge of AIDS," in *Taking Liberties,* eds. Erica Carter and Simon Watney (London: Serpents' Tail, 1989), p. 157.

CHAPTER THREE

1 Perrot, "The New Eve and the Old Adam," p. 5.
2 See Carroll Smith-Rosenberg, *Disorderly Conduct: Visions of Gender in Victorian America* (New York: Knopf, 1985).
3 Linda Dowling, "The Decadent and the New Woman," *Nineteenth-Century Fiction* 33 (1979), pp. 440–41.
4 "The Strike of a Sex," *Quarterly Review* 179 (1894): 290.
5 Ella Hepworth Dixon, quoted in Rubenstein, *Before the Suffragettes,* p. 41.
6 Maugue, *L'Identité Masculine,* pp. 84–85; and Victor Jozé, "Le Féminisme et le bon sens," *La Plume,* no. 154 (September 1895): 391–92; in Debora L. Silverman, *Art Nouveau in Fin-de-siècle France* (Berkeley: University of California Press, 1989), pp. 63–73.
7 G. Stanley Hall, *Adolescence* (New York: D. Appleton, 1904), 2:633; quoted in Russett, *Sexual Science,* p. 120.
8 *Lancet* 2 (1886): 314.
9 Russett, *Sexual Science,* p. 149.
10 T. Clifford Allbutt, "Nervous Diseases and Modern Life," *Contemporary Review* 67 (1895): 210–31.
11 Russett, *Sexual Science,* p. 118.
12 Fraser Harrison, "Introduction," (1914) *The Yellow Book* (London: Boydell Press, 1982).
13 *Autobiography of Sir Walter Besant* (New York: Dodd, Mead, 1902), p. 211.
14 See Gilbert and Gubar, *Sexchanges,* p. 50.
15 Reprinted in *The Daughters of Danaus,* ed. Margaret Morganroth Gullette (New York: Feminist Press, 1989).
16 Anne K. Mellor, "On Feminist Utopias," *Women's Studies* 9 (1982): 243.
17 Walkowitz, "The Men and Women's Club," p. 47.
18 Eleanor Marx and Edward Aveling, *The Woman Question* (London: Swan, Sonnenschein, Lowry, & Co., 1887), p. 15.
19 Quoted in Chushichi Tsuzuki, *Edward Carpenter 1844–1929* (Cambridge: Cambridge University Press, 1980), p. 122.
20 Judith Walkowitz, "The Men and Women's Club," p. 41, and "The City of Dreadful Delight," work in progress. Many thanks to Judy Walkowitz for sharing her important work.
21 Gilbert and Gubar, *Sexchanges,* p. 63.
22 Schreiner, *Letters,* p. 61.

23 Letters of 14 February 1886 and 29 March 1888, in Pearson Collection, University College, London; quoted in Carol Dyhouse, *Feminism and the Family in England, 1880–1939* (Oxford and New York: Basil Blackwell, 1989), p. 165.

24 *Letters*, 9 February 1888, p. 135.

25 See Ruth First and Ann Scott, *Olive Schreiner* (New York: Schocken, 1980), p. 148.

26 Mona Caird, *The Morality of Marriage*, p. 7.

27 Schreiner, *Woman and Labor* (London: T. Fisher Unwin, 1911), p. 287.

28 In Add.Ms. 47449, 18 September 1893, British Library.

29 Pearson, "Socialism and Sex," *Fortnightly Review*, 1887, p. 442.

30 See Schreiner, *Letters*, p. 64.

31 Schreiner, *Letters*, p. 95.

32 See William Robert, *The Novel-Readers Handbook* (Birmingham, 1899), pp. 1–2; quoted in Boumelha, *Thomas Hardy and Women: Sexual Ideology and Narrative Form* (Brighton: Harvester, 1980), p. 136.

33 H. G. Wells, *Experiment in Autobiography* (Boston: Little, Brown, 1934), p. 465.

34 M. G. Fawcett, "The Woman Who Did," *Contemporary Review* 67 (1895): 630.

35 Sarah Grand, "The Woman's Question," *The Humanitarian*, March 1886; quoted in Gillian Kersley, *Darling Madame: Sarah Grand and Devoted Friend* (London: Virago, 1983), p. 87.

36 Walkowitz, "The Men and Women's Club," p. 39.

37 Yvonne Kapp, *Eleanor Marx* (London: Virago, 1979), 2:86.

38 Kapp, *Eleanor Marx*, 2:82.

39 See First and Scott, *Olive Schreiner*, p. 136.

40 Kapp, *Eleanor Marx*, 2:16–17; First and Scott, p. 147.

41 Walkowitz, "The Men and Women's Club," p. 40.

42 Eleanor Marx and Edward Aveling, *The Woman Question*, p. 16.

43 Kapp, *Eleanor Marx*, 2:700.

44 In Schreiner, *Letters*, 2 August 1884, p. 36.

45 See Walkowitz, "The Men and Women's Club," p. 47.

46 Schreiner, *Letters*, pp. 151–52.

47 Schreiner, *Letters*, p. 66.

48 Schreiner, *Letters*, p. 51.

49 Schreiner, *Letters*, p. 208.

50 S. C. Cronwright-Schreiner, *Letters of Olive Schreiner* (London: Unwin, 1924), p. 193.

51 Schreiner, *Letters*, pp. 217–18.

52 For this observation and other useful comments, see Carol Barash, *An Olive Schreiner Reader* (London: Pandora, 1987).

53 Nadine Gordimer, review of First and Scott, *Olive Schreiner, Times Literary Supplement,* 15 August 1980.

CHAPTER FOUR

1 Lillian Faderman, *Surpassing the Love of Men* (New York: William Morrow, 1981), p. 163.

2 Gordon Haight, *George Eliot: A Biography* (Oxford: Clarendon Press, 1968), p. 550.

3 Bonnie Zimmerman, "The 'Mother's History' in George Eliot," in *The Lost Tradition: Mothers and Daughters in Literature,* ed. Cathy Davidson and Esther Broner (New York: F. Ungar, 1980), p. 84.

4 Gilbert and Gubar, *No Man's Land,* p. 166.

5 See Nancy Chodorow, *The Reproduction of Mothering: Psychoanalysis and the Sociology of Gender* (Berkeley: University of California Press, 1978).

6 Haight, *George Eliot,* p. 535.

7 Margaret Oliphant, *The Autobiography and Letters of Mrs. M.O.W. Oliphant,* ed. Harry Coghill (London: Blackwood, 1899), p. 3.

8 Mrs. Desmond Humphreys, *Recollections of a Literary Life* (London: Andrew Melrose, 1936), p. 156.

9 Mary Vivian Hughes, *A London Girl of the 1880s* (Oxford: Oxford University Press, 1978), p. 116.

10 *The Diary of Alice James,* ed. Leon Edel (New York: Dodd, Mead & Co., 1964), pp. 40–41.

11 Rachel DuPlessis, *Writing Beyond the Ending* (Bloomington: Indiana University Press, 1985), ix.

12 Jane Gallop, *The Daughter's Seduction: Feminism and Psychoanalysis* (Ithaca: Cornell University Press, 1982), p. 113.

13 Quoted in Deborah Epstein Nord, *The Apprenticeship of Beatrice Webb* (Amherst: University of Massachusetts Press, 1985), p. 31.

14 Nord, *Beatrice Webb,* pp. 11, 17, 18, 44.

15. Letter, April 1888, in *Marxists on Literature,* ed. David Craig (Harmonsworth: Penguin, 1977), p. 269.

16 Letter to Havelock Ellis, 5 April 1889, in Schreiner, *Letters,* 1, p. 154.

17 Laura Hansson, *Six Modern Women,* trans. Hermione Ramsden (London: John Lane, 1896).

18 Penny Boumelha, *Thomas Hardy and Women,* p. 63.

19 Boumelha, *Thomas Hardy and Women,* pp. 63–64

20 Tickner, *The Spectacle of Women,* p. 183.

21 Martha Vicinus, "Introduction," to George Egerton, *Keynotes and Discords* (London: Virago, 1983), pp. xvi–xvii.

22 George Egerton, "A Keynote to Keynotes," in *Ten Contemporaries,* ed. John Gawsworth (London: Ernest Benn, 1912), p. 58.

23 Grand, in Kerseley, *Darling Madame,* p. 83.

24 Percy Lubbock, *Mary Cholmondeley: A Sketch from Memory* (London, 1928), p. 24.

25 See Boumelha, *Thomas Hardy and Women,* p. 67ff. for an insightful analysis of the contradictions of New Woman fiction.

26 H. G. Wells, "Jude the Obscure," *Saturday Review* 82 (1896): 153; quoted in Boumelha, *Thomas Hardy and Women,* p. 137.

27 Sharon O'Brien, *Willa Cather* (New York: Oxford University Press, 1987), p. 43.

28 Letter of 1 December 1919, in Cherry A. Hankin, ed., *Letters Between Katherine Mansfield and John Middleton Murry* (London: Virago, 1988), p. 228.

29 Simone de Beauvoir, *Memoirs of a Dutiful Daughter,* trans. James Kirkup (Cleveland: World Pub., 1959), p. 148; and *The Prime of Life,* p. 291.

30 Florence Howe, "Feminism, Fiction, and the Classroom," *Soundings* 55 (1972): 372–73; and Lee R. Edwards, "Women, Energy, and *Middlemarch,*" *Massachusetts Review* 13 (1972): 223–24.

31 Marie F. Deer, *Yale Alumni Weekly,* December 1988, p. 69.

32 John Gregory Dunne, "Sweet Liberty," *Esquire* (March 1987): 190.

CHAPTER FIVE

1 Edmund Gosse, *Portraits and Sketches* (London: William Heinemann, 1912), p. 16; and *Aspects and Impressions* (London: Cassell & Co., 1922), p. 1.

2 *Collected Letters of W. B. Yeats,* vol. 1, 1865–1895, ed. John Kelly (Oxford: Clarendon Press, 1986), p. 8.

3 *The Letters of G. M. Hopkins to Robert Bridges,* ed. C. C. Abbott (London: Oxford University Press, 1935), p. 239.

4 Henry James, *Views and Reviews* (New York: Scribners, 1890), pp. 130–131.

5 Quoted in Ernest Earnest, *Silas Weir Mitchell* (Philadelphia: University of Pennsylvania Press, 1950), p. 174.

6 Rachel Bowlby, *Just Looking* (New York and London: Methuen, 1985), p. 7.

7 Gilbert and Gubar, *No Man's Land,* p. 130.

8 Marie-Hélène Huet, "Living Images: Monstrosity and Representation," *Representations* 4 (Fall 1983): 77.

9 Edward W. Said, *Beginnings* (New York: Basic Books, 1975), p. 145.

10 Gerard Manley Hopkins, quoted in Gilbert and Gubar, *The Madwoman in the Attic* (New Haven: Yale University Press, 1979), p. 3.

11 Phyllis Grosskurth, ed., *The Memoirs of John Addington Symonds* (Chicago: University of Chicago Press, 1984), p. 77.

12 *Fortnightly Review* 1887, 410–416; quoted in D. S. Higgins, *Rider Haggard* (New York: Stein & Day, 1981), p. 119.

13 Andrew Lang, "Realism and Romance," *Contemporary Review* 52 (November 1887): 684.

14 J. A. Hammerton, *Stevensoniana* (Edinburgh: John Grant, 1907), p. 243.

15. W. E. Henley, "Modern Men," *Scots Observer*, 27 April 1889; quoted in Peter Ellis, *H. Rider Haggard* (London: Routledge & Kegan Paul, 1978), p. 119.

16 H. Rider Haggard, *The Days of My Life*, p. 220; cited in Higgins, *Rider Haggard*, p. 76.

17 Edward Salmon, "What Boys Read," *Fortnightly Review*, 45 (1886).

18 See Patrick A. Dunne, "Boys' Literature and the Idea of Empire, 1870–1914," *Victorian Studies* 24 (Autumn 1980): 108.

19 John Boswell, *Christianity, Social Tolerance, and Homosexuality* (Chicago: University of Chicago Press, 1980), pp. 28–29.

20 See Patrick Brantlinger, *Rule of Darkness: British Literature and Imperialism, 1830–1914* (Ithaca: Cornell University Press, 1988), p. 231.

21 Ellis, *H. Rider Haggard*, p. 176.

22 Edward Said, *Orientalism* (New York: Vintage, 1979), p. 190.

23 Sir Richard Burton, *The Sotadic Zone* (New York: Panurge Press), n.d.

24 Joseph Boone, *Tradition Counter Tradition: Love and the Form of Fiction* (Chicago: University of Chicago Press, 1987), p. 231.

25 See Wayne Koestenbaum, "A Manuscript Affair: The World's Desire and the Literary Intercourse of H. Rider Haggard and Andrew Lang," unpublished paper, Princeton University, January 1986.

26 Judith L. Sensibar, "Edith Wharton Reads the Bachelor Type," *American Literature* 60 (December 1988): 582.

27 See Norman Etherington, *Rider Haggard* (Boston: G. K. Hall, 1984), p. 84.

28 H. Rider Haggard, " 'Elephant Smashing' and 'Lion Shooting,' " (1894); quoted in Brantlinger, *Rule of Darkness*, p. 239.

29 Koestenbaum, "A Manuscript Affair;" p. 9.

30 Wendy Katz, *Rider Haggard: The Fiction of Empire* (Cambridge: Cambridge University Press, 1987), p. 9.

31 H. Rider Haggard, *The Days of My Life* (London, 1926), p. 64.

32 Haggard, Quoted in Higgins, *Rider Haggard*, p. 3.

33 Peter Ellis, *H. Rider Haggard*, p. 109.

34 Gilbert and Gubar, *Sexchanges*, p. 13.

35 *Recreations of the Rabelais Club 1885–1888* (Guilford: Billing and Sons, 1888), p. 68.

36 See Koestenbaum, "A Manuscript Affair."

37 Margaret Atwood, "Superwoman Drawn and Quartered: The Early Forms of *She*," in Atwood, *Second Words* (Boston: Beacon, 1982).

38 Elizabeth Bowen, "She," in Bowen, *Seven Winters and Afterthoughts* (New York: Knopf, 1962), pp. 235–36.

39 Edmund Gosse, *Century Magazine* (1895), quoted in Roger Lancelyn Green, ed., *Kipling: The Critical Heritage* (London: Routledge Kegan Paul, 1971), p. 105.

40 See Green, *Kipling: The Critical Heritage*, pp. 65, 67. On the friendship of Haggard and Kipling, see Morton Cohen, ed., *Rudyard Kipling to Haggard* (Rutherford, N.J.: Fairleigh Dickinson University Press, 1965).

41 See Lewis Wurgaft, *The Imperial Imagination: Magic and Myth in Kipling's India* (Middletown: Wesleyan University Press, 1983), pp. 135–36. Thanks to Sandra Gilbert for suggesting Wurgaft's remarkable book.

42 See Green, *Kipling: The Critical Heritage*, pp. 302, 305–306.

43 John Huston, quoted in Gerald Pratley, *The Cinema of John Huston* (New York: A. S. Barnes and Co., 1977), p. 188.

44 See Paul Fussell, "Irony, Freemasonry, and Humane Ethics in Kipling's *The Man Who Would Be King*," ELH 25 (1958): 216.

45 George Grella, "The Colonial Movie and *The Man Who Would Be King*," *Texas Studies in Language and Literature* 22 (Summer 1980): 247.

46 Pratley, *The Cinema of John Huston*, pp. 191–92.

47 Quoted in Pratley, *The Cinema of John Huston*, p. 193.

48 Wurgaft, *The Imperial Imagination*, pp. 10, 58, 35, 54.

49 Ellis, *Sexual Inversion*, p. 17.

50 George MacMunn, *The Underworld of India* (London: Jarrolds, 1933), p. 201; quoted in Wurgaft, p. 50.

51 Ian Watt, *Conrad in the Nineteenth Century* (Berkeley: University of California Press, 1979), p. 132.

52 Watt, *Conrad*, p. 131.

53 Nina Pelikan Straus, "The Exclusion of the Intended from Secret Sharing in Conrad's *Heart of Darkness*," *Novel* 20 (Winter 1987): 124.

54 Quoted in *Heart of Darkness*, ed. Robert Kimbrough (New York: Norton Critical Edition, 1963), p. 124.

55 Straus, "The Exclusion of the Intended," p. 134.

56 Edmund A. Bojarski, "Joseph Conrad's Sentimental Journey: A Fiftieth Anniversary Review," *Texas Quarterly* 7 (1964): 164.

57 See Cleo McNelly, "Natives, Women, and Claude Levi-Strauss," *Massachusetts Review* 16 (1975): 6–29; and Nina Pelikan Straus, "Exclusion of the Intended," pp. 128–29.

58 Bronislaw Malinowski, quoted in James Clifford, *The Predicament of Culture: Twentieth-Century Ethnography, Literature, and Art* (Cambridge: Harvard University Press, 1988), p. 96.

59 See *Conradiana*, 13 (1981), pp. 37, 41, 55. 1981. But see also Garrett Stewart, "Coppola's Conrad: the Repetitions of Complicity," *Critical Inquiry* 7 (Spring 1981): 455–74. I am indebted to Garrett Stewart's brilliant and sympathetic analysis of *Apocalypse Now*.

60 Jeffrey Chown, *Hollywood Auteur* (New York: Praeger, 1988), p. 123.

61 Eleanor Coppola, *Notes* (New York: Simon and Schuster, 1979), p. 43.

62 Coppola, *Notes*, p. 44.

63 Coppola, *Notes*, p. 180.

64 Francis Ford Coppola at the Cannes Film Festival, quoted in Chown, *Hollywood Auteur*, p. 126.

65 Chown, *Hollywood Auteur*, p. 126.

66 Coppola, *Notes*, pp. 184, 186, 187.

67 Coppola, *Notes*, p. 177.

68 Chown, *Hollywood Auteur*, p. 126.

69 Chown, *Hollywood Auteur*, p. 127.

70 Griel Marcus, "Journey up the River," *Rolling Stone*, 1 November 1979, p. 56.

71 Coppola, *Notes*, p. 282.

72 Coppola, *Notes*, p. 229.

73 Coppola, *Notes*, p. 212.

74 Coppola, *Notes*, p. 247.

75 Maureen Orth, "Watching the Apocalypse," *Newsweek*, 13 June 1977, p. 63; quoted in Chown, p. 126.

76 Seth Mydans, "In Philippine Town, Child Prostitution, Despite Protests, Is a Way of Life," *New York Times*, Sunday, 5 February 1989, p. 3.

CHAPTER SIX

1 Frederic W. H. Myers, "Multiplex Personality," *The Nineteenth Century* (November 1886): 648–66.

2 Mrs. R. L. Stevenson, "Note," in *Works of Robert Louis Stevenson: Skerryvore Edition* (London: Heinemann, 1924), 4:xvii–xvii.

3 Emile Batault, *Contribution à l'étude de l'hystérie chez l'homme*, (Paris, 1885), author's translation.

4 See Wayne Koestenbaum, "The Shadow Under the Bed: Dr. Jekyll, Mr. Hyde, and the Labouchère Amendment," *Critical Matrix* 1 (Spring 1988): 31–55.

5 Miller, *Doubles*, p. 216.

6 Phyllis Grosskurth, ed. *The Memoirs of John Addington Symonds: The Secret Homosexual Life of a Leading Nineteenth-Century Man of Letters* (Chicago: University of Chicago Press, 1984), p. 122.

7 Regenia Gagnier, *Idylls of the Marketplace*, p. 158.

8 "A Chapter on Dreams," in *The Works of Robert Louis Stevenson* (London, 1922), p. 247.

9 Miller, *Doubles*, p. 213. For discussions of Stevenson's homosociality/ homosexuality, see William Veeder's brilliant essay, "Children of the Night: Stevenson and Patriarchy," in *Dr. Jekyll and Mr. Hyde after One Hundred Years*, Chicago: University of Chicago Press, 1988), William Veeder and Gordon Hirsch, eds. especially pp. 159–60; and Wayne Koestenbaum, *Double Talk: The Erotics of Male Literary Collaboration* (New York and London: Routledge, 1989), pp. 145–51.

10 Andrew Lang, "Recollections of Robert Louis Stevenson," *Adventures Among Books* (London: Longmans, Green, and Co., 1903), p. 51.

11 Jenni Calder, *Robert Louis Stevenson: A Life Study* (New York: Oxford University Press, 1980), p. 65.

12 Quoted in Stanley Olson, *John Singer Sargent* (New York: St. Martin's Press, 1986), pp. 115, 114.

13 Malcolm Elwin, *The Strange Case of Robert Louis Stevenson* (London: Macdonald, 1950), p. 198; quoted in Koestenbaum, *Double Talk*, p. 150.

14 Eve Kosofsky Sedgwick has called the genre to which Stevenson's novel belongs "the paranoid Gothic." According to Sedgwick, "the Gothic novel crystallized for English audiences the terms of a dialectic between male homosexuality and homophobia, in which homophobia appeared thematically in paranoid plots," (*Between Men*, p. 92). Such texts involved doubled male figures, one of whom feels obsessed by or persecuted by the other; and the central image of the unspeakable secret. I am indebted also to Paul Zablocki, and to John Perry's unpublished senior thesis, "Novel as Homotext: A Gay Critical Approach to Narrative," Princeton University, 1987.

15 See, for example, the excellent essay by Stephen Heath, "Psychopathia sexualis: Stevenson's *Strange Case*," *Critical Quarterly* 28 (1986), p. 28.

16 Julia Wedgwood, *Contemporary Review* 49 (April 1886): 594–95; and Alice Brown, *Study of Stevenson* (Boston: Copeland and Day, 1895); quoted in Koestenbaum, *Double Talk*, p. 145.

17 For the manuscripts and publishing history of the novel, see William Veeder, "The Texts in Question," and Veeder and Hirsch, eds., "Collated Fragments of the Manuscript Drafts of *Strange Case of Dr. Jekyll and Mr. Hyde*," in *Dr. Jekyll and Mr. Hyde*, pp. 3–58.

18 James Twitchell, *Dreadful Pleasures: An Anatomy of Modern Horror* (New York: Oxford University Press, 1985), p. 236.

19 Heath, "Psychopathia sexualis," p. 95.

20 Veeder and Hirsch, *Dr. Jekyll and Mr. Hyde*, p. 55.

21 Vladimir Nabokov, "The Strange Case of Dr. Jekyll and Mr. Hyde," in *Lectures on Literature*, ed. Fredson Bowers (New York: Harcourt Brace Jovanovich, 1980), p. 194.

22 Weeks, *Sex, Politics, and Society,* p. 113.

23 Weeks, *Sex, Politics, and Society,* p. 113.

24 See Veeder, "Children of the Night," in *Dr. Jekyll and Mr. Hyde,* p. 159.

25 Miller, *Doubles,* p. 241.

26 Alexander Welsh, *George Eliot and Blackmail* (Cambridge: Harvard University Press, 1985), p. 9.

27 Edward Carpenter, *The Intermediate Sex,* p. 79; quoted in Weeks, *Coming Out,* p. 21.

28 Sedgwick, *Between Men,* p. 88.

29 Veeder, "Collated Fragments," pp. 34–35.

30 Thanks to Paul Zablocki and Gary Sunshine, students in my course on the *fin de siècle,* for their comments on "homotextuality" and suicide.

31 Veeder, "Children of the Night," p. 149. Thanks to Phil Pearson.

32 Anne Harrington, *Medicine, Mind, and the Double Brain* (Princeton: Princeton University Press, 1987), p. 170.

33 Harrington, *Medicine, Mind, and the Double Brain,* p. 94.

34 Paul Maixner, *Robert Louis Stevenson: The Critical Heritage* (London: Routledge Kegan Paul, 1981), p. 215.

35 See Christopher Craft, " 'Descend and Touch and Enter': Tennyson's Strange Manner of Address," *Genders* 1 (Spring 1988): 91–92.

36 J. A. Symonds to Stevenson, 3 March 1886, in *Letters of J. A. Symonds,* eds. Herbert M. Schueller and Robert L. Peters (Detroit: Wayne State University Press, 1968), pp. 120–21.

37 Quoted in Jenni Calder, *Robert Louis Stevenson,* p. 118.

38 I am indebted for this observation to Daniel Jaeger-Mendelsohn in the Classics Department at Princeton.

39 Twitchell, *Dreadful Pleasures,* p. 256.

40 Vicinus, *Independent Women,* p. 297.

41 Virginia Woolf, *The Pargiters,* ed. Mitchell Leaska (London: Harcourt Brace Jovanovich, 1977), p. 37.

42 Vicinus, *Independent Women,* p. 146.

43 Marx and Aveling, *The Woman Question,* p. 9.

44 Weeks, *Sex, Politics, and Society,* p. 115.

45 Nigel Nicholson, *Portrait of a Marriage* (London: Athenaeum, 1973), p. 35.

46 *Parliamentary Debates,* Commons, 1921, vol. 145, p. 1805.

47 Morton Prince, *Psychotherapy and Multiple Personality: Selected Essays,* ed. Nathan G. Hale, Jr. (Cambridge: Harvard University Press, 1975), p. 195.

48 Prince, *Psychotherapy and Multiple Personality,* p. 151.

49 Roberta Smith, "Singular Artists Who Work in the First Person Plural," *New York Times,* Sunday, 10 May 1987. Thanks to Wayne Koestenbaum for this reference.

50 See Rosamond Smith, *Lives of the Twins* (New York: Simon and Schuster, 1987), and *Soul/Mate* (New York: E. P. Dutton, 1989).
51 Sue Roe and Emma Tennant, "Women Talking About Writing," in *Women's Writing: A Challenge to Theory*, ed. Moira Monteith (New York: St. Martin's Press, 1986).
52 Humphrey and Dennett, "Speaking for Ourselves: An Assessment of Multiple Personality Disorder," *Raritan* 9 (Summer 1989): 68.
53 See Michael G. Kenny, *The Passion of Ansel Bourne: Multiple Personality in American Culture* (Washington: Smithsonian Institution Press, 1986), pp. 161–82.

CHAPTER SEVEN

1 Judith R. Walkowitz, "Jack the Ripper and the Myth of Male Violence," *Feminist Studies* 8 (Fall 1982): 544.
2 Gilbert and Gubar, *Sexchanges*, p. 48.
3 See Sander Gilman, *Sexuality: An Illustrated History* (New York: John Wiley & Sons, 1989), pp. 179–90; L. Belloni, "Anatomica plastica: The Bologna Wax Models," *CIBA Symposium* 8 (1060): 84–87.
4 Ludmilla Jordanova, *Sexual Visions: Images of Gender in Science and Medicine between the Eighteenth and Twentieth Centuries* (London: Harvester, 1989), pp. 54, 50.
5 Quoted in Gilbert and Gubar, *No Man's Land*, p. 33.
6 See Renaldo Columbo, *De re anatomica* (1572), book 2, chap. 16, pp. 447–48; and Nicolas Culpepper, *A Dictionary for Midwives; or, A Guide for Women* (1675), both cited in Laqueur, "Orgasm, Generation, and the Politics of Reproductive Biology," *Representations*, p. 14.
7 *Lancet* 1873:223.
8 Robert T. Morris, "Is Evolution Trying to Do Away with the Clitoris?" *Journal of American Obstetrics*, p. 850.
9 Gayatri Chakravorty Spivak, "French Feminism in an International Frame," in *Other Worlds: Essays in Cultural Politics* (New York and London: Routledge, 1988).
10 Wharton Sinkler, "The Remote Results of the Tubes and Ovaries," *University Medical Magazine* (1891).
11 D. MacClean, "Sexual Mutilation," *California Medical Journal* 15 (1894): 382.
12 David Gilliam, "Oophorectomy for the Insanity and Epilepsy of the Female: A Plea for Its More General Adoption," *Trans. of the American Association of Obstetrics and Gynecology* 9 (1896): 319–21.
13 *La Femme* (1981), p. 77; cited in Charles Bernheimer, *Figures of Ill Repute:*

Representing Prostitution in Nineteenth-Century France (Cambridge: Harvard University Press, 1989).

14 Quoted in Jordanova, *Sexual Visions*, p. 1.

15 Gilman, *Sexuality*, pp. 249–50.

16 Jordanova, *Sexual Visions*, p. 57.

17 Michael Kimmelman, "Image Manipulation," *New York Times*, 13 January 1989.

18 James Russell, "The After Effects of Surgical Procedure on the Generative Organs of Females for the Relief of Insanity," *The Canadian Practitioner* 23 (1898).

19 Spencer Wells, "Castration in Mental and Nervous Diseases," *American Journal of the Medical Sciences* 91–92 (1886): 470–71.

20 See Peter Schwenger, *Phallic Critiques: Masculinity and Twentieth-Century Literature* (London: Routledge and Kegan Paul, 1984), pp. 49–50.

21 Bernheimer, *Figures of Ill Repute*, p. 214.

22 This story was brought to my attention through a reference in K. K. Ruthven, *Feminist Literary Studies* (Cambridge: Cambridge University Press, 1984), pp. 46–47.

23 Sigmund Freud, *Dora: An Analysis of a Case of Hysteria* (New York: Collier Books, 1964), p. 136.

24 William J. McGrath, *Freud's Discovery of Psychoanalysis* (Ithaca: Cornell University Press, 1986), p. 299.

25 McGrath, *Freud's Discovery of Psychoanalysis*, pp. 300–301.

26 Sandra M. Gilbert, "Rider Haggard's Heart of Darkness," *Partisan Review* 13 (1983): 451.

27 Amy Taubin, *Village Voice*, October 1987.

28 Karen Jaehne, "Double Trouble," *Film Comment* 24 (September/October 1988): 27.

29 Terrence Rafferty, "Secret Sharers," *New Yorker* 64 (3 October 1988): 92.

30 Stuart Klawans, "Films," *The Nation* 247 (31 October 1988): 431.

31 Brian D. Johnson, "A Fatal Obsession," *Macleans* 101 (19 September 1988): 51.

32 Johnson, "A Fatal Obsession," p. 50.

33 Karen Jaehne, "Visit to the Doctor," *Film Comment* 24 (September/October 1988): 26.

34 Rafferty, "Secret Sharers," p. 94.

35 Johnson, "Fatal Obsession," p. 53.

36 Gordon Burn, *Somebody's Husband, Somebody's Son* (London: Heinemann, 1984); quoted in Patricia Highsmith, "Ripping Time," *Times Literary Supplement*, 25–31 December 1987, p. 27.

37 Highsmith, "Ripping Time," p. 27.

38 Isabel Wilkerson, "Charges against Doctor Bring Ire and Questions," *New York Times*, 11 December 1988, p. 32.

39 "Physician Charged Over 'Love Surgery' Surrenders License," *New York Times*, 26 January 1989.

40 Walkowitz, "Jack the Ripper," p. 570.

41 See, for example, the preface by Catherine A. MacKinnon and the introduction by Jeffrey Masson to *A Dark Science: Women, Sexuality, and Psychiatry in the Nineteenth Century* (New York: Farrar, Straus and Giroux, 1986).

42 David Denby, "Heart of Darkness," *New York Magazine* 21 (3 October 1988): 61.

43 Andrew Dowler, "Film Reviews," *Cinema Canada* 24 (November 1988): 24.

44 Rafferty, "Secret Sharers," p. 94.

CHAPTER EIGHT

1 Mary Anne Doane, "Veiling Over Desire: Close-ups of the Woman," in Richard Feldstein and Judith Roof, eds., *Feminism and Psychoanalysis* (Ithaca: Cornell University Press, 1989), p. 107.

2 Wurgaft, *The Imperial Imagination*, p. 52.

3 Jordanova, *Sexual Visions*, p. 89.

4 Froma Zeitlin, "Cultic Models of the Female: Rites of Dionysus and Demeter," *Arethusa* 15 (1982).

5 Peter Brooks, "Storied Bodies, or Nana at Last Unveil'd," *Critical Inquiry* 16 (August 1989): 29.

6 Maxime Du Camp, *Les convulsions de Paris* (Paris: Hachette, 1889), 2: 189–90.

7 Quoted in Peter Gay, *The Bourgeois*, I: 198.

8 Jordanova, *Sexual Visions*, pp. 96, 110. Jordanova also points out that "dissection was a form of unveiling," and that the word "veil" has the biological meaning of "membrane." (pp. 99–106).

9 Geoffrey Faber, *Oxford Apostles: A Character Study of the Oxford Movement* (1933); quoted in Peter Gay, *The Tender Passion* (New York: Oxford, 1986), p. 236, n. 39.

10 Carl E. Schorske, *Fin de Siècle Vienna* (New York: Knopf, 1980), p. 224.

11 Philippe Jullian, *Esthetes et magiciens* (Paris: Perrin, 1969), p. 132; quoted in Jean Pierrot, *The Decadent Imagination 1880–1900* (Chicago: University of Chicago Press, 1981), p. 199.

12 Richard Ellmann, *Oscar Wilde* (New York: Knopf, 1988), pp. 37–72.

13 Ellmann, *Oscar Wilde*, p. 209; quoted in Worth, p. 65.

14 Quoted in Jane Marcus, "Salome: The Jewish Princess Was a New Woman," *Bulletin of the New York Public Library* (1974): 100, n. 28.

15 Katherine Worth, *Oscar Wilde* (New York: Grove Press, 1983), p. 66.

16 This is taken from a very recent example, Robert C. Schweik, "Oscar Wilde's Salome, the Salome Theme in Late European Art, and Problem of Method in Cultural History," in *Twilight at Dawn*, ed. O. M. Brack, Jr. (Tucson: University of Arizona Press, 1987), p. 129.

17 Marcus, "Salome," p. 106.

18 Elliot L. Gilbert, " 'Tumult of Images': Wilde, Beardsley, and *Salome*," *Victorian Studies* 26 (Winter 1983): 133, 150, 154.

19 Marcus, "Salome," pp. 98, 99.

20 Marcus, "Salome," p. 100.

21 Ewa Kuryluk, *Salome and Judas in the Cave of Sex* (Evanston: Northwestern University Press, 1987), pp. 110–115.

22 Hélène Cixous, "The Laugh of the Medusa," in *New French Feminisms*, ed. Elaine Marks and Isabelle de Courtivron (Amherst: University of Massachusetts Press, 1980), p. 255.

23 "A Keynote to Keynotes," in *Ten Contemporaries*, ed. John Gawsworth (London: Ernest Benn, 1932), p. 58.

24 George Egerton, quoted in Terence de Vere White, ed., *A Leaf from the Yellow Book* (London: The Richards Press, 1958), pp. 23–24.

25 Dijkstra, *Idols of Perversity*, p. 392.

26 Marcus, "Salome," p. 104.

27 Worth, *Oscar Wilde*, p. 64.

28 Peter Wollen, "Fashion/ orientalism/ the body," in *New Formations* 1 (Spring 1987): 20.

29 Wollen, "Fashion/ orientalism/ the body," pp. 19, 18.

30 Michael de Cossart, *Ida Rubenstein: A Theatrical Life* (Liverpool: Liverpool University Press, 1987), pp. 10–15. Thanks to Richard Kaye for telling me about this book.

31 Quoted in Wollen, "Fashion/ orientalism/ the body," p. 19.

32 Worth, *Oscar Wilde*, p. 67.

33 *New York Times*, 23 August 1908; quoted in Judith Lynne Hanna, *Dance, Sex, and Gender: Signs of Identity, Dominance, Defiance, and Desire* (Chicago: University of Chicago Press, 1987), p. 183.

34 Diana Cooper, *The Rainbow Comes and Goes* (Boston: Houghton Mifflin, 1958), p. 82. Thanks to Richard Kaye for this reference.

35 Gagnier, *Idylls of the Marketplace*, p. 199. See also Michael Kettle, *Salome's Last Veil: The Libel Case of the Century* (1977).

36 See Ethan Morrden, *Movie Star: A Look at the Women Who Made Hollywood* (New York: St. Martin's Press, 1983). Thanks to Jennie Kassanoff for this reference.

37 Robert I. Sherwood, *The Best Moving Pictures of 1922–23* (New York: Small, Maynard, and Co., 1923), p. 103.

38 "The Screen," *New York Times,* 10 January 1923, p. 139.

39 See Simon Callow, *Charles Laughton: A Difficult Actor* (New York: Grove Press, 1987), pp. 721–22. Laughton was "openly contemptuous of the proceedings."

40 Roland Barthes, "Striptease," in *Mythologies,* trans. Annette Lavers (New York: Hill and Wang, 1972), p. 85.

41 David Lodge, *Small World* (London: Secker & Warburg, 1984), pp. 26–27.

42 Laurence Senelick, "Changing Sex in Public: Female Impersonation as Performance," *Theater* (1989): 6–11. I am grateful to Laurence Senelick for sharing his research on cross-dressing, and for lively discussions during the Salzburg Seminar on "Gender and the Humanities" in the summer of 1988.

43 Joy Melville, "The Ladies Let It All Hang Out," *The Guardian,* 19 July 1988.

44 Worth, *Oscar Wilde,* p. 67.

45 Hanna, *Dance, Sex, and Gender,* p. 219.

46 See Paul Taylor, "Divine Decadence," *The Independent,* 9 November 1989, p. 44; and Allan Kozinn, "A New 'Salome' at the Met: Brutal and Corrupt, with a Feeling of Twilight," *New York Times,* Sunday, 19 February 1989.

47 See Joan Riviere, "Womanliness as a Masquerade" (1929); reprinted in *Formations of Fantasy,* eds. Victor Burgin, James Donald, and Cora Kaplan (London and New York: Methuen, 1986), p. 36.

CHAPTER NINE

1 Marcus, "Salome," p. 95.

2 Sandra Siegel, *Degeneration,* p. 210.

3 "A Defense of Cosmetics," *Yellow Book,* 1 (1894): 78; quoted in Dowling, "The Decadent and the New Woman," p. 44.

4 John R. Reed, *Decadent Style* (Athens: Ohio University Press, 1985), p. 7.

5 See Jean Pierrot, *The Decadent Imagination,* p. 10.

6 Dowling, "The Decadent and the New Woman," p. 447.

7 Harrison, *The Yellow Book,* p. 27.

8 Gagnier, *Idylls of the Marketplace,* p. 144.

9 Harrison, *The Yellow Book,* p. 25.

10 See Ellen Jordan, "The Christening of the New Woman, May 1894," *Victorian Newsletter* 63 (Spring 1983): 19–21.

11 See Dellamora, *Masculine Desires,* p. 146.
12 *Westminster Gazette,* 6 April 1895; quoted in Ed Cohen, "Writing Gone Wilde: Homoerotic Desire in the Closet of Representation," *PMLA* 102 (October 1987): 80.
13 Sander L. Gilman, *Disease and Representation,* p. 160.
14 The phrase "intermediate sex" is from Edward Carpenter, *Love's Coming of Age.* The quotation is from Eve Kosofsky Sedgwick, "Across Gender, Across Sexuality," *SAQ* 88 (Winter 1989): 58.
15 Noel Grieg, introduction to *Edward Carpenter: Selected Writings* (London: GMP Publishers Ltd., 1984), I: 64.
16 *My Days and Dreams,* in *Edward Carpenter,* 1:86.
17 Benedict Friedlander, quoted in Donald Mager, "Gay Theories of Gender Role Deviance," *SubStance* 46 (1985): 35–36.
18 Sedgwick, *Between Men,* p. 207.
19 See Sedgwick, *Between Men,* p. 213.
20 Gagnier, *Idylls of the Marketplace,* p. 160.
21 Dellamora, *Masculine Desire,* p. 108.
22 Marx and Aveling, *The Woman Question,* p. 12.
23 See Walkowitz, "The Men and Women's Club," p. 48.
24 Dora Marsden, *The New Freewoman,* 1 September 1913, p. 115.
25 Schreiner, *Letters,* pp. 88–89.
26 Sedgwick, *Between Men,* p. 217.
27 H. G. Wells, "Preface to *The Island of Dr. Moreau,*" *The Works of H. G. Wells* (New York: Atlantic Edition, 1924), 2:ix.
28 The gender elements of the story are muted in the two modern film versions, both of which stress metaphors of imperialism, slavery, and revolution. In the imperialist reading of the story, the Beast People are the colonized who revolt against their master. In *The Island of Lost Souls* (1930), with Charles Laughton and Bela Lugosi, the Beast People rise up against Moreau and take him to the House of Pain, a horrifying reversal both expected and shaped by the iconography of class revolution. Images of revolution are also important in the more recent film of the story with Burt Lancaster and Michael York, in which Moreau looks like a Civil War plantation owner in a white suit, with a panther-girl consort in a frilly white gown; when the Beast People rebel, they break into the compound and release all the imprisoned animals, like the storming of the Bastille. Finally, they burn the buildings in a conflagration that signals the end, the apocalypse, the beginnings of a new life.
29 Christopher Craft, "Kiss Me With Those Red Lips: Gender and Inversion in Bram Stoker's *Dracula,*" in *Speaking of Gender,* ed. Elaine Showalter (New York and London: Routledge, 1989), p. 220.
30 Dr. William J. Robinson, quoted in Dijkstra, *Idols of Perversity,* p. 334.
31 Craft, "Kiss Me With Those Red Lips," p. 231.

32 Wendy O'Flaherty, *Women, Androgynes, and Other Mythical Beasts* (Chicago, University of Chicago Press, 1980), p.87.

33 Jane Halstead, quoted in Ines Rieder and Patricia Ruppelt, eds., *AIDS: The Women* (San Francisco: Cleis Press, 1988), p. 145.

34 Marj Plumb, quoted in Rieder and Ruppelt, *AIDS: The Women*, p. 147.

35 Marilyn Frye, *The Politics of Reality: Essays in Feminist Theory* (Trumansburg, N.Y.: The Crossing Press, 1983), pp. 129, 132, 133, 137.

36 Alice Jardine, *Men in Feminism*, eds. Alice Jardine and Paul Smith (New York: Metheun, 1987), p. 244.

37 Janet Todd, *Feminist Literary History* (London: Polity Press, 1988), p. 118.

38 Edmund White, "The Artist and AIDS," *Harper's Magazine*, 30 (May 1987): 22.

39 Sontag, *AIDS and Its Metaphors*, p. 76.

40 Rieder and Ruppelt, *AIDS: The Women*, p. 145.

41 See Dennis Altman, *AIDS and the New Puritanism* (London: Pluto Press, 1986), p. 170.

42 David Leavitt, "The Way I Live Now," *New York Times Magazine*, 9 July 1989, p. 32. Thanks to John Perry for this reference.

43 Leavitt, "The Way I Live Now," p. 82.

44 Mort, *Dangerous Sexualities*, pp. 219–22.

CHAPTER TEN

1 Alain Corbin, "Le péril vénérien au début du siècle: prophylaxie sanitaire et prophalaxie morale," *Recherches* 27 (December 1977): 245–83.

2 Allan Brandt, *No Magic Bullet: A Social History of VD in the United States Since 1880* (New York: Oxford University Press, 1985), p. 26.

3 Charles Mauriac, *Leçons sur les maladies vénériennes professées à l'Hôpital du Midi* (Paris: J. B. Bailiere, 1883), pp. 186–87; quoted in Alain Corbin, *Les Filles de Noce* (Paris: Auber Montaigne, 1978), p. 364. See also Bernheimer, *Figures of Ill Repute*.

4 Corbin, "Le péril vénérien," p. 252.

5 Stephen Kern, *Anatomy and Destiny: A Cultural History of the Human Body* (New York: Bobbs-Merrill, 1975), p. 42.

6 Lyndall Gordon, *Eliot's Early Years* (London: Oxford University Press, 1977), p. 27.

7 Lady Cook, *A Check on Libertines* (London, 1890); quoted in Boumelha, *Thomas Hardy and Women*, p. 20.

8 Brandt, *No Magic Bullet*, pp. 16–17.

9 Howard Kelly, "Social Diseases and Their Prevention," *Social Diseases* 1 (1910); quoted in Allan Brandt, "AIDS: From Social History to Social

Policy," in Elizabeth Fee and Daniel M. Fox, eds., *AIDS: The Burdens of History* (Berkeley: University of California Press, 1988), p. 169.

10 Fee, "Sin Versus Science: Venereal Disease in Twentieth-Century Baltimore," in Fee and Fox, *AIDS: The Burdens of History*, p. 122.

11 Altman, *AIDS and the New Puritanism*, p. 13.

12 *New York Times*, 7 June 1987, p. 1.

13 Dr. Donald Louria, chairman of the Department of Preventive Medicine at the University of Medicine and Dentistry of New Jersey, quoted in Ralph Ginsburg, "Prostitution Up, Despite AIDS," *New York Times*, 2 February 1987.

14 Ned Rorem, "Photographs Before a Birthday," *The Advocate*, 29 September 1983; quoted in Altman, *AIDS and the New Puritanism*, p. 168.

15 William F. Buckley, "Identify All the Carriers," *New York Times*, 18 March 1986, sec. A, p. 27.

16 "Panic in the Streets," *NFT Programme* (August 1988), p. 10.

17 Judith Williamson, Programme Notes, "Panic in the Streets," NFT (August 1988).

18 Paula Treichler, "AIDS, Gender and Biomedical Discourse," in Fee and Fox, AIDS: *The Burden of History*, p. 200.

19 Altman, *AIDS and the New Puritanism*, p. 311.

20 Simon Watney, *Policy Desire* (Minneapolis: University of Minnesota Press, 1987), p. 9.

21 Grover, "A Matter of Life and Death," *Women's Review of Books* (March 1988): 3.

22 Brandt, *No Magic Bullet*, p. 27.

23 George Melly, "Let the Thoughtless Man Here Pause," *New Statesman* (1 March 1963), pp. 317–18.

24 Alain Corbin, "Commercial Sexuality in Nineteenth-Century France: A System of Images and Regulations," *Representations* 14 (Spring 1986): 212.

25 Jean-Noël Jeanneney, "La Syphilis . . . avant le SIDA," *Le Monde*, 16 July 1987, p. 9.

26 Quoted in Claude Quêtel, *Le mal de Naples: Historie de la syphilis* (Paris: Seghers, 1986), p. 184 (author's translation).

27 Quoted in Laura Engelstein, "Morality and the Wooden Spoon: Russian Doctors View Syphilis, Social Class, and Sexual Behavior, 1890–1905," *Representations* 14 (Spring 1986): 174.

28 Josephine Butler, quoted in Judith Walkowitz, *Prostitution and Victorian Society* (Cambridge: Cambridge University Press, 1982), p. 130.

29 See Charles Bernheimer, *Figures of Ill Repute*, p. 235.

30 Brandt, *No Magic Bullet*, p. 16.

31 Alain Corbin, "Le péril vénérien au début du siècle: prophylaxie sanitaire et prophalaxie morale," in *Recherches* 27 (December 1977).

32 William Acton, *A Practical Treatise on Diseases of the Urinary and Generative Organs in Both Sexes* (London: John Churchill, 1851), pp. 602–03.

33 Stefan Zweig, *The World of Yesterday* (London: Cassell, 1943), p. 77.

34 Cecily Hamilton, *Marriage as a Trade* (New York: Moffat, Yard, and Co., 1909), p. 73.

35 Sigmund Freud, *Dora: An Analysis of a Case of Hysteria* (New York: Collier Books, 1964), p. 35, n. 6.

36 Walkowitz, *Prostitution and Victorian Society*, p. 128.

37 Pankhurst, *The Great Scourge and How to End It* (London: David Nutt, 1913), pp. 133, 124.

38 See C. F. Marshall, *Syphilology and Venereal Disease* (New York: Wood, 1906), p. 306. See also James N. Hyde and Frank Montgomery, *Manual of Syphilis and the Venereal Diseases* (Philadelphia, 1895); and William J. Brown et al., *Syphilis and Other Venereal Diseases* (Cambridge: Harvard University Press, 1970).

39 See Roger Williams, *The Horror of Life* (Chicago: University of Chicago Press, 1980).

40 See George Pickering, *Creative Malady* (London: George Allen & Unwin, 1974), p. 295; Leon Edel, *Henry James: The Middle Years* (New York: Avon, 1978), p. 177; H. Montgomery Hyde, *Oscar Wilde* (New York: Farrar Straus & Giroux, 1975), pp. 181, 184; Phyllis Grosskurth, *Havelock Ellis* (New York: Knopf, 1980), p. 335.

41 See *Phoenix: The Posthumous Papers of D. H. Lawrence*, ed. Edward D. McDonald (New York: Viking, 1968), pp. 552–55.

42 See Michael Mayer, *Ibsen: A Biography* (New York: Doubleday, 1971), pp. 657–59; and Michael Egan, *Ibsen: The Critical Heritage* (London: Routledge & Kegan Paul, 1972).

43 Siegfried Sassoon, *Siegfried's Journey* (London: Faber & Faber, 1945), p. 30.

44 Jeffrey Weeks, "AIDS, Altruism, and the New Right," in *Taking Liberties*, eds. Erica Carter and Simon Watney (London: Serpents' Tail, 1989), p. 127.

45 Leavitt, "The Way I Live Now," p. 29.

46 Michael Denneny, quoted in Edwin McDowell, "After a Slow Start, AIDS Books Are Coming Out in a Rush," *New York Times*, 11 June 1987.

47 See Dennis Altman, *AIDS and the New Puritanism*, p. 23.

48 Michael Denneny, quoted in David Kaufman, "The Creative Response," *Horizon* 30 (November 1987), 14.

49 Quoted in Douglas Crimp, *AIDS: Cultural Analysis, Cultural Activism* (Cambridge: October Press, 1988), p. 5.

50 Edmund White, "The Artist and AIDS," *Horizon,* 30 (November 1987): 22.

51 Crimp, *AIDS: Cultural Analysis, Cultural Activism,* p. 7.

52 D. A. Miller, "Sontag's Urbanity," *October* 49 (Summer 1989): 101.

53 Paul Monette, "The Very Same," *Love Alone: 18 Elegies for Rog* (New York: St. Martin's Press, 1988).

54 Dominique Fernandez, *Le Rapt de Ganymede* (Paris: Grasset, 1989), p. 302.

55 Jacqueline Piatier, *Le Monde,* 20 February 1987; quoted in Jeanneney, "Le syphilis avant le SIDA," p. 9.

56 Fernandez, *Le Rapt de Ganymede,* p. 291.

57 Fernandez, *La Gloire du Paria* (Paris: Grasset, 1987). Author's translations.

58 Fernandez, *Le Rapt de Ganymede,* p. 233.

59 *Le Rapt de Ganymede,* pp. 297, 298, 300.

60 *Le Rapt de Ganymede,* p. 300.

61 Susan Sontag, "The Way We Live Now," *New Yorker,* 24 November 1986, pp. 42–51.

62 Ellmann, *Oscar Wilde,* p. 71.

63 See Gregory Woods, *Articulate Flesh: Male Homo-Eroticism and Modern Poetry* (New Haven: Yale University Press, 1987), pp. 28–30, and Paul Fussell, *The Great War and Modern Memory* (New York: Oxford University Press, 197), p. 285.

64 Susan Sontag, *AIDS and Its Metaphors* (New York: Farrar, Straus, and Giroux, 1989), p. 29

65 Anatole Broyard, column in *New York Times Book Review,* 13 December 1987: 11.

66 Leavitt, "The Way I Live Now," p. 30.

67 Edmund White, "The Artist and AIDS," *Harper's Magazine* (May 1987), p. 25.

68 The term "cruel muse" comes from a review by Stephen Koch of a biography of the novelist Djuna Barnes.

69 Paula Treichler, "AIDS, Gender, and Biomedical Discourse," 217.

70 Leavitt, "The Way I Live Now," p. 28.

71 Leo Bersani, "Is the Rectum a Grave?" in Crimp, *AIDS: Cultural Analysis, Cultural Activism,* p. 203.

72 Lynne Segal, "Lessons from the Past: Feminism, Sexual Politics, and the Challenge of AIDS," in *Taking Liberties,* p. 144.

73 Schreiner, *Woman and Labor* (New York: Frederick Stokes, 1911), pp. 296–97.

Index

Page numbers in *italics* refer to illustrations.